WHITE DIAL CLOCKS
The Complete Guide

WHITE
DIAL CLOCKS
The Complete Guide

Brian Loomes

DAVID & CHARLES

Newton Abbot   London

Frontispiece Thirteen-inch arched dial showing moonwork with tidal times, an unusual feature on a white dial. The longer pointer gives the lunar date, the shorter one tidal times. The dial was made c 1790 by James Wilson; the clock is by Thomas Husband of Hull, who died in 1812. Note the quality of the moon dial painting. The restorer has not attempted to pen in the two global maps. This clock has repeating-work. The hands are original in steel. The motto means 'Thus is the life of man'.

British Library Cataloguing in Publication Data

Loomes, Brian
    White dial clocks.—2nd ed.
      1. Clocks and watches—Great Britain—History
    I. Title
    681'.113   TS543.G7

    ISBN 0-7153-8073-7

Printed in Great Britain
by Butler & Tanner Ltd, Frome and London
for David & Charles Publishers plc
Brunel House Newton Abbot Devon

I dedicate this book to my dear wife for her tolerance and understanding during the many hours of work which its preparation involved

Contents

List of Illustrations

Foreword
to the First Edition

This book is about grandfather clocks with painted dials. I use the term 'white dial' as this covers all the various types, although many later examples, far from being white, are extremely colourful. Furthermore, this is the term the dialmakers themselves used at the time. These dials are not true enamel, although they are sometimes incorrectly referred to as such. (Longcase clocks with dials of true enamel are very rare indeed.) The dials have a japanned surface, which is basically decorative paint, hardened by a heat process.

I have often searched for authoritative written comment about this type of clock, and have usually met with disappointment. I found a frequent tendency on the part of southern English writers of the past to pre-date northern clocks, and then to compare them unfavourably with southern clocks of an earlier period.

As I handle clocks of this type every day, a certain pattern of development in styles began to form in my mind. For amusement I made a detailed analysis of 100 clock dials, selected at random, and although I had begun this with some half-formed opinions already, I was amazed at the clarity of the progressive stylistic pattern which emerged: a far stronger pattern than I had expected. Continuation of this analysis gradually threw up a list of features indicative of the period, in other words a set of 'rules', which one could not expect to hold good for every single white dial clock, but which do seem to apply to a surprisingly large proportion of British longcase clock dials. Since British dials were exported to America, it follows that dial-style developments there are almost identical, in the early period at least. So far as I am aware, none of these developments in dial styles are mentioned in any existing horological work.

This is not intended to be a technical book about the mechanics of clocks: there are plenty of books on this aspect already. It is about the ordinary, household, grandfather clock of the type met with in thousands of homes and antique shops.

Some of the views I express may well be controversial, but as far as possible I have tried to support them with factual examples; and a high proportion of the clocks I illustrate are dated positively by the maker. Many of the clocks illustrated are ones which have passed through my hands, and therefore I have been able to make a close personal examination of them. I have tried to use examples which are typical and not exceptional: clocks one might meet with every day rather than rare museum pieces which one might never come across again in a lifetime.

No one person's experience can ever be fully comprehensive, and I do not for one moment regard this work as pronouncing final conclusions. My observations relate essentially to longcase clocks; and while some bracket-clock dials were produced by the same processes and probably the same dialmakers, the developments I outline do not relate to bracket clocks.

If even a fraction of the pleasure I derived from writing this book is shared by the reader, it will have been very worth while.

B.L.

Foreword
to the Second Edition

The first edition of this book has been enthusiastically received by a public eager for information about this kind of clock, which was not covered in any other book and still today (1980) has not been dealt with in any books but my own. In describing the typical styles, the first edition covered mainly the cheaper, humbler examples, and may have left the reader with the impression that there were very few better ones. In this new edition some better-quality examples are illustrated too, both of dial painting and of casework.

Since the first edition, too, more facts have come to light, especially on dialmakers, where Roy Gault has made a painstaking investigation and has allowed his findings to be incorporated into my original list for the sake of completeness. The new edition represents the latest research and opinion as far as I personally know it.

The first edition was written in 1972, and eight years on it has been interesting to see the degree to which my initial opinions have stood the test of a longer period of observation and occasional opposing views. Books have since been published (if principally my own) which have made available further facts on some of the makers mentioned. In these cases I have let the wording of the first edition stand, and have added the new facts in an extra paragraph. This has been done deliberately so that the reader can see that the principles of dating by style should not be too greatly affected by new data on the maker's life. Where new research has shown some slight variance with my original datings, I felt it was more honest to leave this to be apparent rather than to revise my datings and let it appear that I was correct all along.

Since the first edition, and largely because of it, there has been a considerable change of attitude on the part of the clock world. No one with any knowledge of clocks would now challenge my view that the clockwork behind japanned dials was no different from that behind the same maker's brass dials, yet when I first suggested this it was regarded as heresy. I could point to writings by 'horologists' who wrote off in ignorance the 'Birmingham-bracket' clocks as poor quality, mass-produced, made-in-Birmingham tickers, when in reality some of the best clockwork ever produced can be found behind Birmingham dials.

Another result of the first edition has been that many a clocklover who previously kept secret his personal fondness for some of these clocks today no longer feels ashamed to admit his liking for them, even in horological circles where 'painted dial' used to be dirty words.

If the first edition has removed some misconceptions and prejudices, I am delighted. Another result has been that with increasing public awareness and interest, prices have rocketed. Inflation has helped this along, obviously, but white dial clock prices have soared way above any inflation rate. In some ways this is a pity, for it keeps many of them out of our financial reach and this affects me as a dealer just as much as, or even more than, the private buyer, because dealers have to raise the finance to keep a stock of them. But it does mean that a clock purchased today will be valued seriously by its purchaser who has had to pay out real money to acquire it, and that we are unlikely ever again to see the terrible neglect and destruction of white dial clocks which took place before about 1970.

Today's high prices also mean that people now consider restoring white dial clocks, a thing undreamed of twenty years ago. Today a small group of skilled dial restorers has grown up who actually understand these clocks and can restore the dials sympathetically, a strong contrast to the heavy-handed 'restorers' of twenty years ago, who meant well but did more harm than good. Inflated prices have, therefore, been beneficial in some ways.

Who knows, one day we may even see the time when museums will actually consider buying white dial clocks. If I am hard on museums it comes as a result of having been scorned for offering 'undesirable Birmingham-ware' to museums who did not notice Birmingham-made movements behind a seventeenth-century London master's dial, or as a result of hearing local masterpieces derided as 'distinctly provincial' whilst London-made mediocrity was, and still is, cherished. I have never been able to adjust to the fact that

I have found more interest and enthusiasm for British white dial clocks in American museums than in British ones.

Thank heavens a new generation of clock enthusiasts is coming along who both appreciate and attempt to understand our clock heritage, including white dial clocks.

B.L.
Nidderdale, 1980

I

Neglect

Until the publication of the first edition of this book, existing horological reference books had told us little or nothing about white dial clocks, except that their authors usually regard them as very inferior country cousins, almost a different species from brass dial longcase clocks. Some authorities say that the white dial appears shortly after the middle of the eighteenth century; some say 1760; some 1770; some 1780. The disturbing thing about this variance is not so much that it indicates a difference of opinion among experts, as that it is really an indication that no one knows.

In a way this is understandable. Many of the standard clock books were written around the turn of the last century, when white dial clocks were only just out of production. At that time this type of clock, which had been in existence just over 100 years, was not old enough to have an antiquarian interest. In just the same way today we hardly think it important enough to write about furnishing objects made in the early twentieth century. They are not antique, not valuable generally, not in demand. They are simply old-fashioned and in that no-man's-land between junk and antique: the sort of thing which our grandparents bought as new for their homes.

In 1894, then, when the first edition of F. J. Britten's *Former Clock and Watchmakers and Their Work* was published ('for more than half a century the standard work on horological history'), brass dial clocks by provincial makers could be bought for very small sums. Few people wanted the white dial ones in this situation. They were dumped in outbuildings, pushed into attics, the cases chopped up for firewood. In the early years of this century second-hand furniture dealers would deliver a white dial clock in perfect order and set it up in one's home for less than £1. In this situation it is not surprising perhaps that Britten did not devote much space to them—maybe half a dozen lines.

Subsequent writers gradually began to include a little information in their books, but the pattern had been set and I cannot recall any book where the author even begins to whet the reader's appetite to own a white dial clock. The precise period at which the white dial clock first appeared was not a problem of great importance then, and does not seem to have been looked at seriously since.

Understandable as this may be, it is none the less surprising when we think a little more about it. One day in the 1760–80 period a man or group of men, or several men independently, had the courage to try to make and sell a clock with a painted dial. It was new, simple, colourful, legible; and it became popular. From that moment the brass dial clock died rapidly. The introduction of the white dial was to prove one of the most important and far-reaching innovations in the history of clockmaking in Britain and America. The white dial enjoyed a period of popularity that lasted 100 years. I know that several reference books state that longcase clocks died out by 1820. Don't believe it! They were still being made even fifty years after that date. In fact, by 1820 they were just reaching their height of popularity.

So great was the impact which the new white dial made on the clock trade, that with many provincial clockmakers the change to white dials was not only rapid but permanent. I have data on the clocks of one particular country clockmaker, typical of thousands of similar men, which show that once he began to use the new type of dial (about 1774 in this case) he instantly dropped the use of brass dials, and very few brass dial clocks by him are known later than the date of his first white dial one. What can be discovered about one clockmaker will no doubt ultimately be discovered about many others, if we take the trouble to investigate.

It seems to me amazing that the introduction of the new white dial has been regarded as a regrettable event by writers about clocks. I can only imagine that this sort of attitude originates from indoctrination through those books on horology which regarded London as the centre of clock design, exerting its influence on the rest of the country. True as this may have been in the earlier periods of clockmaking, it is no longer true in longcase clock production of the later eighteenth century, when it was in the *provinces* that longcase clocks were really popular, with Birmingham as the centre for the new white dial fashion. What London clockmakers did in this direction at that time had little bearing on the designs or fashions popular in the provinces. It is perhaps for this same reason that London writers

2 An interesting, unrestored late dial, from c 1835, the dialmaker unknown. The clockmaker was William Moorehouse of Wetherby. The white dial centre is of the dished (convex) type, surrounded by a brass pipe-like bezel. The paintings outside the brass ring are on an unusual and effective *black* background.

are unsympathetic towards later provincial clock casework, apparently failing to realise that provincial cases of the late eighteenth and early nineteenth centuries fail to resemble earlier London cases simply because they were never intended to resemble them.

It has been, and apparently still is, fashionable for writers to glorify the brass dial and to decry the painted one because it is not made of brass; though the same people do not normally decry the painted moon dial filling the arch of many a brass dial clock. No one seems to have a kind word for the painted dial. No one, that is, except the countless thousands of clockmakers in Britain and America who began to use painted dials in the last quarter of the eighteenth century to the relatively rapid and ultimately complete exclusion of the brass ones. If the appearance of the white dial did mark the beginning of the end, then that end was almost 100 years in coming, since the painted-dial longcase clock was popular for almost as long as the brass dial one had been. Anyone who looks at a provincial white dial clock of 1800, expecting it to resemble a London brass dial one of fifty years or more earlier, need hardly be surprised at his failure to appreciate it. However, it seems to me to indicate a lack of modesty if such a person ascribes this to an absence of good taste and design in clockmakers and their customers over the best part of a century.

The white dial clock was to find its way into perhaps the majority of homes in the country, cottages and farmhouses as well as mansions and town houses, in a way that the brass dial clock never did. Yet the revolution began so quietly that its originator was soon forgotten, and has remained forgotten. It is unlikely that we shall now establish for certain who made the very first white dial clock, and when. We can, however, make a reasonable assessment of when this took place; I shall cover this aspect in detail later. Occasional attempts were made to produce longcase clocks with dials of true enamel, but because of the problem of applying enamel to such a large surface area, these were not very successful; and when speaking here of producing white dial clocks, I am thinking of the serious and continuous production of them as a regular trade item.

What we are only just beginning to appreciate is that for the vast majority of clockmakers in Britain and America most of the longcase clocks after about 1780 *were* built with white dials. Brass dials after this date were the exception rather than the rule; perhaps not quite so much applicable to makers in the far south, but holding true particularly of the Midlands and northern clockmakers. In one or two regions there persisted a fondness for the single-sheet type of engraved brass and silvered dial, so that late examples of these, outside their normal period—even occasionally up to half a century out of period—do appear. These late ones are found in London, in the West Country (that is the south-west corner of England) and in Scotland, especially western Scotland. It is important to realise that these late examples are exceptions to the national trend, and nationally the brass dial was virtually obsolete by 1790. We now know that the white dial is to a large extent an indication of the period of a clock rather than of the quality. By 1790 the longcase clock had the new type of dial as standard, except in those unusual instances where local demand specified otherwise. Rather than being a cheaper

3 The terminology of brass dials. The features indicated may be met with on brass dials over widely varying periods. *1*, moon dial; *2*, engraved corner decoration; *3*, dotted minutes; *4*, engraved dial centre; *5*, leaf-shaped winding arbor; *6*, curved date aperture; *7*, seconds dial; *8*, chapter ring; *9*, dial plate; *10*, cup and ring turnings; *11*, herring-bone engraving, sometimes called 'wheatear' engraving; *12*, square date-box; *13*, name-plate signature; *14*, matted dial centre; *15*, ringed winding hole; *16*, plain winding arbor; *17*, engraving between spandrels; *18*, half-hour marker; *19*, half-quarter marker; *20*, spandrel; *21*, arch spandrel; *22*, full minute band; *23*, Halifax moon, or halfpenny or penny moon; *24*, arch; *25*, name boss in arch.

21

alternative to the brass dial, we now know that the japanned dials were in fact more costly, but I will deal with that aspect later.

Until very recently white dial clocks have been generally regarded by the trade as cheap 'shipping goods' and sold to dealers from America, Holland, Germany, Scandinavia and Australia. Some buyers, such as the Americans, buy in vast numbers to try to fill containers and thereby make shipment as economical as possible. Others, like the Dutch and Swedes, come in their own vans on regular trips every three or four weeks and return home with a dozen or so long-case clocks from each trip, along with other antique and semi-antique 'décor' items. Only when one begins to imagine the scale on which this takes place throughout Britain does one appreciate how many hundreds of clocks leave the country every week, probably for ever.

'Why', people often ask, 'do so many white dial clocks go abroad?' There are three reasons. First, the grandfather clock was essentially a British product. While some other countries made them with their own national variations, nowhere in the world were they made on the same vast scale as in Britain, where almost every village had its own clockmaker or clockseller; and nowhere in Britain were so many made as in the north of England.

Second, being more uncommon in these other countries, British clocks fetch a better price there than here, which situation is also helped by the higher cost of living in many of the importing countries. Therefore there is plenty of room for profit, despite costs of transport and duties. Third, and this is perhaps the main reason, white dial clocks (the main type to be exported) simply have not had the same popular appeal here in the present day as the brass dial ones.

Foreign buyers seem to go especially for white dial clocks, partly because they are cheaper than brass dial ones, and because they can probably get a similar price at home for either type. Hence they prefer the type with the higher profit. The American public tends to prefer painted dials to brass dials anyway.

Price trends in recent years have reflected a greater appreciation of white dial clocks by the public at large. I like to think that this book (still the only one on this subject) has played some part in removing older misguided attitudes towards them. As public awareness in Britain grows, there seems to be a falling-off in overseas shipment. The situation today is very often that the overseas bulk buyer takes the junk that the informed buyer here would not want. Most overseas buyers buy them 'by the yard' with no attempt to ascertain genuineness or originality; as long as it is cheap, ticks and looks like a clock, they usually neither know nor care whether it is a genuine 200-year-old item or was cobbled together last week from bits by some backyard bodger. With these kinds of buying criteria we need not worry about any great loss of national heritage. Of course, there are some discriminating buyers from overseas, but not many.

The fact that lack of understanding left many white dial clocks unwanted and therefore cheap, relative to brass dial ones, caused them to be plundered in large quantities over the years as a source of spare parts. If a brass dial clock movement was worn or damaged, it became common practice to replace it with one taken from a white dial clock, and many white dial clocks were spoiled in this way, mostly during the period from about 1890 to 1960, the era of neglect.

Laziness on the part of owners of thirty-hour brass dial clocks caused a great demand for eight-day (white dial) movements for conversion. I know of old-established and highly respected antiques dealers who still today regard thirty-hour clocks as of no use to anyone until converted to eight-day ones, which of course means substituting a totally different 'works' from some other clock and could be regarded as akin to putting Victorian legs on a Queen Anne table. They are not unaware that an eight-day clock is more valuable than a thirty-hour one. If the supposedly respectable dealers will do this, what can we expect of the disreputable? Fortunately, as clocks get more costly, it seems likely that the public will become better informed and therefore less gullible.

Probably the biggest single way in which the white dial clock has suffered is in having had its cases stolen, in the same way as its eight-day movements have been, for the benefit of the brass dial clock. It is simply not correct to imagine that in its day the white dial clock was regarded by the clocksellers or clockbuyers as in any way inferior to the contemporary brass dial one. The white dial clocks were the newest and most fashionable kind. This contemporary view of its equality, indeed of its superiority, is supported by the fact that it was made to accompany some really splendid cases. Over the years very many of these fine cases have been taken to rehouse brass dial clocks to satisfy the modern customer's desire for fashion. It happened a great deal in the past and it still happens frequently today.

Eventually a good white dial clock in a good original case will be a vastly rarer thing to obtain than a similar brass dial one. Then

4 A very fine mahogany pagoda-top case dating from c 1810–20, and housing a clock by Robert Rowntree of York. Many cases of this high-quality type and style were later divorced from their clocks in order to accommodate brass dial clocks that were regarded as 'better' by an ignorant public.

perhaps the situation will begin to reverse itself, and cases will be stolen from brass dial clocks to be put onto white dial ones. Not that I would advocate that practice either!

These then have been the fates of many white dial clocks over the years, and some of these practices continue. There are signs now that the tide is turning, and rapidly, as antique clocks become scarcer almost by the hour. People today are much more conscious of their responsibilities towards the past, and there is a far deeper and more widespread interest today than at any time before in antique objects of all kinds. Perhaps the impersonal nature of modern mass-produced goods causes us to find greater satisfaction in and affection for the works of earlier times; we share something of the pride and pleasure which a craftsman took in his work. White dial clocks are now beginning to take their rightful place in the scheme of things; while few will appeal to the old school of 'collectors', vast numbers will find appreciative homes among this wider public which loves antiques for their own sake, and also *cares*.

2

The First White Dials

Before the introduction of the white dial, all longcase clocks in this country had dials made of brass, usually with separate features such as chapter ring, name boss, etc, superimposed on the dial sheet. The whole dial was made of brass; but in general any engraved part was silvered over when new. The effect was that the dark, 'blued' steel hands (one seldom sees original *brass* hands on a brass dial clock, by the way) stood out well against the silvered background, on which engraved details such as hours and minutes were filled with black wax for clarity. This was the form of the longcase clock from its very beginnings.

Later in its development, however, a new type appears. On this the dial is made out of a single sheet of brass with all the details engraved on it, and the whole sheet silvered over—a one-piece silvered dial. This appears always to have been regarded as a natural development of the ordinary brass dial clock, arriving on the scene late in the eighteenth century, though not many authorities seem anxious to suggest a date for its appearance. It does appear round about the same time as the white (painted) dial clock, and at a distance the two resemble each other superficially.

The one-piece silvered dial seems to be largely a product of the south of England. I have seen very few north-country ones of this type and period. Here I am thinking of normal longcase clocks, not austere regulators and regulator-types of clock, which are usually timepieces (ie non-striking) only, and which often have circular dials. It should be explained that a regulator was a clock made particularly for its precision in timekeeping, often with complicated escapements for greater accuracy or special devices to counteract the influences of temperature changes. Regulators were sometimes made by the clockmaker for his personal use in setting the timekeeping of his other clocks. Sometimes they were made for offices and public buildings, for scientists and astronomers, or wherever extreme accuracy

5   A good high-quality early dial after restoration, the dial having no identification marks. The clock is by Robert Swan of Bridlington and probably dates from c 1780. The calendar is an engraved and silvered brass disc, which makes this an early experimental dial. The globes are unusual being cut at the equator.

was especially demanded. By their very nature they were uncommon items, and while white dial regulators do exist, not only are they seldom met with, they are far from typical of clockmaking of the period. For this reason I have not illustrated one in this book, where my aim is to show what is normal and typical.

I show as an example of the one-piece silvered dial a clock by Daniel Dickerson of Eye, made about 1780 (see page 28).

As far as I am aware, those books which mention the subject at all have suggested that the painted dial began its life as an imitation in cheaper form of the one-piece silvered dials of the Dickerson kind.

6 A single-sheet brass dial, the surface engraved and silvered, by Daniel Dickerson of Eye, c 1780. This type of dial is sometimes called a one-piece dial. There is a close resemblance between these and some types of early white dial.

This is an understandable view. Longcase clocks had always had dials of brass, and it is perhaps reasonable to assume that such a clock with a dial in a new material succeeded those in the traditional material. This view is logical but it has not been proved; and it is one with which I certainly disagree.

Such a view of course fails to take note of the fact that the one-piece dial was almost exclusively a product of the south of England. I am not suggesting that the one-piece silvered dial was unknown in the north; but it was very uncommon there. In this situation how could northern clockmakers readily take to the painted dial as a cheaper *alternative* to a type of clock virtually unknown to them? That the northern clockmakers did take to the painted dial, there is absolutely no doubt. What I would question is whether they took to it as an *alternative* form.

As we shall see, the white dial was already being marketed by 1772. The question I am raising is whether the one-piece silvered dial was known as early as that. I personally do not know of examples so early, and certainly most of the one-piece brass dials one sees are of the 1790–1800 period or later. It is possible that *after* the introduction (about 1770–2) of the painted dial, there began an immediate attempt on the part of dial engravers to copy this new white dial style but in the traditional material (brass) and thereby to retain the engraving work which they had always been accustomed to receive from the entire clockmaking industry. Faced with the possible loss of such a large portion of their business, the engravers could naturally be expected to retaliate by attempting to make dials which looked like the painted ones but which had the durability of brass.

As to which type came first we cannot be sure, unless a one-piece silvered brass dial comes to light that can be proved to be a pre-1770 one. Neither is it very important which type came first, except in relation to the stigma which has always been attached to the painted dial clock: that of its being an 'inferior imitation' of a brass dial one. It is this accusation (without trial or proof) which has led to an almost total lack of interest in white dial clocks, on the part of informed clock enthusiasts, for almost 200 years.

If, as a parallel example, I could prove that the one-piece silvered dial was in fact an imitation of a painted one, that would be no argument for rejecting one-piece silvered dial clocks as being unworthy of attention. It would seem to me to be much more sensible to treat each type independently of the other, for certainly the dial of both types is simply covering up examples of the *same* kind of clockwork. At the time we are concerned with (1770–90), I do not think anyone would suggest that the movements of ordinary longcase clocks would be anything but similar, regardless of which form of dial they were attached to.

The cases of longcase clocks from, say, 1770 onwards, were no better on brass dial clocks than on white dial ones. If, therefore, both brass dial and white dial longcase clocks from 1770 onwards have movements which are largely indistinguishable one from another, and if they differ only in so far as the dial is concerned, then surely to class either one as superior to the other is to judge in a superficial way.

I find it very difficult to accept that the beauty of engraving surpasses the beauty of painting. If this were so, would not every home be filled with engravings rather than paintings? In fact, the popularity of paintings greatly surpasses that of engravings and always has done, and this very factor may have been one reason why the painted dial clock rapidly replaced the brass dial one.

As I see it, the white dial originated as a new type of clock dial which not only served its purpose in the same way that the traditional brass dial had done, but in fact did the job better. So well did this new dial perform its function, that it rapidly outgrew the brass dial in popularity to the extent of the eclipse of the previous kind. Surely if it had done its job less satisfactorily than the brass dial, it would never have caught on at all.

Before outlining the known facts I must make reference to an example of a white dial clock supposedly made in 1761. In his book *Chats on Old Clocks* published in 1917, Arthur Hayden illustrates a white dial clock 'dated' 1761. It has a most unusual dial of oval shape. One of the few such that I have seen is that by James Lomax of Blackburn. Of course, a dial of this type could have been made in any shape at all. Perhaps tradition and commonsense established that the white dial was most often made in square and arched shape, and somewhat less frequently in circular shape. I say commonsense, since a square and even arched dial is far simpler for the casemaker to deal with than is an oval, egg-shaped one of the type which Hayden shows, or even a circular one. The oval dial illustrated by Hayden bears the name of Marston of Salop. The date of 1761 is claimed for it by virtue of a brass plaque on the case door bearing this date, but it should be borne in mind that a clock dated genuinely by a plaque attached to it is very rare, and evidence of this kind should be regarded as doubtful, in the absence of other proof of the clock's age.

The clock by Marston of Salop is typical in its case and dial features (except for the dial shape) of about 1780–5. The only known information on the maker is that he was listed in the directory of 1795. Those authorities who give his date as 1761 do so on the basis of the clock shown by Hayden. I would put the date no earlier than about 1780, and certainly it is *not* proof of a white dial clock's having been made as early as 1761.

Some longcase clocks exist which have dials of true enamel, but they are exceedingly rare. This real enamel is a white opaque glass fused on to thin copper at red heat. True enamel dials had long ago appeared in watches and, I am told, by 1750 they were standard.

7 Oval dial from the eight-day clock by James Lomax of Blackburn made c 1790, dial by James Wilson of Birmingham. The double dot-and-dash borders to the flowers are typical of Wilson dials. In restoration the globes have not been re-penned with maps. Hands appear to be original, of non-matching steel pattern.

On longcase clock dials, however, enamel was not a success because of the very large dial areas involved. Both sides of the dial had to be coated to prevent distortion, and some panelling to give strength was desirable, though this was not possible for longcase dials.

These rare examples of true enamel dials seem to be in the period 1770–80. One exists by John Green of London, having the arched portion made separately and then attached to the square, presumably to reduce the size of the individual sheets for enamelling. Another interesting example is thought to have been made by Richard Comber of Lewes: the name has worn off over the years. Made about

1770, it has a three-train movement chiming the quarter hours on twelve bells and striking the hours on a thirteenth bell. It is basically a brass dial clock with corner spandrels, but it has a circular, ena- melled centrepiece for the numerals and a smaller, similar one in the arch for a strike/silent feature. In other words it reflects the begin- nings of the move away from the brass dial to the more legible white form. This clock is an attempt at combining the best features of both the brass dial and the white dial. From the photographs I have seen of it, it is a superb clock in a similar case far above average and must have been made for a wealthy customer. The *painted* white dial clock on the other hand had enormous potential because it was reasonably cheap to produce.

Recently I saw a clock combining the two kinds of dial in a dif- ferent way. This was an eight-day, arched dial clock by Dollif Rolli- son of Halton, near Leeds, Yorkshire. The dial sheet, painted in a Chinese design, was deep red with gold decoration in the manner of a red lacquered cabinet. Superimposed on this dial were a *brass* chapter ring, a brass date ring and a brass seconds ring. The appear- ance was most effective, and this seems to be a different approach to the same problem of combining the best features of both brass and white dials. Unfortunately, no dialmaker's name was marked. The clock was probably made about 1775. Such a combination of dial types is very unusual, but was sometimes found in America.

It may even be that this was a normal brass dial clock, which the owner later decided should be 'modernised' by having the dial sheet japanned over, and its spandrels and chapter ring put back again.

All we can deduce is that, while attempts were made at true enamel, such dials were so unsatisfactory or perhaps so costly to produce in commercial numbers that the idea was soon dropped. Many owners of white dial clocks describe the dials as being 'enamel', 'porcelain', 'Devonport porcelain', 'Battersea enamel', and so on. The vast majority of these are mistaken descriptions by the owners, perhaps not surprisingly so. In 1799 the famous cabinetmaking concern, Gil- low's of Lancaster, ordered a thirty-hour clock dial and movement from Newby's of Kendal, at a cost of £2 11s 0d, to go into a case they were making; and they describe it as a 'china dial'. Newby's would almost certainly have obtained this dial from the Birmingham manufacturers, as I shall explain later. These mistaken identifications simply show how realistic these painted dials were 'in imitation of enamel'. Perhaps such descriptions as 'china dial' were deliberately inaccurate sales names used to make this new cheaper dial seem to be a more delicate and more choice item than the term 'painted' would suggest. Longcase clocks with true enamel dials are so rare that the known examples can probably be counted on the fingers of one hand.

The emphasis in this book is upon white dial clocks, so let us imagine that we are looking at clocks of this kind for the first time. Let us further imagine that we have never read anything about them before.

The story begins in Birmingham in 1772. In that year the *Birmingham Gazette* carried the following advertisement in its issue of 28 September:

White Clock Dials
Osborne and Wilson, manufacturers
of White Clock Dials in Imitation of Enamel, in a Manner entirely new, have opened a Warehouse at No. 3, in Colmore-Row, Birmingham, where they have an Assortment of the above-mentioned Goods. Those who favour them with their Orders may depend upon their being executed with the utmost Punctuality and Expedition.
N.B. The Dial Feet will be rivetted in the Dials, and such Methods used as will enable the Clock Makers to fix them to the Movements.

This is the earliest indisputable evidence I know of regarding the making of white dials. It is reasonable to assume that white dials cannot have been made for long before this advertisement appeared. If they had, Osborne would hardly have been able to describe them as being made 'in a Manner entirely new'. We can assume, then, that white dial clocks cannot have been made much earlier than 1770, even 1772. Further evidence in support of this argument is that no white dial clock is yet known which can be proved to have been made before 1772.

The last line of the advertisement is an interesting one, in that an explanation is given that the dial feet will be riveted into the dials, yet in such a way that they can be attached to the movements without difficulty. Of course the dial feet *had* to be fixed to the dials *before* they were 'enamelled', so that the ends of them were hidden by being covered with the paint finish. On a brass dial clock the feet could be fixed by the clockmaker anywhere into the dial where they best fitted in with the movement frontplate. Very often the ends of the feet met the brass dial behind the chapter ring and so were hidden.

8 Head and shoulders of an eight-day clock of c 1790 by Richard Boyfield of Melton Mowbray, Leicestershire, the dial by James Wilson of Birmingham. The mahogany cross-banding and dog-tooth mouldings (dentil mouldings) make this oak case a handsome example.

The difficulty with ready-fixed dial feet was that they might fit in with the movement at an awkward spot, where they were perhaps in the way. To set their customers' minds at rest on this point, Osborne & Wilson specify that there will be no problem in this respect. They do not say how, but it must have been done by using a 'falseplate', which is an intermediate plate-fixing between dial and movement. The falseplate is explained more fully later in this book, but it is interesting to note that by no means all the dialmakers who followed on after Osborne & Wilson used falseplates, at least not all the time, as one sees considerable numbers of dials without falseplates for long after 1770. Perhaps it was that dials without falseplates (ie with long standard dial feet fitting directly to the movement) were supplied by those dialmakers who also supplied the movement to go with them.

Five years later, Osborne & Wilson decided to part company. In the *Birmingham Gazette* for 29 September 1777 they announce that the partnership is being dissolved and that Wilson will carry on alone:

> Birmingham Sept. 29. 1777.
> The Partnership lately subsisting between Messrs. T. Osborne and J. Wilson, Manufacturers of Clock Dial Plates, was on the 27th Instant, dissolved; of which the Public are requested to take Notice; and also that this Branch of Business will be carried on by Wilson alone, at No. 11, Great-Charles-Street, Birmingham, who hopes for the Continuance of the Favours of his Friends and the Public ... All Persons having any Demands on the said Partnership, are desired to send an Account of the same, as above; and all Persons who stand indebted to the aforesaid Partnership, are desired to pay the same.

> *Clock Dials*
> The Partnership between Thomas Hadley Osborne and James Wilson, Manufacturers of Clock Dials, is this Day mutually dissolved:— They have authorised Mr. John Walker, of Colmore-Row, to receive and discharge all Debts due to, and by, the said Partnership.
> Birmingham Dec. 24, 1777.

It was, maybe, that Osborne was failing in health. However, in the issue of 19 January 1778, we learn that Osborne has decided to carry on after all:

> T. HADLEY OSBORNE, thinks it necessary to aquaint the Public, that he intends to carry on the Manufactory of CLOCK DIALS as usual, when the Favours of his Friends will be punctually attended to, and gratefully acknowledged by their Obedient humble Servant,
> T. Hadley Osborne.
> No. 20, Cherry Orchard, Birmingham.

> JAMES WILSON respectfully informs his Friends and the Public, That he continues the Clock Dial Manufactory, (late Osborne and Wilson's) at No. 11, Great-Charles-Street, where Orders will be gratefully received, and executed in the most expeditious and complete Manner, by their obedient Servant, Birmingham, Jan. 5, 1778.
> JAMES WILSON

Evidently this indicates a change of heart on the part of Osborne, since the earlier notice said that Wilson would carry on *alone*. It would seem that by now a once amicable partnership was turning sour; and henceforth these men must have been determined rivals. Osborne then continued his own business, but not for long, as he seems to have died in 1779, after which time his widow, Ann, continued for some years.

James Wilson, however, appears to have prospered until his death in 1809. Recently I was able to track down his will, dated 20 March 1809 and proved at London 15 June 1810. In it he describes himself as a clock *dialmaker* (not a clockmaker), and this appears to be confirmation of the fact that he supplied dials only, not complete clocks. He seems to have been a widower as he mentions no wife. His two daughters and one son were minors in 1809. Among those appointed trustees and executors was one Edward Simpson, japanner, a man who produced applied painted decoration of the type used on a white dial clock. Osborne & Wilson,* then, probably without realising it, started a revolution in the clock world. We cannot say for certain that they were the very first white dial makers, but they are the first we know about. Instead of becoming famous their names were forgotten the year they died, and it is doubtful whether even one clock enthusiast in a hundred has ever heard of them.

Today this situation is changing however. In the past ten years a great many clock enthusiasts have come to know the names of Osborne and Wilson, and indeed of many of the other more prolific dialmakers. (At the risk of sounding immodest, I feel tempted to point out that this could only have come about through the first edition of this book!) A whole new generation of clock enthusiasts has sprung up, keen devotees of the white dial. To these people Osborne and Wilson stand out as just as important a landmark in the history of the white dial clock as Ahasuerus Fromanteel did in the history of British clocks when he introduced the pendulum in 1658.

---

* Since I began writing this book, my attention has been drawn by Mr Kenneth Roberts of Bristol, Connecticut—himself author of several works on American horology—to an article in *Antiques* in September 1931 by Penrose R. Hoopes, entitled 'Osborne & Wilson, Dialmakers'. The article is written with special reference to the use of these dials on American clocks. An article in *Apollo*, vol 48 (1948) by W. A. Seaby also refers to them briefly. I mention these two articles to acknowledge that I am not the first to write about Osborne & Wilson. I believe that Hoopes was mistaken in his assumption that falseplates were introduced to prevent chipping on the dial feet ends, as I shall explain more fully in Chapter 3.

3

British Dialmakers

Most people are aware that the clockmaker did not make the case: he bought it ready-made from a cabinetmaker. What is not quite so well known is that he did not usually make the dial either. Dialmaking was a specialist business and it was seldom the clockmaker's own province. This applies to brass clock dials, where the engraving was done by a specialist engraver, possibly working to the clockmaker's instructions. Engraving was a highly skilled trade, and in relatively few instances would a clockmaker also have the skill to engrave his own dials.

Now when the white dial clock appears about 1770, from its very beginning dial supplying is a separate trade. Because dialpainting is so obviously quite distinct from clockmaking, many people are already aware that such dials are 'factory' made, and that they simply had the name of the retailer painted on them. But they often regard this as an indication of the inferiority of the product, being quite unaware that brass dials could also be said to be 'factory' made, in just the same way that pinion wire, spandrels, dialplates, hands, and even complete clock movements could all be bought in by the retailer from the trade suppliers certainly by the 1770s and for a good number of years before that too. By a 'factory' is meant a specialist workshop, the size being not so important as the fact that they were specialist component suppliers.

When they first made the new white dial, the men who had the ingenuity to produce it also hit upon another idea to help sell more of their products. This was to sell the dials in such a way that almost any normal movement would fit them, regardless of who had made or supplied the movements. In other words, the smaller clockmakers in country areas, the men who worked alone or who, by traditional methods, made much of their own clockwork, could now if they wished buy these new white dials in just the same way as could the larger town clockmakers who may have been using standard–sized movements (that is, 'factory' made movements). The smaller countryside makers were of course the men in whom true 'craftsmanship' lingered by virtue of their making much of their own product; while the larger town makers, who employed several apprentices and journeymen, merely kept a supervisory eye on their workers, and might never have laid a finger on the product which bore their names. This universal fitting was achieved by use of an iron 'falseplate'.

The traditional dial (white or brass) fitted on to the frontplate of the movement by means of three or four feet of about 1 in in length. The disadvantage of these of course is that in trying to fit any movement to such a dial which was not purely designed for it, one finds the feet cannot always fit into the frontplate because the movement pillars (or some other part of the movement itself) are in the way. By attaching a falseplate between dial and frontplate this problem is overcome. The falseplate is already fixed to the dial when supplied, naturally on shorter ($\frac{1}{2}$in or so) dial feet. Then by drilling holes at any convenient positions into the falseplate one can attach almost any conventional movement without problems.

The falseplate system of fitting the dials has another advantage in that there is less tendency for the short-fitting feet to bend and thereby chip off enamel at the point where they are attached—something which not infrequently happened with the longer-fitting feet of dials without falseplates, especially when in transit (see opposite). This advantage of the shorter dial feet preventing chipping was only a secondary one. It was not, as is sometimes stated, the main reason for the use of falseplates. Osborne & Wilson make this clear in their advertisement of 1772: that the main purpose of the falseplate is for ease of attaching the movement. Further evidence that the primary purpose of the falseplate was not for the prevention of chipping can be seen from the fact that falseplates appear only on eight-day clocks and never (or exceedingly rarely) on thirty-hour ones of the same period—this despite the fact that chipping is far more likely to occur on the normal three feet of a thirty-hour dial as opposed to the normal four feet of an eight-day one. The falseplate was attached to the dial to accept the movement more easily, not, as is sometimes incorrectly stated, attached to the movement to accept any dial.

The benefit as far as we are concerned in studying the age of clocks rather than the technicalities of them is that the falseplates very often have the name of the dialmakers cast or perhaps stamped into them.

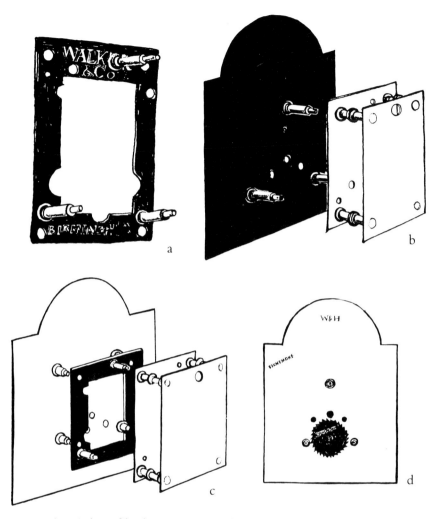

9   a A typical iron falseplate seen removed from its dial. The name of the dialmaker was usually boldly impressed into the falseplate.

b Exploded diagram to show the method of fitting of dial and movement *without* a falseplate, in this example by means of three long dial feet.

c Exploded diagram showing the relationship of dial, falseplate, and movement. A falseplate dial has short dial feet.

d A dial seen from the back and showing the positions where one might normally see the dialmaker's name impressed.

Many were boldly impressed with letters perhaps half an inch tall. Much can be discovered about some of these dialmakers, most of whom worked in Birmingham. The falseplates can often therefore be of assistance in dating a clock.

One point I had best clarify before going further. It is not true, as is sometimes stated, that the falseplate dial will fit *any* movement. This depends ultimately on the position of the winding squares and hands in relation to each other, since the four points involved must relate to each other at the same angles and positions in the movement as the four holes in the dial (hole for seconds hand, hole for main clock hands, two holes for the two winding squares). This applies only on an eight-day clock, as on a thirty-hour clock there is only one hole, that for the main hands, there being no winding holes on a thirty-hour clock and very rarely a seconds hand. On an eight-day dial, then, four holes must line up with four points on the movement; on a thirty-hour dial only one hole must line up. In practice a falseplate dial will fit many types of movement, while the normal dial without a falseplate will fit only the movement which was made for it (or one very similar to it).

The 'problem' of fitting together a falseplate dial and a movement depends on which came first, the chicken or the egg. If we assume the clockmaker began with the dial, and then built his movement so that it would fit it, there is no problem. If we think of the clockmaker starting with the movement and hoping to come by a dial which will fit, then we are beset with all kinds of difficulties—on brass dial clocks as well as white dial ones.

In fact we now know that the clockmaker began with the dial—from the method whereby he allowed his customer to select the dial of his choice from his available range prior to building a movement for it (or fitting a pre-built one, but pre-purpose-built). This was the commonsense way of going about it and is supported by evidence that clockmakers carried a stock of white dials far in excess of their stock (if any) of movements.

Birmingham was the main centre for the manufacture of white dials. The dial is basically a sheet of iron of the required shape: this generally followed the traditional shape of brass dials—ie square or square with an arched top, which I refer to as an arched dial, though sometimes they are called 'break-arch dials' or, less appropriately, 'broken-arch dials'. 'Arched dial' was the term used in the eighteenth century by the dialmakers themselves, which would seem to be

10 Simple oak case c 1820 of the second Palliser clock (see page 171). This hood style is known as a break-arch top. The door on this example fits inside its frame rather than overlapping it, an unusual treatment. The base looks large in proportion to the rest of the case, but this is probably exaggerated in the photograph. Height about 7 ft.

another good reason for us to keep it. One commonly sees circular dials, which were popular in south Yorkshire, Derbyshire, Leicester-shire, Scotland, and London in the nineteenth century.

The iron sheet was treated on the face side with a red-lead type of base-paint, presumably to prevent rust. The back was often painted black, sometimes red. One can sometimes see the runs of red-lead or white paint spilling over on top of the black backing. Then the dial face was painted white, probably by being dipped into a vat of prepared paint. It was not enamel in the true sense, as on the dial of a watch. It was a paint of a hard and durable nature baked on by a heat process. Whatever state of deterioration these dials may now be in, one very rarely seems to see the white background *worn* off. It sometimes chips off, it sometimes shells off through rust, but it never seems to wear off with normal use.

A few early white dials, perhaps of an experimental nature, were made of brass, not iron. These sometimes have falseplates too. With these japanned brass dials the backs were usually left untreated. I do not know which concerns made these, but they were obviously specialist japanners. Moon wheels and calendar wheels for iron dials were usually made of brass, though occasionally one sees an iron moon disc. We have to be careful to avoid confusing a japanned dial on a brass baseplate with a brass dial clock which was later japanned over.

Examination of almost any English dial will reveal traces of white base-paint having spilled through all the holes during the dipping process, as well as lapping over at the edges. This illustrates that the vital holes for winding squares, seconds, calendar, etc were drilled prior to japanning, not afterwards (but see Chapter 14 on American dials for further discussion of this point).

The painted scenes superimposed on this white background, and the painted numerals, were obviously of a far less durable finish. One does see these wearing off, the numbers especially. It is confusing to call such a dial an enamel dial, and similarly confusing to call it a painted dial, though both terms are frequently used to mean just the same thing as a white dial. The makers themselves referred to it as a white dial, and this is probably a further indication (as we shall see later) that the earliest dials were of the all-white or largely white kind.

Before I list the names of known dialmakers, I must explain one or two points about the sources of this information and the dates, since this is vital to an understanding of how to use the list. Most of the dates for these men come from directories, and because of this they do not indicate either the beginning or the end of a man's career. The fact that Christopher Wright is known to have been working from 1835 to 1845 does not mean that he could not have worked before 1835 and after 1845. It normally means that he is listed for the first time in the 1835 directory and not in the previous one of 1830. He could possibly have been there by 1831, or even before then, if by any chance he had been omitted from the earlier directory.

Quite possibly people like Wright of Birmingham were subject to erroneous entries in directories, and without the convenience of twentieth-century communications it was probably difficult to have such errors corrected. I know of instances of clockmakers still being listed in directories two or three years after they had died. It is therefore essential always to appreciate that lists of this type are only a guide and that the dates given are not definite.

Sometimes the falseplates themselves have no names on them and in these cases the dialmaker's name is often found stamped into the back of the dial itself, usually in the top left-hand corner, looking from the back. Sometimes this is punched at the back of the arch centre. Now at first glance many dials show no signs of having a name stamped into them on the reverse. But very often the reverse is covered with a layer of thick black paint, so thick that it can easily obscure such a stamping, and sometimes the stamped name can just be made out faintly beneath the paint and rust.

On dials with an aperture date (ie a painted date disc showing through an aperture) the back of the date disc is very often stamped too. The anonymous dial of a Dawlish (Devon) clockmaker is stamped this way on both the dial and the date disc—made by Wright's of Birmingham (see over). Some dials have unstamped falseplates, unstamped datewheels and no stamping on the dial itself. Perhaps some dialmakers did not care to leave their marks.

On the subject of unstamped dials another possible explanation occurs to me, but one which is rather difficult to investigate. When a dial was being made, prior to painting the front and back were interchangeable. The side eventually to be the dial face was coated at least twice with various paint layers prior to the application of coloured paint. On those dials which are name stamped, the name is usually in a corner or in the arch. If the white background were applied to the wrong side (ie the side with the name-stamping on)

11 Unrestored dial in very worn condition from a clock by a maker in Dawlish, Devon, c 1835. The hour hand is broken on this original matching pair in brass. The dialmakers were Wright's of Birmingham, their imprint being punched into the dial back and the calendar wheel back.

this name would be obscured in the process and the slight impression remaining would be hidden by the final hand-painted details. In other words, many of the apparently unstamped dials may in fact have names *beneath* the dial surface. It is a theory which is difficult to test, as one cannot scrape down dial faces to find the answer. But at least it is a theory worth considering. It seems to me more of a possibility than that a dialmaking firm did not bother to mark its products with identification (and therefore advertising) marks of some sort.

By no means all dials had falseplates. They seem to be more frequently found on eight-day clocks; very rarely on thirty-hour clocks. In fact, I know of no example of a falseplate on a thirty-hour clock, except on those where dummy winding holes were used, and these, whilst thirty-hour clocks, used eight-day dials. As I have already said, thirty-hour clocks were less of a problem, having only a single hole in the dial. If we assume that movements were built to suit the pre-purchased dial rather than dials being bought to fit to pre-made movements, then it was an easier task fitting one to the other, whether of the eight-day or thirty-hour type. It would seem to me from records I have examined concerning the stocks of two northern clockmakers that this was the system operated, a stock of dials being held and movements made up to fit the dial of a customer's choice.

It seems possible that most early eight-day dials were sold with falseplates, to encourage the smaller clocksellers, who still made their own movements, to use them. Later on, particularly after about 1830, one seems to see fewer falseplates on dials. Maybe the later ones were sold as complete clocks—dials and movements together— in which case, of course, the need for a universal fitting was removed. I must not make too much of this point, as it is one where further research is needed before a positive solution can be established; but it can be said with certainty that many early eight-day clocks have falseplates and many late ones do not. It is not unusual to come across very early examples of white dials without falseplates, often it seems at the start of the white dial period and perhaps even before the false-plate system became widely used.

Birmingham was not the only centre where dials were made, but it was the main centre. At one time I found it very hard to accept that local clocksellers in remote parts of the Yorkshire Dales, for example, would even dream of sending halfway across the country for their dials when there were dialmakers nearer to home. But I know from studying many white dial clocks that they did buy Birmingham dials. As we shall see in the chapter on white dial clocks in America (Chapter 14) the Birmingham dialmakers could draw in orders from much further afield than Yorkshire, and they shipped their dials not only halfway across Britain but halfway across the world. This fact must be a measure of the successful selling techniques of such concerns as the Osbornes, the Finnemores and the Wilsons whose falseplates one sees frequently. How many engravers of brass clock dials could claim to have sent regular consignments of engraved dials across the Atlantic? Was there even one?

It must also be largely because of this centralised industry that the orderly progression in dialpainting styles took place. If local artists

12 This photograph shows the back of an eleven-inch thirty-hour dial of c 1785 from a clock by Hepton of Northallerton. It shows two of the three long feet typical of a thirty-hour dial and the method by which it attaches to the movement, which is of plate-framed type with an unusual system of pin-wheel striking, using a variation of the more usual notched countwheel. Individual characteristics such as this are proof that the clockmaker was still making his own clocks, not simply buying in pre-made parts. The main purpose of this illustration, however, is to show the tiny dialmaking processing form stuck on the white paint stripe behind the dial. The black figure 4 may have had a temporary significance during manufacture.

here and there throughout the length and breadth of the country had all been busy painting dials, there could be no steady development in dial styles, but an absolute hotchpotch of them expressing the whims of each individual artist.

We cannot be certain that all dials were sold in a fully finished state. They could have been sold numbered and not painted. They could have been sold as blank white sheets. It is likely, however, that the majority were sold fully finished, as this is consistent with the orderly progression of painting styles, which I shall examine in detail later.

I discovered a dialmaker's order form, pasted on the back of a dial of c 1785 by Hepton of Northallerton, Yorkshire; this suggests that the type of painted decoration was specified in the order from the clockmaker to the dialmaker, thereby supporting the idea that the dials were sold fully finished.

In all I have since come across perhaps seven or eight examples of these printed dialmakers' order forms. Mostly the makers of the dials were unknown, but two were on dials positively identified as being made by James Wilson of Birmingham. It may be that these forms were used only by Wilson—we do not know. The printed forms are very small, maybe half an inch by an inch and a half, and are ruled into tiny boxes giving details of what seem to be lettering instructions. Because of the tiny size, the years of dirt over them and also the fading of the ink-written information, I have not yet managed to read one fully. Attempts at cleaning the paper label usually result in the ink being further erased or smudged or the paper rubbed away, making the problem more difficult. However, from what I have been able to decipher, the labels contain processing instructions at the dial factory, a sort of job-ticket, presumably stuck on at the start of its journey on the production line. Generally a casual brush-stroke of white base-paint (measuring about four inches long by two inches wide) is striped on the blackened dial reverse (probably to draw attention to it) and the label is stuck casually in the middle of this whitened strip, apparently using the wet paint as an adhesive. An impression of such a label is shown in the figure below.

The sort of information given seems to have been instructions to the artists on the colour and style of designs to go on the dial, corners, arch, etc. The one on the Hepton dial (actual size on right) reads as follows:

Arch				Sq. y.	
	straight	moon			
	gilt	common			
	painted	name			
	(illegible)	month			
	(illegible)	sil: strike			
	(illegible)	(blank)			
	gilt	(blank)			
	painted	(blank)			

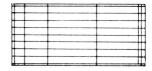

These words were hand-written in ink inside the printed boxes but whether these instructions represent the choice of features from which the required ones were to be selected is not clear. One might think that only the desired features would be penned in, but apparently not so, because this dial was an eleven-inch square thirty-hour dial with gold corner decoration, no colour at all, and curved mouth-type calendar aperture—no question of an arch with moon or common, no question of strike/silent feature. It seems therefore that this list showed the alternatives, eg arch to be moon or common type. But on this order form there were no obvious markings, ticks, etc, to indicate which of the features were to apply in this instance. How the job-ticket system worked is still a matter of conjecture, but at least we know there was a system.

The way I imagine it worked is along the lines of, for instance, the print-publishing concerns who employed colourists. In the famous Currier and Ives print shop the prints were hand-coloured by a dozen or so young ladies. They worked at long tables as a sort of production line with a model set up in the centre which they could all see. Each artist applied only one colour, the first perhaps pink, the second green, and so on, passing the print along the row. At the end of the row a supervisor would check it over and add any final touches. That is how print colouring worked and that is the way I picture dialpainting in the dial factories, but it is only my impression.

Somewhere identifiable dials must survive with job-tickets which are clearly legible (with a magnifying glass perhaps). If readers come across these I would very much like to hear of them as this will help uncover how the system worked.

At this time retail clockmakers or clocksellers would not generally make up a large selection of clocks to sell from a showroom. Rather they might have the odd one or two ready, and on sale for a chance customer, but normally they would make a clock, or buy one in, for a specific order. They must have had some method of describing to a customer the range of available dials. If this was by means of printed leaflets showing dial patterns, none seem to have survived. Perhaps it is more likely that the customer made his choice from the clockmaker's stock of perhaps a dozen dials and then the movement was made up to suit the clock, bearing in mind any special features requested. Indeed recent research has shown that this is almost certainly the way it worked.

Perhaps an exception to my comment about clockmakers not keeping a large stock is in those instances of men to whom clock-making was a secondary business. There were very many of these. Some clockmakers were shopkeepers having such goods as ironmongery, hardware, umbrellas, barometers, jewellery, silverware, watches of course, rings, cutlery, buckles and fancy goods of this kind. This type of merchandise has long been associated with the clockseller's business; and I do not mean to classify *these* men as part-time clockmakers, although clocks formed only a part of their total trade. Recently I saw a printed label pasted on the inside of a clock door sold about 1830 by Richard Blakeborough of Otley, Yorkshire. It gives an indication of the wide variety of goods handled by a man who appears in the directory as a 'clockmaker'. The list includes: hardware, jewellery, weatherglasses, bottlejacks, ear-rings, thimbles, cutlery, spoons, guns, pistols, pans, kettles, files, saws, hammers and other tools, brushes, copper scales and beams, teatrays both paper (ie papier mâché) and japanned, japanned bread baskets, umbrellas, knobs, escutcheons, locks, keys, hinges, *'stringing & shells for enlaying'* (ie for cabinetwork), walking sticks and canes, fifes, flutes, violin strings, looking-glasses, black lead pencils, rat- and mouse-traps, scythes and sickles, and ... *'the best price given for old gold & silver'*. Many of these items would normally be associated with the stock in a nineteenth-century clockmaker's shop, though such a dealer might seem to us today more appropriately described as a hardware dealer. Richard Blakeborough, however, was not a part-time clockmaker. John Manby of Skipton, Yorkshire (1815–50), sold an equally varied range of goods.

By a part-timer I mean a man whose main occupation left him certain quiet periods, during which he made clocks. Examples I can think of are the farmer-clockmakers, of whom there were many. During the quieter winter months they worked on clocks and perhaps built up a stock which they would take to sell in the markets when the finer spring weather arrived. Men like Will Snow of Padside, near Otley, Yorkshire, and his three clockmaking sons were first and foremost farmers, and clockmakers in their spare time. Some were blacksmiths, seaside boarding-house keepers or cabinetmakers. Men in all kinds of trades made clocks to provide a supplementary income. This is why so many clocksellers appeared in tiny out-of-the-way villages where you might think they would not sell one clock in a year; and the clocks they made need not be in any way inferior to those made by a full-time city clockseller and his employees. This type of farmer-clockmaker would make up stocks ahead of his requirements according to the time he had available.

The fact that many of the examples I illustrate are of Yorkshire clocks is because I have tried to select examples of each particular style, and in some cases could not obtain illustrations from each part of the country of exactly the datable types that I wanted. However, what is true of one area in dial styles is equally true of another, with the proviso that Yorkshire was the largest clockselling county of all, and that white dial clocks were generally more popular in the northern, than in the southern, counties of England. However, because of the main concentration of dialmaking in Birmingham, the styles of dial are not so very different whatever the name of the 'maker' and the town written on them. The chapter on American clocks (Chapter 14) will illustrate this point even further.

But I am not suggesting that dials are the same all over the country at any one time. Southern clocks tend to have smaller dials than northern ones, and their styles progress more slowly in some respects. East Anglia, for instance, seems to have had a liking for the almost-all-white dial, like that by Juler of North Walsham, Norfolk. Such dials occur in Essex too, but would be very unusual on, say, a Yorkshire clock.

What this means of course is that if there were fashions or preferences in certain parts of the country, then the dialmakers must have been wide awake to this fact, and must have known which type of dial would sell in which areas. Alternatively we must assume that each clockmaker specified the dial style each time he placed an order, or else left the supplier to send what he thought was most suitable. Recent research suggests that dial ordering was a bit of a hit-and-miss affair, as we shall see more clearly in Chapter 5.

Another feature is that one never sees the same dial twice—at least I have not done so personally. One sees dials which resemble each other in various ways, sometimes closely, but with some variation in the painted decoration. How much easier it would have been for a 'factory' system to have had people sitting in a row, each one repeating the same design over and over again. They did this in the pottery factories; but not with clocks. Was this done intentionally to make each clock unique? Presumably it was.

In the pottery factories, of course, the designs on many items were

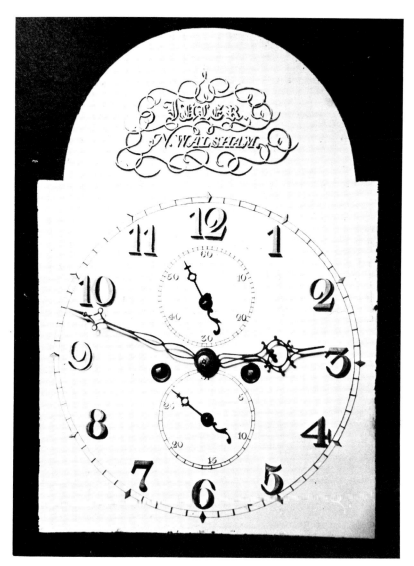

13   Unusual dial of c 1820 from a clock by one of the Juler family of North Walsham, Norfolk. The lettering is in gold with black outline on a plain white background. The dial was made by Finnemores of Birmingham and has a falseplate carrying their imprint. The hour and minute hands look odd and may be replacements; seconds and calendar hands are thought to be original.

transferred on, sometimes with additional hand-painting over the transferred pattern. This is not usually the case with clock dials, though there are exceptions. Very occasionally I have seen a dial with transfer patterns. One I can think of depicted hunting hounds in the corners and a hunting scene in the arch, apparently very casually touched up here and there with hand-colouring, but the transfer had been left plain for the most part. The result was very effective and it is surprising that more dials were not decorated by this method, which must have been simpler and cheaper than hand-painting. Perhaps it was avoided because of this very factor of repetition, and because white dials were intended to be 'one-off' jobs, each one being unique.

While still on the subject of transfers, the following item occurs to me. Surrounding the painted areas on most clocks one can usually see what has been described to me very effectively as a kind of 'halo'. One sees it around a painted corner decoration and also around or sometimes just below the arch scene. It shows up mostly where the painting ends and the white of the dial begins. This halo, which is present on very many painted dials, might seem to suggest that the painted scene is transferred on, as it resembles the sort of halo around a transfer. All it is in fact is the edge of the coat of varnish which was applied over the painted scene to seal it. The varnish discolours at a different rate from that of the white area of the dial, and over the years it becomes a different shade, usually yellower. The varnish was applied originally over the painted areas only, not over the entire dial. This is why the numbering and lettering frequently wear off while the paintings are less prone to erasure.

Many early dials (like those by Osborne and by Wilson) appear not to show this varnish halo, so perhaps these were not varnished. One does see it regularly on those dials with fully-painted corner and arch scenes.

Now some readers, I hope, may challenge my statement that one never sees the same dial twice. Perhaps I had better enlarge on this a little. In the early period (Period One), with a square dial clock particularly, I accept that dials can look very similar to one another. There are often only the painted corner decorations by which to judge. The numbering certainly will be similar, and the corner decoration can often be a single flower such as a pink rose or a spray of flowers. In the 'gold spandrel' type of dial, as in the Terry and Nicholas clocks (see Chapter 6), there is naturally not a great deal of scope for variety. I suppose, therefore, that it is by no means impossible to find two identical dials belonging to Period One.

I was really thinking of the post-1800 arched dial clocks which have painted scenes in the corners and arch. The same themes certainly recur, but in many varied forms and styles, and even two dials showing the same theme will show it with some variations. I said that I hoped some reader might disagree, and I mean that. I am willing to be instructed if anyone can show me photographic evidence of two identical dials. It is impossible for our memories to store visual details of dials and do it correctly. Therefore while we might *think* we have seen the twin of a certain dial before, the comparison of photographs of each would probably show differences. In this connection I have collected many photographs of white dial clocks, and I have no two which are exactly alike. Naturally no man's experience can ever be comprehensive: I am quite ready to be proved wrong, but it must be with photographic evidence.

4

Names and Identification

The following list of dialmakers is, I believe, fairly complete. I compiled this list from directories for the following years: 1777; 1791–8; 1800; 1803; 1815; 1816–17; 1819–20; 1822; 1828; 1830; 1835–6; 1839; 1841–2; 1849–50; 1858; 1860; 1862; 1865; and 1880.

The list has been revised since publication of the first edition, and it also now includes the results of more protracted research by Roy Gault, whose help in this connection I am glad to acknowledge.

ENGLAND

Aaron, Solomon, & Son	Birmingham	1803	Watch dials
Abbott, —	Not known	c 1810–c 1820	Clock dials
Alldridge, Edwin	Birmingham	1860	Clock dials
Allen, Joseph	Birmingham	1867–70	Clock hands and bezels
Ashwin & Co	Not known	c 1790	Clock dials
Bagley, Samuel, & Son	Birmingham	1851–61	Enamellers
Baker & Son	Birmingham	1846	Clock dials
Baker, Richard	Birmingham	1850–66	Clock dials
Baker, Samuel	Birmingham	1823–50	Clock dials
Baker, Samuel, & Son (= Richard?)	Birmingham	1858	Clock dials
Baker, Thomas	Birmingham	1839–50	Also clockmaker
Baker, William I	Birmingham	1822–31	Clock dials
Baker, William II	Birmingham	1854–67	Also clockmaker
Batkin, William, & Son	Birmingham	1803	(?Printed dials)
Beach, Joseph (Senior)	Birmingham	1849–63	
Beach, Joseph (Junior)	Birmingham	1849–80	
Beilby & Hawthorn	Newcastle-upon-Tyne	c 1798–c 1815	Clock dials
Beilby & Hawthorn & William Whittaker	Halifax & Newcastle	c 1790–c 1800	
Bingham, Charles	Birmingham	1808–18	Church clocks & sundials
Bingham, Charles, & Son (= Thomas?)	Birmingham	1821–5	Church clocks & sundials
Bingham, Thomas born c 1798	Birmingham	1841–61	Church clocks & sundials
Blood, Richard	Birmingham	1813	Dial artist
Bolton, C.	Birmingham	1866	Watch dials
Boucher, Daniel	Birmingham	1808–12	Clock dialpainter
Brooke, Thomas	Birmingham	1812	Also clockmaker
Brown, William	Birmingham	1851	Dial writer
Byrne, F.	Birmingham	c 1780–c 1810	Clock dials

Carter, Joseph	Birmingham	1854	
Clarke, Henry	Birmingham	1851	
Clarke, Richard	Birmingham	1851	
Cohen, Morris	Hull	1849–58	Clock dials
Cooke, James George (of Howell & Cooke?)	Birmingham	1858–88	
Cooper, William	Birmingham	1808	Clock dialpainter
Cox	Taunton	c 1810	Clock dials
Crow, Edward	Birmingham	1822–39	Also clock hands
Crow, Thomas	Birmingham	1841–52	Also clock hands
Denniston, John	Halifax	1834	Clock dials & painter
Dugmore & Foster	Birmingham	1816	
Eaves, Thomas (Senior)	Birmingham	1865–7	Clock bezel maker
Eaves, Thomas Arthur	Birmingham	1865–70	Clock bezel maker
Edwards, William	Birmingham	1870	Engraved & silvered dials
Egginton, Thomas	Birmingham	1851	
Egginton, Thomas & James	Birmingham	1841–2	
Felton, Eli	Birmingham	1808–31	Also button maker
Field, William	Birmingham	1854	
Finnemore, George	Birmingham	1846	Clock dials
Finnemore, William I	Birmingham	1812–25	Clock dials
Finnemore, William II	Birmingham	1849–52	Clock dials
Finnemore, William & George	Birmingham	1839–46	Clock dials
Finnemore, William & Son	Birmingham	1828–36	Clock dials
Fletcher, John Wright	Birmingham	1841–50	
Francis, Sarah (widow of William?)	Birmingham	1835–43	Clock dials
Francis, William	Birmingham	c 1810–31	Clock & watch dials
Griffiths, Richard	Birmingham	1867–70	
Griffiths, William & Richard (successors to Finnemores)	Birmingham	1854–66	
Guest, Joseph (or James)	Birmingham	1864	Also gun cases
Hand, Samuel	Birmingham	1851	Clock dial writer
Harden, John	Birmingham	1816	
Hayes, Josiah	Birmingham	1800–31	
Hayes, Josiah, & Son	Birmingham	1835–6	
Higgins, William	Birmingham	1839	
Hipkiss & Har(r)old	Birmingham	1797–1805	Clock dials
Hipkiss, Richard	Birmingham	1805–10 (–1816?)	Clock dials
			Clock dials
Hitchens, Samuel	Birmingham	1861	Clock dial worker
Hitchens, Thomas	Birmingham	1858–88	
Hobson & Hodgkins(on)	Birmingham	c 1815 or later	Clock dials
Hobson, L.	Birmingham	c 1830	Clock dials
Hobson & Todd	Birmingham	1800	Clock dials
Hobson, Todd & Hodgkinson	Birmingham	1808	Clock dials
Howell, Edwin, & Cooke (James George?)	Birmingham	1845–67	
Hughes, William	Birmingham	1845	Clock bezel makers
Hunt, S.	Liverpool	Late 19thC	Clock dials
Jones & Carter	Birmingham	c 1810	Clock dials
Jukes, John	Birmingham	1839–70	Clock dials
Jukes, Josiah	Birmingham	1839–42	Clock dials

Keeling, Thomas	Birmingham	1800–25	
Kempson & Felton (Eli?)	Birmingham	1812–c 1815	Clock dials
Leighton, Thomas	Birmingham	1870–84	Clock bezel maker
Leighton, Thomas, & Son	Birmingham	1884	Clock bezel maker
Longmore & Fairfax	Birmingham	1815–18	Brass rings for clocks (bezels?)
Longmore, Thomas (Junior)	Birmingham	1825	Brass bezels for clocks
McIntyre, Martin	Birmingham	1854	
Mansell & Allen	Birmingham		
(probably Joseph)	Birmingham	1865	Bezel makers
Meeke, Joseph	Birmingham	1864	
Minshull, John	Birmingham	1816–31	
Moon, Henry	Birmingham	1870–88	Bezels & materials
Neal, Thomas	Birmingham	1785–1803	Watch dials?
Nicholas, William	Birmingham	1793–1825	Also clockmaker
Osborne & Wilson (partnership)	Birmingham	1772–7	Clock dials
Osborne, Thomas Hadley (alone)	Birmingham	1777–9	Clock dials
Osborne, Mrs Ann (widow of Thomas)	Birmingham	(1779?) 1793–1800	Clock dials
Osborne, Ann & James	Birmingham	1800–03	Clock dials
Osborne, James	Birmingham	1808–13	Clock dials
Owen, Edward	Birmingham	1803–21	Clock dials
Owen & Price	Birmingham	1800–1	Clock dials
Parkes, S., & Son(s)	Birmingham	1861–4	Sundials & toys
Porter, Nathaniel	Birmingham	1812	
Potter, John	Birmingham	1835	
Prince & Forrest	Birmingham	1870	
Prince, Henry	Birmingham	1880–8	
Pyke, T.	Bridgwater	c 1820–c 1825	Clock dials
Rainer, James	Birmingham	1841–51	Dialpainter
Riding, John	Birmingham	1816	
Roberts, —	Not known	Not known	Clock dials
Robinson, Thomas	Birmingham	1865–7	Clock bezel maker
Schwanfelder, James & John	Leeds	c 1810–37	Dialpainters (& makers?)
Shreeve, William	Halifax	d 1817	With Whittaker, qv
Shuker, Aaron	Birmingham	1870	Clock bezel maker
Smith, Richard	Birmingham	1777–85	Dialmaker (but none recorded)
Smith, W. H.	Not known	Not known	Clock dialmaker (error for Richard?)
Solomon & Co	Birmingham	1815	Also materials
Solomon, Eve	Birmingham	1818–21	Also materials
Swinden & Sons (F. C. & Francis & Edwin Charles)	Birmingham	1851–88	Also materials
Swinden, Francis Charles	Birmingham	1835–58	
Symonds, Charles	Birmingham	1851–61	Dial artist with John Jukes
Totley, Mrs Elizabeth	Birmingham	1851	Clock dial (worker?)
Turner, I.	Birmingham	c 1830–c 1840	Clock dials
Vann, Joseph	Birmingham	1865–70	Clock bezel maker
Walker & Finnemore	Birmingham	1808–11	Clock dials
Walker & Hughes	Birmingham	c 1811–35	Clock dials
Walker, G. G.	Birmingham	1823–5	

Waterhouse, George	Birmingham	1818–25	Also pawnbroker
Westwood, Samuel	Birmingham	1880–8	Also engraver
Whittaker, Sarah	Leeds	1834–7	Dialpainter (& maker?)
Whittaker, William	Halifax	c 1809–c 1815	Clock dials
Whittaker & Shreeve	Halifax	(c 1800) 1815–1817	Clock dials
Wilkes, B., & Co	Birmingham	Not known	Clock dials
Wilkes & Baker	Birmingham	1815–20	
Wilkes, John, & Son (Samuel?)	Birmingham	1820–31	Clock dials
Wilkes, John	Birmingham	1803–15	
Wilkes, Samuel	Birmingham	1829–52	Clock dials & clockmaker
Wilson, James (earlier with Osborne)	Birmingham	1777–(d 1809)	Clock dials
Winn, Robert	Birmingham	1815–45	All sorts!
Wood, —	Birmingham	c 1810–c 1820	Clock dials
Wood & Cooke	Birmingham	c 1810–c 1820	Clock dials
Wright, B., & Co	Birmingham	c 1805–c 1820	Clock dials
Wright, Christopher	Birmingham	1835–45	Clock dials

SCOTLAND

Adam, Joseph	Glasgow	1837	Clock dials
Bell & Meudell	Edinburgh	1832–(c 1845?)	Clock dials & ironmonger
Bell, P. (with 'Finest Fancy' dials)	Edinburgh	1832–52	Clock dials
Burnet, J.	Edinburgh	1898	Japanner
Cameron, John, & Sons	Edinburgh	1898	Japanner
Coats, Andrew	Glasgow	1818–20	Clock dials & japanner
Craig, Peter	Glasgow	1837	Clock dials
Crawford, Maurice, & Co	Edinburgh	1773	Japanned ware (but prob not dials)
Dallaway, William (first dialmaker there)	Edinburgh	1775–93 (& later)	Clock dials
Dallaway & Son	Edinburgh	c 1797–1812 (& later?)	Clock dials
Drew, John (later Shearers)	Glasgow	1835–68	Clock dials
Johnston, Alexander	Edinburgh	1898	Japanner
Laing, John	Edinburgh	1848	Japanner
Paterson, James	Perth	c 1820–(d 1852)	Clock dials, japanner & painter
Peterkin, J.	Edinburgh	1824	Japanner
Russell & Bell, then:	Edinburgh	1824	Ironmongers
Russell & Anderson, then:	Edinburgh	1832	Ironmongers
Russell & Clark, then:	Edinburgh	c 1835–c 1840	Dialmakers
Russell, Thomas (alone)	Edinburgh	1848	Ironmongers
Scott & Co	Glasgow	1837	Dialmaker
Shearer, D. L., & Co	Glasgow	1868–88	Clock dials
Sinclair, D.	Edinburgh	c 1840	Japanner/clock dialmaker
Smith, T., & Stevenson	Edinburgh	c 1815	Clock dials
Stewart, J.	Edinburgh	1848	Japanner
Walker, John	Edinburgh	1824?–1832	Japanner, clock dialmaker
Walker & Watson	Edinburgh	1824	Japanner
Wright & Bethume	Edinburgh	(Est 1832)–1898	Japanners
Wright, J. & W.	Edinburgh	1848	Japanners

The monogram 'W. H.' or 'W. & H.' impressed into the rear of some dials represents the firm of Walker & Hughes. Sometimes this appears in the top right-hand corner (when seen from the back of the dial), sometimes it appears in the centre of the arch back. This monogram is also seen cast or stamped into clock bells, and suggests the firm also made these.

On the back of some English dials there appears a number, punch-lettered, usually into the back of the arch or back of the dial centre. The number '14' appears between about 1785 and 1805 and the presence of the Maltese cross sign (below) on some of these '14' dials suggests they are by Wilson. The number '15' has been noted similarly punched into dial backs and moon disc backs of about 1820, and these are thought to be by the Wilson firm too. Some with the number '16' are known to be by Wilson. Just what these numbers mean is not known, but they do not refer to the dial size, nor to the year the dial was made.

On the rear of some Wilson dials (sometimes in addition to the above-mentioned features) can be seen a blob of white base-paint with a black-painted initial R, sometimes a black initial W. Often there are scratch marks cutting through this white base-paint marker. This may represent some sort of checking-out technique, or may even indicate the original presence of a dialmaker's order ticket, perhaps indicating its removal by scratching off after the dial had passed through the processing system.

On some clocks, particularly on the bells, can be seen the word 'Ainsworth-' or 'Ainsworth-Warrington'. This is George Ainsworth who supplied many clock parts around 1810, particularly bells with his name cast on them. He is not known to have made white dials, but he is mentioned here as his name may be seen when examining white dial clocks.

While Birmingham was the main centre of dialmaking, there were others. At Halifax, Yorkshire, the partnership of Whittaker and Shreeve grew up. William Whittaker, a japanner and clock dial-maker, worked there c 1809–c 1815. His name is seen stamped on falseplates, sometimes in full, sometimes as 'W. W. Halifax'. It is difficult to pin down the period when he worked there because he was at one time in partnership with William Shreeve, a painter. The partnership of Whittaker and Shreeve is listed in directories between about 1815 and 1817, but clocks bearing their falseplates (stamped Whittaker & Shreeve, Halifax) seem to date from as early as about 1800. If this is correct then Whittaker must have worked both independently and in partnership with Shreeve during the same period.

Shreeve, an account of 1869 recounts, was 'a housepainter and did business in clock faces, himself being the chief embellisher. Mr Shreeve used to prepare his own varnish, and he was manipulating the mixture when by some accident it was thrown over him and he was burned to death.' Another account, of 1875, reports that 'he was burned to death with boiling oil which he used to use in his trade.' Shreeve died on 15 August 1817 aged 43. I have seen movements on other makers' clocks punched with Whittaker's name, so evidently he also supplied movements to the trade. Whether this is the same William Whittaker who was still working in Halifax as a clockmaker in 1866, I cannot say for certain. Strangely enough, a Sara Whittaker was in business in nearby Leeds from 1834 to 1837 as 'painter, clock dial enameller and japanner'. Japanning was another term for this form of imitation enamelling. She must have been connected in some way with the Halifax man, but I do not know the connection.

Another provincial dialmaking concern was the firm of Beilby & Hawthorn, Newcastle upon Tyne. They appear in directories from 1801 to 1811 as watch-glass manufacturers and Lancashire tool warehouse. Exactly during what period they produced painted dials is not known, but falseplates exist bearing their name. As they do not appear in the directories for 1795 or 1821, we might set their working period as c 1798–c 1815.

In the period 1770–1800 a great many dials have what I call 'strawberry corners'—delicate painted decorations usually in pink of flowers or fruit or both, often including strawberries, many of which look superficially similar though made by a variety of dialmakers. Quite often for amusement I have tried to guess the maker of a dial from looking at the front only, and later checking behind the dial for possible confirmation. It is a good way to test your expertise. I have usually found that I could guess Wilson dials more easily than others, perhaps because they are fairly common, probably the commonest of the early period.

On some early Wilson dials the flower or strawberry decoration in the corners is edged by a raised border, originally picked out in gold. This border follows a curved dot-dot-dash pattern, as shown below (actual size):

Often the straight corner edges have a six-dash border, sometimes an eight-dash one, or even five or seven, but the sweep of the curving dot-dot-dash pattern seems consistent. This typical Wilson border can be seen clearly in the oval dial by Lomax.

The borders on some Osborne dial corners look very similar to this. In practice there is a slight difference, but this is so slight, and the problem so much more complicated where a dial has been restored and a slight flourish of the brush can confuse, that we probably have to accept that some Osborne dials have virtually this same pattern.

The borders on other Osborne dial corners seem to follow a more straight line dot-dash pattern as shown below:

It has as many as twelve dashes to the corner straight edge.

Dials by the Beilby & Hawthorn/Whittaker team apparently copy the theme of Wilson with a dot-dot-dash system, but lacking the distinctive sweep of Wilson's borders.

An unidentified American-made dial of c 1790 which I saw recently obviously copies the Wilson theme too with a dot-dot-dash border, but the sweep is far more pronounced than on a Wilson dial, and with a distinctive comma-like tail to the dash as shown below:

Another American dial I noticed had this sweeping dot-dash pattern:

(In any case we are unlikely to see many American copies in Britain.)

I cannot claim that this dot-dash recognition system always works, but it is worth a try. Of course not all these 'strawberry corners' have borders—quite a few of Osborne's do not, and also some by Wilson and no doubt by others too.

Some named falseplates carry more than one name. For instance, whilst some named falseplates are lettered 'Wm. Whittaker' at the top and 'Halifax' at the bottom, some exist which bear the names of 'Beilby & Hawthorn—N'castle' at the top and 'W. W. Halifax' at the bottom. This presumably indicates some sort of business partnership and these Whittaker/Beilby dials appear to date from around 1790–1800. There is perhaps nothing remarkable about this except that we seem not to have picked up this partnership from directories and they do seem rather far apart to have had a close working relationship. These Beilby/Whittaker dials are often in the Wilson style. Was this partnership before the Whittaker and Shreeve one and before Beilby and Hawthorn worked on their own? We do not know, but it looks that way.

What is much more puzzling is that some falseplates exist with one name on one side and a different name on the other! For example I have seen falseplates with 'Osborne & Wilson' on one side and 'Wilson' alone on the other side. This might suggest that after the partnership broke up Wilson decided to have his inherited stock of falseplates re-stamped with his own, more personal, imprint. Presumably this was done by heating up the iron falseplate and stamping it with a steamhammer. If our reasoning is correct then such a dial would date from the very first years of Wilson's independent period, ie late 1777 to early 1778, because when he ordered new stocks of falseplates, he would see that they were personalised from the start. This is just theory but it would explain an otherwise puzzling occurrence.

More difficult to explain are falseplates with names on both sides such as several noted with 'Wilson' on one side and 'Walker & Hughes' on the other; one with 'Wilson' on one side and 'William Francis' on the other. It is possible that Walker & Hughes bought up the old Wilson stock c1809–11 and re-stamped it before use. If so this would probably date these dials at the earliest Walker & Hughes period—c1809–11. The same applies to William Francis—did he buy up some of the old Wilson stock and re-impress them c1809–10? More difficult to explain is one reported with 'Walker' on one side and 'Finnemore' on the other.

In my opinion the iron falseplate was a device invented and sold *attached to the dial*, purely on white dial clocks. Opinions seem to differ in this respect, however. My view is supported by the simple fact that one finds many a white dial impressed with the same maker's name as on its falseplate, thereby indicating that the two were sold

14   Movement of the clock by Lomax of Blackburn showing position of falseplate (James Wilson) between dial and movement. Two of the four short dial feet show up here as do the longer falseplate feet.

together. In fact some white dials could not have been sold without the appropriate falseplate, since the date discs are sometimes fixed between dial and falseplate and *attached* to each.

One school of thought is that falseplates were sold as separate items for use on white or brass dials. It is possible that some may have been sold separately, though I cannot see the point of it. I do not incline to the view that they were ever intended for use on brass dials. There had never been a need in the past for such a device on a brass dial, where there was no problem in attaching dial feet between movement and dial. There seems nothing to be gained by using a falseplate to attach a brass dial to its movement. I have never seen one used in this way that did not look very suspicious to me. A falseplate of course can serve as a very useful device to assist someone in fitting a dial (white or brass) to a wrong movement.

All the brass dial clocks that I have ever seen that did use a falseplate fitting fall into one of the following three categories. Firstly those used in America, where early clockmakers often worked in unconventional ways. Secondly outright fakes, where the falseplate has been used to make it easier for some bodger to fit together a dial and movement that did not start life together. I have sometimes heard it said in mitigation that such a conversion may have been made long ago, but my own view is that a fake does not cease to be a fake because it happens to have been faked a hundred years ago. Most of these falseplate/brass dial fakes are very obviously 'wrong' to anyone who takes the slightest trouble to look. In fact sometimes they are ludicrously wrong, where a falseplate bearing the name of, for example, Walker & Hughes (whose business did not begin until about 1811), may be found behind a brass dial bearing the name of a clockmaker who perhaps died in the 1780s. How dealers can keep a straight face when trying to sell this sort of 'eighteenth-century' clock I do not know, but I have seen a number manage it.

The third category is a little difficult to describe. It consists of clocks made new towards the end of the last century, often by a clock-jobber or enthusiast who wanted to make one of the old-style brass dial clocks. By this time brass dial clocks were virtually forgotten (except for some single-sheet brass dials) and so there were no dial parts to be had which were 'in period'. Therefore such a person had to use old parts—old spandrels, old chapter rings, sometimes an old dial sheet but more often a new dial sheet. So the end result was a hotch-potch of old dial parts dating from the 1780s or before, often mixed with new engraving of perhaps the 1890s. Onto this the 'maker' might fit a new movement, perhaps one he had made himself even, and he might use a falseplate in doing so. The end result will be a hotch-pot dial plus falseplate plus late nineteenth-century movement, but is that a genuine clock or a fake? The maker may have had no intention to deceive, but may have used these parts simply for convenience. Well, such clocks do exist and people buy them, and it is difficult to say they are outright fakes. I would not want one and, as far as the use of falseplates is concerned, this is not the use for which (I think) they were made. I would not accept this type of clock as offering valid evidence for the use of falseplates with brass dials.

The view that falseplates were supplied with the movement and not with the dial was expressed by E. L. Edwardes in *The Grandfather Clock*. It is reiterated by Anthony Bird in *English House Clocks*, and by Eric Bruton in *The Longcase Clock*. This view seems not to take account of these facts: many dials bear the same names as their falseplates; these names are of *dial* not *movement* makers (though I would not quibble against the possibility that an occasional dialmaker might also have made movements, especially after 1840); not all movements on falseplate dials are of the 'factory-made' type, but considerable numbers of earlier white dial clocks have movements bearing features indicative of the clockmaker's own handiwork, such as scoring and marking out wheel positions on the plates; some dials have the datewheel pivoted between dial and falseplate; movements appear to have been made or at the very least assembled by the clockmaker himself to fit on to ready-purchased dials even as late as the 1830s (see end of Chapter 9), while it is usually suggested that the dials were bought to fit on to pre-made movements; the meaning in the 1772 advertisement by Osborne & Wilson, when they say 'such Methods used as will enable the Clock Maker to fix them to the Movements', can hardly apply to anything but falseplates, especially as falseplate dials bearing their names are well known; and finally, no British brass dial clock of unquestionable originality seems to have been shown to have a falseplate fitting: the Birmingham dialmakers are not known to have made brass dials and therefore a Birmingham falseplate would immediately seem to be 'wrong' on a brass dial.

Since the above lines were written (for the first edition) I have come across a scarce little booklet by Samuel Harlow called *The Clock Maker's Guide* which was published in Birmingham in 1813.

In it Harlow suggests that benefits would derive from standardisation in movement-making and dialmaking—from which we can conclude that standardisation in these fields had not yet arrived.

Harlow refers twice to falseplates, which he calls 'backplates'. In the first instance he mentions 'the backplate, *generally put on by* the Birmingham dial makers ...'. On the second occasion he refers to 'the backplate, *commonly used by* the Birmingham dial makers, which, if put on correct, might save the workman a great deal of trouble ...' (the italics are mine).

Here then is contemporary evidence that falseplates were 'generally put on' by the dialmakers, but more has come to light just recently. When the workshop and materials of the Deacon family of clockmakers were re-housed in Leicester Museum, amongst the tackle was a number of clock dials, about a dozen of which had falseplates (though unfortunately the dialmakers cannot be identified). What is interesting is that these dials had never been used, never been fitted to a clock. They were obviously the leftovers of a batch bought in advance of immediate requirements and from which customers might make their choice, but these particular ones had never been selected.

Not only had the falseplates never been drilled to take pillars to fit them to movements, but they were already attached to the dials, hence confirming the view that these were supplied with the dials—indeed attached to the dials. It also confirms the view that clockmakers bought dials by the batch ahead of their actual needs to enable the customer to select one from the available stock.

Another important point on which I feel these three writers may be mistaken is their implication that all movements on falseplate clocks must be 'factory-made' ones, since this carries with it an unfair suggestion of inferiority to those made (or assembled) by the clockmaker himself. I know of clockmakers whose movements on their early white dial clocks are indistinguishable from those on their (usually earlier) brass dial ones and which also have distinctive features enabling one to recognise them as the handiwork of the makers concerned. Such movements appear on falseplate dials and there is no question of their having been made in Birmingham. Note for instance Samuel Deacon's famous 'pecking bird' movements (page 79). The work of Will Snow of Padside, Sam Deacon of Barton or Jonas Barber junior of Winster, for example, bears absolute testimony of this because these men had highly distinctive styles, but individual handicraft must be recognisable in a less obvious way in the work of many hundreds of our local clockmakers. Three-train musical clocks, scarce as they are, perhaps more frequently appear behind white dials than behind brass ones. Surely no one would suggest that such musical movements were Birmingham-made, despite their being attached to Birmingham falseplate dials.

I would not go so far as to say that a falseplate dial would never have a factory-made movement attached to it. Nevertheless it would seem more likely that in very late clocks of the late 1840s and 1850s the *absence* of a falseplate is much more likely to be an indication that movement and dial were supplied together. After all, if one workshop were supplying dial and movement what need would there be for a falseplate, when standardised dial feet could be made to fit into standardised movement plates?

As with all hints on identification of objects, one must use the available facts with care. Information on dialmakers can be an extremely valuable reference guide to establishing the age of a clock. But one should take it along with other guiding features, not on its own as firm evidence. For instance, a falseplate on a clock could conceivably be a replacement, in which case it would have no bearing at all on the age of the clock. Similarly, a stamped date disc could be a replacement standing in for a damaged original one. It is very unlikely that a falseplate *will* be a replacement, as it is a sturdy object hardly likely to suffer damage; just the same, this possibility must be borne in mind. A date disc is more prone to damage and it is not unusual for a replacement one to be fitted. In the case of a replacement date disc (of the aperture date type), the colour of the white background will often vary in shade from the rest of the dial, and the style of numbering can vary too.

The dialmakers have left us a whole series of clues and guiding features which give us a completely independent field for identification. If you simply take the trouble to look, the information is usually there, and you can observe it without even getting your fingers dirty. You don't need to dismantle the clock: just look closely with the aid of a torch or a good light. The evidence, however, should be used alongside the other dating evidence you have available to you, ie the dial style; the facts on the maker's life; and the case.

Whilst thirty-hour clocks do not normally have falseplates, there is one category that is an exception. A thirty-hour clock would not usually have a seconds dial. If it did it would tick anticlockwise unless

15   Very worn dial from a clock by Thomas Snow of Knaresborough c 1835, the dial
by Wright's of Birmingham. The artwork is crude and clumsy. This is an eight-day dial
but used here on a thirty-hour clock, with dummy winding squares visible (at rakish angles)
protruding from the winding holes.

the movement were specially built with an extra wheel in the train to reverse the direction and produce a clockwise-rotating seconds hand. There were always some customers contrary enough to want a seconds dial on a thirty-hour clock and to cater for them the clockmaker would sometimes find his easiest solution was to use an eight-day dial, which would already have the seconds lettering on it. Therefore where a thirty-hour clock has a seconds dial it may well have a falseplate, but only because the clockmaker has used what was really an eight-day dial. Sometimes such thirty-hour clocks were also given dummy winding squares to complete the superficial resemblance to an eight-day clock, and such dummy winders were sometimes attached for convenience to the falseplate. The clock by Thomas Snow is one such example with dummy winders.

5

How the Clockmaker Got His Dials

To most clockmakers dials were a headache. The dial was the part the customer saw, the package if you like, behind which the clockmaker's talents in the form of the movement were hidden from all but the very curious. The average clock owner or buyer today has precious little knowledge of, or interest in, what goes on behind the dial. It is sad but true that the criterion by which he often decides what constitutes a 'good' clock is the dial alone or, even worse, the case, which was not made by the clockmaker at all!

How much more this must have applied in the past, when the clock's 'works' were regarded by the masses as an absolute mystery, a magic box—much as the workings of a computer are regarded today.

So the dial was very important as the bit that showed, and to most clockmakers dials were always a problem, a real nuisance, unless they were amongst the few who were skilled engravers. A clockmaker was of course an engineer, and to expect him to be an engineer *and* a first-class artist was asking a lot. Clockmakers who were skilled engravers were in a small minority.

Those who were not had two choices. They could have a go at engraving their own dials and accept a less-than-perfect job—and a good many were content to do this—or they could pay a skilled engraver for a first-class dial, but that forced up the price of their clocks. One of the few examples of known engraving costs, now widely quoted, is the late eighteenth-century advertisement of Charles Blakeway of Albrighton who engraved 'Dyal Plates' at 2s 6d each (12½p); this may seem little money to us, but when even the best provincial clockmakers were doing well to earn £1 a week, 2s 6d was a very good day's wages.

It is hard for us to establish the original cost of a brass dial with its engraving because few people bothered to record the sum, and most records would have been thrown away years ago anyway. The only one I had discovered in twenty years of searching was that by Samuel Roberts, a Montgomeryshire clockmaker working in the late eighteenth century who made an eleven-inch square brass dial for a customer, perhaps to replace a damaged one, at a cost of 12s 0d (60p) (see my *Country Clocks and their London Origins*).

Recently, however, I had the chance to have a brief look at the account books kept by Samuel Deacon, a clockmaker at Barton-in-the-Beans, Leicestershire, and these revealed a few surprises. Samuel Deacon was born in the village of Ratby, Leicestershire, the son of a carpenter (Samuel's father later made clock cases for his son's clocks at £1 a time). His mother died when he was four. At eleven he left home to be a farm servant, which work he did for $4\frac{1}{2}$ years. Then, in 1762, he heard that Joseph Donisthorpe, a clockmaker at Normanton, wanted an apprentice and surprisingly Samuel got the job, although his education had been so lacking that he did not even know his multiplication tables. Even later in life he used to have his tables written out in full at the back of his notebook for easy reference.

His master, it seems, was an accomplished man, accomplished in all the vices according to Samuel Deacon's account. Then, late in life, he was converted to the ways of the Church, and became as fervent a champion of religion as he had been formerly of debauchery. Deacon stayed with him for nine years until in October 1771 he moved to Barton to set up on his own account. Probably one of the first things he did was to build his own shop clock, which registered time on a wooden dial overlooking the village street and was inscribed 'Deacon – 1771'.

From the very first moment it seems that he was keen to record his activities, although his first account book is lost. He probably borrowed the money to set himself up, perhaps from Joseph Donisthorpe, for in October 1773 Samuel had probably repaid the loan and, feeling a weight removed from his shoulders, wrote in large letters across his notebook 'MY OWN MASTER'. It is clear that he began in 1771, for in October 1774 he begins the year's accounts with 'the beginning of my 4th year for myself'.

This series of notebooks started by Samuel Deacon was continued by his son John and his descendants and runs in an almost unbroken series until the late nineteenth century, as the Deacon family of

16 Restored dial of a clock by Deacon of Leicester dating from c 1805–c 1810. It could be by Samuel Deacon or his son, John, or a joint product. The dial was made by William Whittaker of Halifax and has his stamped falseplate. This is an example of tumbling numbers, where the numerals are inverted between 4 and 8.

clockmakers occupied the same workshop premises until 1951. Then Mr John Daniell of Leicester Museum, hearing that the Deacon property was to be sold, investigated and found that not only were the record books preserved, but Samuel Deacon's workshop and forge had survived virtually intact after almost two centuries. Workshop, forge and records are now in the custody of Leicester Museum.

This unique series of record books numbers perhaps forty volumes, some in a poor state, difficult to read and sometimes used as jotting books at such widely varying periods that they are difficult to understand. So voluminous were they that even Samuel Deacon himself had to make a rough index to find his way through them. They contain all the day-to-day transactions, lists of jobs taken in hand, for whom, when, and the amount charged for the work. The majority of his time was spent on small cleaning and repair jobs of 1s 0d and 1s 6d a time (5p and 7½p), servicing watches, clocks or virtually any mechanical device. Here is an example of the way he summed up his earnings for the year 1810:

Sold 42 clocks at	£242	2s 6d
profit average 10%	25	0s 0d
cleaned 438 clocks, average 1s 6d	32	17s 0d
	57	17s 0d
clock repairs, etc.	5	0s 0d
	£62	17s 0d

Samuel Deacon became a superb clockmaker, way above the level of his contemporaries or his old master, Joseph Donisthorpe. But what is so important about him from our point of view is that his records give a uniquely detailed background to his clockmaking skills, which can be examined through surviving examples. No other similar records are known to survive for any British clockmakers at this time, and in the study of white dial clocks this is the absolutely vital period, for within a year of Samuel Deacon's setting up shop at Barton, Osborne & Wilson, dialmakers, were advertising their new dials only a few miles down the road in Birmingham. Surely Deacon as a young and enthusiastic craftsman would want to try these new dials. We ought to be able to study this transition from brass to japanned dials through Deacon's records, and we can.

But to return for a moment to brass dials, Deacon was one of the few makers who was a highly skilled engraver and consequently he received orders for brass dial work from other local makers who perhaps were not engravers. From his notebooks we read: '15 May 1773, Engraved clock face for Sam Clark, Hinckley, and finished it—10 shillings'. Sam Clark was a Hinckley clockmaker here apparently buying a complete brass dial for only 10s 0d—a sum not unlike the 12s 0d that Sam Roberts charged. Later in 1773 we read: 'Sold Sam Clark 12inch face, rough set of heads & dolphins, 4lb 12oz—six shillings'. What this means is that he sold a complete dial, including castings of corner spandrels of head pattern and dolphin spandrels for the arch, for 6s 0d. 'Rough' probably means not cleaned of the casting rag, which needed filing off. The weight is given because worked brass was sold by weight of worked materials. This dial is so cheap that it must have been without engraving work.

Another entry later that year shows a charge for engraving work alone: 'Grave'd 14inch face for Heafield—moon, day, month, minutes, hours, secs—5 shillings'. John Heafield was a clockmaker at Ashby, and this sounds like the dial of quite a complex clock. But we can arrive at a cost for supplying a normal brass dial, say a twelve-inch square dial, of 10–12s 0d to those clockmakers who chose not to produce their own.

The first example of a japanned dial that I could spot in the Deacon records was this entry: '16 May 1774 Had an arched face japanned from Lindley for Wm. Hall—£1. 4s. 0d.' Perhaps Lindley was a wholesaler and presumably Hall was the customer. However, there was a Thomas Lindley, a clockmaker, working in Leicester at this very time and it could even be that Deacon got the dial from him, perhaps just so that he could try out the new type of dial. The price is *twice* that of the brass dial.

The brass dials quoted may perhaps have been square dials and so not quite a fair comparison with the arched japanned one, but even much later a square thirty-hour japanned dial cost 11s (and an eight-day 18s) as we can see from the 1820 price list on page 84, and if anything the prices of these dials fell over the years, due to increasing mass production and competition.

So, far from being a cheaper product than the brass dial, we can see from the Deacon books that japanned dials cost more! We shall see further proof of this in the 1782 advertisement of John Benson of Whitehaven, who pointed out that his bargain offer was to supply clocks with japanned dial plates 'at the same price as those with Brass

Plates, which is a great advantage to the Purchaser...'. In other words, by 1782—only ten years after the new dials first appeared—it was common knowledge that you would normally expect to pay *more* for clocks with japanned dials than for those with brass ones.

This evidence calls for a complete revaluation of attitudes, for the japanned dial has always been thought of in the past literature of horology as the poor relation of the brass dial, an inferior alternative which became the dominant type because it was cheaper. In fact it must be an indication of its status in the eyes of the clockmaker and clockbuyer of the period, that it soon became the dominant type in spite of the fact that it was more costly than the brass version!

But let us leave prices aside for a moment and come back to the Deacon papers. On 13 November 1774 is an entry: 'Had faces came from Birmingham as per bill + carage (= carriage) one shilling—£4 6s 8d'. So by 1774 Deacon not only knew about the Birmingham makers of the new dials, but he was obviously sufficiently impressed by them to order them in bulk. After only two years of production the Birmingham japanners had converted a top craftsman to their new dials.

One might well imagine that the run-of-the-mill clockmaker who could not do his own engraving might jump at the chance of these new dials, because here was his opportunity to wipe out instantly the disadvantage at which his work stood when compared with that of a Samuel Deacon. The new dials could make all clockmakers equal overnight to the average buyer who was buying just a pretty face and neither knew nor cared about the quality of what lay behind the dial. But even the Samuel Deacons of this world were converted, men who had the edge over their contemporaries because they could do not only their own engraving but could take in engraving work for others too ... if these men took so rapidly to the new dials, then they *must* have been good!

But how did the clockmaker select his dials? Hitherto we have had no idea how he knew what patterns were available, what qualities. A memorandum in the Deacon records (standard practice before the days of carbon paper and photocopiers) gives a clue, dated 10 December 1805:

Ordered the following dials:
12—12inch square, varied, neat corners, open mouth, written figgers, 30hours, Deacon-Barton.

4—12inch arched 30hour, open mouth.

3—13inch arched 30hour, two with figgers in arch, one with an urn.

1—13inch arched with moon.

Let some of the 12inch have a bird above the centre.

So at last we have discovered how it was done. The basic size and type were specified and this, plus a few vague suggestions, was all the supplier had to guide him—'Let some . . . have a bird above the centre'. The choice was largely up to the supplier. They were to be lettered 'Deacon-Barton'. The term 'open mouth' means the curved aperture type of calendar feature. But what if the selection did not please? We will see what happened later.

Samuel Deacon, and his son John after him, dealt for many years through a Mr D. Anderson of Birmingham, who was presumably a wholesaler of dials—we will see later that Anderson stocked dials by several different dialmakers. Here is a copy of a complete letter to Anderson:

To Mr. Anderson, Birmingham.
    Sir, I want a 13inch arch moon 8days with seconds
two 13inch 8days no moon with second
three 13inch 30hour no seconds, Good cullour & month plates
    The last 5 have sorted neat 2inch figures in arches
Six 12inch 30hours, neat painting, not extra price
12 square 12inch, neat flowers in middle
    All the lot written figures. be sure to see to the collour & the last parcel of 12inch were very bad. Some must be returned.
See also to the packing, some of the last are spoiled.
    18 pair of good giltt hands 12 & 13 inches, sorted, small centre holes.
    24 bushes.
    Send the wole (= whole?) soon as you can, the arches are much wanted.
Barton   Yours in haste
Jany 16 1816   S. Deacon

One or two points may need explanation. Month plates are the japanned calendar discs to fit behind the mouth apertures. Notice that he specifies with or without seconds features on both eight-day and thirty-hour dials, which shows that he had the option with either type. Notice too that he asks for them with numbers on, which suggests he could have had them without numbers if he wanted. The bulk of his order was for thirty-hour dials, which probably made up most of his normal output. The term '24 bushes' is a little puzzling. As there were 24 dials ordered, these presumably were the tension washers which held the hands fast—we usually call them 'hands collets' today.

What he meant by insisting on 'good cullour' we do not know—perhaps he meant strong colours. Anyway, some of the previous batch were not to his liking in this respect and would be returned later. We also notice the problem of the dials getting damaged in transit through inadequate packing—a feature we meet again in Chapter 14.

From Birmingham to Barton is about twenty miles by road. The dials took seven weeks to arrive. In the 'goods-in' book against Anderson's name is written: 'Mar 8 1816 Rec'd 24 dials, 18 pair clock hands gilt—£10–16–2'.

A note to Anderson's in 1820 complaining about a certain shipment reads: 'The above dials were not Walkers and so must have more discount. NB These dials were W. Frances.' Anderson's therefore must have previously supplied dials by Walker & Hughes and it seems that theirs were costlier than those by William Francis and, whilst Deacon would accept Francis dials, he would not accept them at the Walker & Hughes price.

Names of dialmakers with whom the Deacons dealt and which were noted from the records were Hipkiss, Wilkes & Son, Walker & Hughes, F. C. Swinden, William Finnemore & Sons and Cohen of Hull. We also know that they used dials by Wilson and by William Whittaker of Halifax. The dealings with Hipkiss seem not to have been too successful, for in March 1809 is an entry: 'Returned 8 dials, 4 12inch & 4 13inch. Also returned the boxes they came in (that were charged 3/- to 5/6 each).' Whether this was due to inappropriate selection or damage we cannot tell.

The wholesalers obviously catered for the straightforward thirty-hour and eight-day dials, but suppose you wanted something out of the ordinary such as a dial with three winding-holes for a three-train clock such as a musical clock? This would clearly have to be a special order. No doubt the dialmakers would have made one specially for you, but then such a clock was a very costly affair anyway and perhaps one might want to be more fastidious than usual about the choice of dial.

The Deacon records contain the following entry:

May 27 1813 chime clock for Mr. Wilson, 7 tunes on ten bells, (one fiddler?). Mr. W. to find hands and painting of the dial and weights. Price £15.

This note suggests that Deacon could buy a blank dial, not yet painted, and perhaps even not yet drilled. Whether it would be a bare iron sheet or already whitened with base-paint, we do not know. Obviously the customer could (and perhaps wished to) arrange for his own artwork and this is what he intended when the clock was ordered. Something must have made him change his mind, however, for a later note adds:

The dial to be painted by Mr. Richard Blood, No 41 Newhall St., Birmingham. Tunes:

1. Easter Hymn
2. Highland Laddie new
3. (illegible) Machree
4. Baker's Hornpipe
5. Blewbell
6. Gavott by Green(ton?)
7. Handalls march

Presumably Richard Blood was an artist and a dial of this type would need to have the tunes named on the dial for a selection lever, sometimes positioned in the arch.

In concluding our evidence about japanned dials as seen through Samuel Deacon's work, we can see that he was using these new, costlier dials by 1774. No doubt he still made some of the cheaper brass dial clocks after that time, but increasingly he was converted to white dials.

Samuel Deacon numbered and dated many of his clocks, engraving the number and date onto the movement frontplate. Some numbered examples known to me include:

No 44 dated 1773 30 hour brass dial
No 84 dated 1777 30 hour brass dial
No 127 dated 1778 30 hour white dial (circular dial)
No 135 dated 1779 (no details)
No 149 dated 1778 30 hour white dial (circular)
No 160 dated c 1780 30 hour brass dial
No 224 dated 1783 8 day arched white dial (by Wilson?)
No 228 dated 1783 30 hour square white dial (single-hander)
No 338 dated 1789 8 day arched white dial by Wilson

These numbers and dates can be confusing. No 160 also bears the number 110; No 149 also bears the number 100; No 135 also bears the number 87. The date of 135 falls considerably out of sequence with the rest, though it is correctly read from the clock. Samuel's son, John Deacon, also made clocks, at least some of which were numbered. One of John's has the movement signed Samuel Deacon No 67 dated 1791, a number and date plainly out of step with the others above. As Samuel Deacon made many clocks for others in the trade, he may have kept more than one numbering sequence running. There is no register of numbers preserved amongst Deacon's records, and in his job book he seems to have numbered every job series anew each year, so it is not possible to consult his records by taking, for example, 1777 and looking up job No 84 to trace the clock listed above.

The name on his clock dials varies as 'Sl. Deacon-Barton' and 'Deacon-Barton'. John's were 'Deacon-Leicester' or 'J. Deacon-Leicester'. An examination of several Deacon movements reveals that he had three or four grades of clock varying in quality from the very ordinary to the very fine. His best ones are said to incorporate his 'pecking bird' feature.

If it took two years for the white dial to become firmly accepted by a local master craftsman of Deacon's stature, we may expect its acceptance further afield to have taken a little longer. But obtaining evidence of this acceptance is extremely difficult because most clockmakers did not date their clocks and we need evidence, not opinions, about a clock's age. However, a few years ago I did a little research into a northern clockmaker who, like Deacon, numbered his clocks and dated some of them.

This was Jonas Barber junior of Winster, Westmorland, a third-generation clockmaker who was born about 1718 and died in 1802. Barber was a superb craftsman who could and did perform his own engraving work. His major product was, like Deacon's, the simple country thirty-hour clock. We will not go into great detail about Barber here—his full story can be read in my book *Westmorland Clocks and Clockmakers*. What is interesting for our purpose here is that Barber was numbering and dating his clocks right through this vital transitional period of the 1770s. Before he retired in 1799 he had made (with his small workforce) close on 1,450 clocks. Incidentally there is no question but that men like Deacon and Barber did actually *make* their clock movements. Anyone who has ever seen one

17 Top-quality eight-day movement by Samuel Deacon of Barton, No 224 dated 1783, showing his famous 'pecking bird' feature. The tall vertical bladespring on the extreme right is a repeater spring operated by a cord attached to its top. The scoring-out lines show up clearly on the frontplate. These were for marking out the positions of wheels, etc, and are almost always an indication of handcraftwork.

by either of these men will see that they incorporate features so highly individual that one can recognise their movements even if seen without dials. The clock movement by Will Snow (page 81) shows how individualistic some makers could be.

Barber's first clocks with white dials that I know about can be seen to date from 1774. We know that Barber bought some of his dials from James Wilson. A few brass dial clocks of his are known after 1774, but these are by that time exceptions to his general rule.

If we sidetrack momentarily to John Chapman, a clockmaker at Loughborough, Leicestershire, who had been a fellow apprentice of Sam Deacon, completing his apprenticeship under Joseph Donisthorpe in 1774, we find that no example of Chapman's clocks yet recorded is a brass dial type. So when the new dial took hold, it was a firm hold.

So it took two years to convert the top craftsmen in the land at a distance of up to 150 miles. A little further up the road from Jonas Barber was John Benson of Whitehaven, situated perhaps 200 miles from Birmingham. Benson was another top-flight clockmaker, a man of thirty-odd years' standing in the trade, who is known to have made, amongst others, a thirteen-tune longcase clock with an annual calendar hand recording important feast days. Within ten years of its introduction, Benson was converted to the superiority of the new dial, as his advertisement in the *Cumberland Pacquet* for the year 1782 demonstrates:

> John Benson (who makes all sorts of plain, repeating, musical and astronomical clocks at reasonable prices) begs leave to return his most sincere thanks ... he has an assortment of the best japanned clock dial plates which he makes up to any sort of clocks, at the same price as brass plates, which is a great advantage to the purchaser, as they will never want silvering, but still be the same, keep as well and clean as soon as glass. Smoke, steam & damp does not affect them, which soon dissolves the best silvering and lacker that can be laid on brass;— and the expense of renewing the silver and lacker comes high or the clock looks bad and more so where they are exposed to the sea air; the japanned plates are still the same and the expense saved ... His abilities are unquestionable having carried on the clockmaking business in all its different branches during a period of thirty years in Whitehaven ...

Just across the Irish Sea in that same year (1782) a Belfast clockmaker named James Wilson (not connected with the Birmingham

18   Movement from the Will Snow clock on page 94. His movements were highly distinctive having skeleton plates, ie all non-essential areas of the brass plates were cut away.
On the back of the dial can be seen the typical Wilson white brush strokes here marked
with the initial 'R'. White paint splashes and runs can be seen lapping over the dial edges.

dialmaker of the same name) advertised in the *Belfast Newsletter*: 'He also has a few clocks with white enamelled dial-plates, very strong and beautiful, that will never stain or tarnish, being the first plates ever imported into this port ...'. So after ten years the first white dials had just reached Belfast, though in all likelihood they had been imported through Dublin earlier than this.

The new dials had also penetrated into Scotland by 1780 to the point where by 1785 William Dallaway had set up his own japanning business in Edinburgh, though how many years he had been in the business there prior to that we do not know. An estimate would be about 1780. The Dallaway Japan Manufactory is dealt with more fully in Chapter 13.

Records of clocks which are precisely dated are very hard to uncover. The examples quoted above are probably no more than the tip of the iceberg in illustrating the rapid spread of the new dials, but even that tip is evidence of how rapid was the fall from favour of the old-fashioned and (as we now know) cheaper brass dial.

But what about those people who had bought their clock before the new dials appeared? Their reaction must have been similar to that of the buyer of a new TV set shortly before colour TV arrived. Who wants to watch black-and-white once colour has proved itself? These clock owners wanted the new colourful dials too. Probably a great many would buy new clocks with the new dials. But a few dials survive of the traditional brass type, which were *later* japanned over! In other words they had been converted to colour. Illustrated is one made about 1775 as an engraved brass dial with spandrels, chapter ring, etc. Perhaps ten or twenty years later the owner had it japanned. Spandrels and chapter ring were removed, unwanted holes were plugged up (eg where the spandrel screws had been), the engraving levelled off with filler, and the result looks very much like a normal japanned dial. In other words the clock was 'modernised'. I can think of another longcase clock and a bracket clock that had been through this same treatment but these are the only three that I can recall.

One reason one seldom sees these 'modernised' dials is perhaps because it was less troublesome (though maybe more costly) to have a completely new white dial fitted, and if a new japanned dial had been fitted carefully in, say, 1790 to the movement from a brass dial clock of, say, 1770, the likelihood is that we would never recognise this alteration today.

19   An example of a brass dial of c 1775, 'modernised' later by japanning, taken from a clock by Hardaker of Salem. The spandrels were removed, holes plugged, engraving filled and the whole dial japanned. Parts of the original engraved brass surface can be seen showing through below XII and I. There are several Salems in West Yorkshire and the exact one has not been identified.

Another reason, however, may well be that if such a clock today comes into the hands of a dealer, he may well wonder whether he should restore the japanned surface or strip it down to the original brass dial, add replacement spandrels, and refurbish the clock as it originally was—a brass dial one. Given the fact that a brass dial version is much more valuable in today's market than a japanned one, there is considerable financial advantage in restoring it as a brass dial clock, and this may well have happened to a good many of these 'modernised' dials. From our point of view such clocks are interesting evidence of the desire of the period to switch to the new white dials.

So the clockmaker got his initial contact with the dialmaker or wholesaler perhaps by seeing advertisements such as the Osborne & Wilson ones, perhaps through word of mouth in the trade, or by seeing other clockmakers use them. Perhaps he tried a sample order or two and eventually he built up a relationship with his supplier.

Some dialmakers issued price lists but, being of only temporary use, these were probably destroyed within a year or two of printing. Recently one was discovered by Mr Alan Treherne when researching amongst the business archives of Peter Stubs, toolmakers and merchants, of Warrington, Lancashire.

Birmingham, January 1820

Prices
of
JAPANNED CLOCK DIALS
manufactured
by
WILKES & SON,
Whittall-street, Birmingham.

Fourteen inch Arch Moon dial	£1 4s 0d
Thirteen inch ditto ditto	£1 2s 0d
Twelve inch ditto ditto	£1 0s 0d
Fourteen inch Square ditto	£1 2s 0d
Thirteen inch ditto ditto	£1 0s 0d
Twelve inch ditto ditto	18s 0d
Fourteen inch Solid Arch Eight Day	16s 0d
Thirteen inch ditto ditto	14s 0d
Twelve inch ditto ditto	12s 0d
Fourteen inch Square ditto	14s 0d
Thirteen inch ditto ditto	12s 0d
Twelve inch ditto ditto	11s 0d
Fourteen inch Round ditto	13s 0d
Thirteen inch ditto ditto	11s 0d
Twelve inch ditto ditto	10s 0d
Thirteen inch Arched Thirty-hour	13s 0d
Twelve inch ditto ditto	11s 0d
Eleven inch ditto ditto	10s 0d
Fourteen inch Square ditto	13s 0d
Thirteen inch ditto ditto	12s 0d
Twelve inch ditto ditto	10s 0d
Eleven inch ditto ditto	8s 6d
Ten inch ditto ditto	7s 0d
Fourteen inch Round ditto	12s 0d

Thirteen inch	ditto	ditto	10s 0d
Twelve inch	ditto	ditto	9s 0d
Six inch Round Spring Dial			7s 0d
Eight inch	ditto	ditto	8s 0d
Six inch Arch		ditto	8s 6d
Eight inch	ditto	ditto	10s 0d

Oval and Round Dials of all Sizes.

Additional Paintings and Movements charged as follows:-

Seasons, Quarters, Virtues, Elements, Etc	8s 0d
Landscapes or Figure Pieces in Arch	4s 0d
Single Figures painted in Arch	2s 0d
Adam and Eve to move	7s 6d
Ditto, if Serpent to move	10s 0d
Ship to move, Old Time, Etc	6s 0d
Swan's Neck to move	6s 0d
Boy and Girl swinging, Harlequin & Columbine, Etc	7s 0d
Shuttlecock and Battledore to move	7s 0d

Movements and Paintings of every Description.

. . . .

Printed by R. Peart, Bull-street, Birmingham.

Wilkes preferred to call them japanned dials and this was probably the most widely-used term. Personally I like to keep the term 'white dial' because it was used by Osborne & Wilson in their advertising, the oldest so far discovered.

One could hardly wish for a more detailed break-down of the availability of designs and features—almost any combination you could want of size and pattern in eight-day and thirty-hour versions, the latter usually a shilling cheaper than the former, probably because no falseplate was supplied with the thirty-hour. The price structure compares very closely with Jonas Barber's stock list on page 138.

As we might expect, dials with a fixed arch (or solid arch as it was sometimes called) were cheaper than those with a moon or moving figure; square ones were cheaper than arched ones, round ones cheaper than square—smaller dials needed less metal, less artwork. Spring dials (those for spring-driven bracket clocks) were cheapest of all. Notice that oval dials were offered but infuriatingly were not priced.

The optional extras may need a word or two of explanation. Seasons, Quarters, Virtues, Elements, refer to the themes for the dial corners—the four seasons, the four quarters of the world, ie the four continents, the four virtues (faith, hope, charity and justice) and the four elements (earth, air, fire and water). All these are common corner motifs in Regency times. Presumably they cost eight shillings extra because there was more detail to be painted than in a simple geometrical or flower-patterned corner.

'Adam and Eve to move' refers to the type mentioned on page 139. 'Old Time' means a rocking Father Time. Rocking figures could apparently be made to the customer's own request and specification, and of course a painted scene would always be supplied to order if the customer had some particular theme he wanted.

An example of custom-made painting was drawn to my attention recently by Canon Miles-Brown, the authority on Cornish clocks. It is on the clock which was formerly in the Levant Mine counthouse. This is a Walker & Hughes of Birmingham falseplate dial with a scene in the arch showing a mine—enginehouse, winding engine, cables, shaft, etc, and entitled 'Levant Mine, St. Just'. Now the interesting thing is that this is plainly not a true depiction of the Levant Mine which stands on a clifftop, nor is the winding engine remotely like any used in the region. The artist had apparently only the vaguest idea of what a real mine looked like. Nevertheless the dial must have been ordered specially and painted specially—'One arched dial please, the arch to show the Levant Mine'.

Occasionally one does see custom-ordered paintings on these dials, usually lettered with the name of the actual place. One of the Leeds Cloth Hall comes to mind, also one by Johnson of Cowbridge (South Wales) c 1860 with a scene in the arch of a castle, entitled 'Carisbrooke Castle' (in the Isle of Wight), yet this bears no resemblance at all to the real Carisbrooke Castle. It is the same sort of situation which resulted in clocks sold in the Yorkshire Dales, for example, bearing on their dials thatched-roof cottages quite unlike anything in the locality where the clock would be sold. It arose through the centralised industry in Birmingham which offered the Birmingham version of a cottage, a castle or of the Levant Mine.

6

Dial Progression:
Period One, 1770–1800

Among the earliest types of white dial clock must surely be those with an all-white dial and gold-painted corner decorations, which resemble the rococo spandrels of a brass dial clock. I cannot prove that these were of the very earliest type, but it would seem reasonable to assume so, since later developments indicate that, as a general rule, the more colour the later the date of the clock. The dialmakers themselves called them *white* dials, not coloured dials. On these clocks the gold-painted corner decorations are obvious attempts to copy the traditional spandrel corners of a brass dial clock. This is not, however, to contradict my earlier remarks about the one-piece brass dial, where *engraved* corner decorations appear to copy white dial corner patterns. The clock by Pannel of Northallerton (page 106) does have all-gold corners, but here an actual object is featured rather than just gold scrollwork, and the Pannel clock is clearly later.

The full potential of what an artist might do to a clock dial is not yet realised. Here he is working in one colour only. He cannot achieve very much when colour, which is the essential factor of his medium, is denied him. To express the situation that way, however, is to put the cart before the horse. In considering dials of this type, we must imagine that we have never yet seen a coloured dial. The white dial of this gold-corner type has certain advantages over the brass dial, the principal one being its superb legibility.

The prime function of a clock, of course, to which any other consideration is secondary, is its ability to tell one the time at a glance. This kind of dial is clearly legible, legible in a way which will never again be seen to be matched in later longcase clocks. A disadvantage of course is that the white dial is more prone to damage such as chipping. The advantage was claimed for them that these dials would resist tarnishing.

20 Thirty-hour dial from a clock by William Terry of Bedale in Yorkshire, signed and dated 1787.

The examples illustrated are interesting in several ways. The Terry one is a typical country clock; the Nicholas one a town clock. I use these terms in their original meaning, not in the way that they are sometimes used, where 'town' means 'London'. By a country clock I mean one made for a country cottage or house (generally by a country maker). By a town clock I mean one made for a town house (generally by a town clockmaker). The former is a thirty-hour clock in a traditionally simple case. The latter is an eight-day clock in a

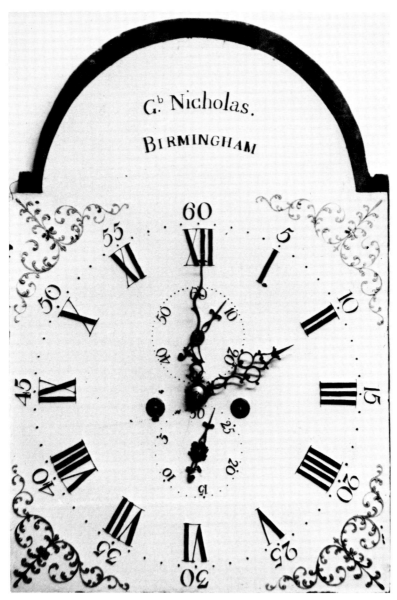

21 Unrestored dial from an eight-day clock by Caleb Nicholas of Birmingham c 1785. These all-white dial types were clearly legible and the gold corner decorations are vaguely reminiscent of the spandrels on brass dial clocks. At this time hands were of steel and of non-matching pattern.

more sophisticated case with a large amount of brasswork, all entirely original. The minute hand on the Terry clock is a replacement. The Terry clock is actually signed and the date inside is 1787, engraved by Terry into the brass frontplate. There is no name anywhere on it which might identify the dialmaker—not a falseplate dial. Terry is known to have worked at Bedale from at least 1770 to 1820 when he died.

The Nicholas clock was made about the same time, say 1785. It has a falseplate, but unfortunately one which is not stamped. The dial shows no impressed maker's mark. The date disc on this clock cannot help us with the dialmaker's name, as it is a replacement: I am certain about this, as I had it fitted, the original one being missing when I bought the clock. (A date disc on this type of clock is one which fits behind the pointer and by which the pointer is driven.) Known dates for Nicholas's working in Birmingham run from at least 1787 to 1808, but of course these are not terminal dates.

The Elliott of Whitby clock has an Osborne dial. The maker married at Whitby in 1788 and worked there till at least 1792. I would date this dial c 1785–90. The Swan clock (page 27) has an unmarked dial, which is in some ways an experimental one retaining the older-type engraved and silvered brass calendar disc (*not* believed to be a wrong replacement). This is a large dial (fourteen inches) and I would date it c 1780–90. Dials of this size are usually later but several features suggest this may be a locally made dial and it is a pity that no dialmaker's marks are present. Robert Swan married for the first time in 1757 and most of his clocks are brass dial ones. The two main hands may be later replacements but could perhaps be an early example of the use of brass hands.

Apart from their all-white dials with gold-painted corners, the Terry and Nicholas clocks both have certain features in common with other clocks of the earliest white dial period. The hands are of steel and non-matching (except the Swan clock). The original Terry minute hand would have been like the Nicholas one, or perhaps like the one by John Day of Wakefield, Yorkshire. Minute markings are indicated by *dots*, not by a continuous minute band. The minutes are numbered at intervals of 5, 10, 15, 20, etc. The hours are marked by *Roman* numbers. All these features are pointers which, when taken together, indicate the age of the clock. In the case of the arched dial a further indication is the largely undecorated arched part, bearing the name. In later clocks, as we shall see, the arch is filled completely by an oil-painted scene.

22 Thirteen-inch arched dial by Osborne, movement by William Elliott of Whitby, made c 1785. Note superior quality of moon dial painting. The non-matching steel hands are original. The globes are unusual in being cut at the equator.

23 Dial by James Wilson of Birmingham from a clock by John Day of Wakefield, c 1780–5. The steel hands are original and of non-matching pattern. The restoration of this dial has not been well done, for many of the finer details of the flower decorations are missing and the two flowers inside the centre circle are very faded.

While this type of dial was among the earliest styles of white dial, I do not mean to indicate that it was the only early style. Contemporary with this type was another, a little more colourful but with many similar features, which I shall examine next. There are maybe as many dial patterns as there are clocks. One often sees very similar dials but never in my experience any two identical ones, a possible exception being the Terry type where decoration is so sparse that there can be little variety. Also of course it was not a case of changing in 1770 to style B, then again in 1800 to style C, and so on. Obviously changes take place gradually and designs overlap from different periods. This is one reason why it is always difficult in any work on antiques to give actual dates for styles, for there are exceptions to every rule. My aim in this book is to outline the normal, the usual; and it must be assumed that the exceptions by their very nature are less likely to be encountered.

This is the first book which attempts to give serious guidance on the progression of and dating of white dial clocks. The reader may take it that before writing it I looked at what existing horological works say on the subject. If dates I suggest differ from those which any other writer may indicate, this is absolutely intentional; and as far as possible I shall give evidence to support my dates.

Now look at the other early type of white dial clock, as an example of which I have chosen a dial by John Day of Wakefield. The lettering says 'I. Day', but at the time 'I' was often used for 'J', especially in 'John'. The clock was made about 1780–5. It differs from the first two only in one essential: coloured painted decoration in the arch and corners replaces the gold 'spandrels' (and the name-plate on the Nicholas clock). It is of course a thirty-hour clock and therefore we expect no seconds dial. Thirty-hour clocks very rarely have seconds dials, though on later examples they sometimes have dummy ones. Eight-day clocks on the other hand usually do have seconds dials.

The dial by William Snow is very similar to the Day one and is probably also a Wilson dial. The Snow dial is unrestored and can be seen to be wearing thin in parts as far as the decoration goes, the lettering crudely touched in again. Craze marks show up clearly on both dials. William Snow senior died in 1795 and clocks by William Snow junior are believed not to have had the skeleton form of the father's movements. This dial dates from about 1780–5.

The minute hand of the Day clock is different in design, being of a slightly earlier style than that of the Nicholas clock. The Day dial has two concentric black circles, which the Terry clock also has, but which do not show on the Nicholas one. This last feature is not, however, an important one, and I shall explain why. I know all these clocks, as I have owned them. Over the years the black-painted numbering tends to wear off with cleaning and today one often has to restore some of this lettering. All three of these dials have been retouched in varying degree. The Nicholas one has not had its circles repainted, though they *were* there when it was new. I explain these small differences to avoid confusion, but they are really unimportant.

24 Unrestored thirty-hour dial probably by James Wilson of Birmingham, c 1780, from a clock by Will Snow of Padside, North Yorkshire. Birds and flowers were very popular themes at this time.

The Day clock, like the Terry one, shows the date through an aperture, not with a pointer as the Nicholas clock does. These early clocks more frequently do have aperture dates rather than pointer date-hands, but on eight-day clocks a pointer is sometimes used to balance, ie visually, the seconds pointer. The Day clock is typical in style of very many clocks, but on each similar one the corner and arch designs will vary. Sometimes the corners depict flower sprays, or fruit such as strawberries. The arch may show a bird, or a flower, or a spray of flowers, or fruit. The position of the man's name may vary as will the style of script; but the dial pattern, its overall outline, is the same. The pattern of numbering in particular is an important

25 Eight-day dial from a clock by John Bancroft of Scarborough, c 1780–90. The dial
has been 'restored' though not particularly well. Notice that the globes are worn very
faint and the artist has not attempted to renew the worn details.

factor. The special popularity of strawberries as corner decorations
has led to this general type of dial being described as a 'strawberry-
corner' type.

John Day is known to have worked at Wakefield from at least
1770 to 1801, in which year he died there. This dial is stamped 'Wil-
son-Birmingham', which dates it as post-1778. A reasonable
assessment would be 1780–5, maybe 1790.

Illustrated is the dial of an eight-day clock by John Bancroft of
Scarborough which at one time belonged to me. It was made about
the same time as the Day clock, perhaps just a little later, say 1780–
90. Apart from the arch, the dial is very similar to the Day clock,

95

though of course it has the normal (with eight-day clocks) seconds dial and matching date pointer. The hands are of non-matching pattern in blued steel, the serpentine minute hand dating from just a little later than the straight one by Day. The corner decorations are enclosed by double ruled lines, which again may suggest a slightly later date, but this detail is not really significant. The arch carries a moon dial showing the lunar date (here it is 21) and the shape of the moon in the sky. As the month progresses the moon wanes by disappearing behind the right-hand 'hump', and as it fades away completely a new moon face begins to appear from the left. This type of moon dial is used for about fifty years or so from the start of white dial clocks; in exceptional instances longer. Those clocks without the moon are more common than those with such a dial, but when they have a moon dial this is the type they usually have, right through the period without changing. Moon dials are dealt with in detail in Chapter 15. John Bancroft worked at Scarborough prior to 1807, and probably died before 1820.

Another type of moon dial appears on some square-dial clocks where a semicircular aperture below the numeral XII shows the moon's phases. This type was often made around the turn of the century, about 1790–1820.

The dial by James Lomax of Blackburn (see page 91) is almost identical in style to the Bancroft one, differing from it in one respect only: the shape of the dial. This may give it a superficially different appearance, but it is not really an important difference, at least as far as stylistic dial progression and dating are concerned. Presumably a dial of such unusual shape had to be ordered and made specially for the customer in question. It is an extremely unusual *shape* of dial, but the features on it are almost exactly the same as on the Bancroft one. The dial has a Wilson falseplate, which we know limits it to the period 1778–1809. James Lomax was born in 1749 and died in 1814, which does not help in narrowing down the period. My own estimate would be 1785–95.

The clocks by Day and Bancroft represent the stock types of dial (with or without moon disc) used during this early period of white dial production, 1770–1800, during which time there is not a great deal of change in the appearance of dials. The Day and Bancroft types of clock appear to begin contemporary with the Terry and Nicholas ones, but to have become much more numerous and, presumably therefore, more popular. Many clocks one sees have this type of dial

26 Eight-day dial by Osborne of Birmingham from a clock by Rowlands of Berwick-on-Tweed, c 1780–90. The restoration of the lettering is not well done and even the numbers are heavier than the originals. The minute hand is a replacement of a much later style.

and most would fall into the period 1770–90.

An eight-day clock by Rowlands of Berwick on Tweed, North-umberland, is illustrated. Several men of this name worked there in overlapping periods so in this instance the maker's name is not a great help in dating. It is very often the case that, when a clockmaker signs with his surname only, it may well be a family concern (perhaps just father and son); when he works alone he usually adds his first name or initials. He does not 'sign' it with his own hand of course, but has the name painted on the dial for him by the dialmaker.

This clock by Rowlands was made about 1780–90. It has a false-plate by Osborne of Birmingham, and must therefore be pre-1803.

The hands are of a non-matching steel pattern: the minute and seconds hands are both later replacements. Even where only the hour hand remains of the original two hands, it is apparent from the style of that hour hand as to whether the clock had matching or non-matching hands. As we shall see later, the hour hand from a matching pair is considerably different in style.

The dial is similar to the one by Day: notice the familiar themes of birds and flowers. These must obviously have been favourite themes with the public of the day, bringing a touch of the beauty and colour of nature into the home. This is something the brass dial clock could never do, nor did it attempt to. 'Not only can we make more legible clocks', the white dial makers must have claimed, 'we can give you something altogether more colourful and picturesque, bringing the brightness and colour of a spring day into your home all the year round.' True, when one remembers that these clocks were seen in candle-lit homes, which could be rather gloomy and drab, especially in the months of winter, with dreary days of rain and mist.

Today some people have a superstition about its being unlucky to have pictures of birds in the house. This cannot be a very old superstition, as vast numbers of these white dial clocks depict birds as a favourite theme. Probably the majority of the earlier-period white dials have as their theme either flowers or birds or both, to the extent that this in itself is almost a feature by which one can date a clock.

The dial by Forster of Sheerness, Kent (see page 159), shows nothing new. It illustrates the type of dial we have already examined as used on a southern clock. The strike/silent indicator in the arch is an interesting variation, and seems to have been a feature used much more often in the south than in the north. It is not really indicative of a particular period, though it would probably be unusual after 1820 or so. By rotating the pointer, one can 'switch off' the strike at night time or permanently if one wishes. A strike/silent dial was an optional extra and must have put up the initial cost of the clock slightly, by virtue of there being additional work in the clockmaking. This clock was made about 1790. G. H. Baillie in *Watchmakers and Clockmakers of the World* lists the maker as a member of the London Clockmakers' Company and also gives this same approximate date. It is interesting that a maker with London connections should have bought his dials from Birmingham: the falseplate on this dial is stamped 'Wilson' of Birmingham. This suggests that this type of japanned dial was not made in London.

Before going further it might be as well for me to mention the position of the square dial in relation to the arched one. The arched dial was always the more numerous type and presumably the most popular one. Square dials were used as well as arched ones from the very beginning of the white dial period. Generally, the square dial is more of a country or village product while the arched dial could apply to either town or country. The square dial was cheaper to make, if only because there was less decoration to paint on, and the case hood for the square dial clock must have been easier and cheaper to make. While the square dial begins alongside the arched one, it does not survive for as long. Presumably its popularity waned in favour of the more colourful arched type, and/or dialmakers found it economical to stick to the one type of dial. The square dial is seldom used in the north later than about 1820 to 1830; in the south it survived a little later. The square dial was dying out about fifty years after its introduction; the arched dial had almost a further fifty years to run.

During the first thirty years of these clocks, from about 1770 to 1800, the basic dial styles remained more or less unchanged in so far as there was little progression during that time. With the opening years of the new century, however, things began to happen. As with almost all such evolutionary changes, the main thing to bear in mind is that throughout the period one of the most important factors influencing such progression was the saving of time in order to keep costs down and compete more strongly against rivals · rivals both in the sense of other clockmaking concerns and also other types and nationalities of clock. All the time then, changes were occurring partly to follow the whims of fashion, but more particularly where those whims could be exploited to save work, time and cost. The dialmakers themselves must have created fashion.

An interesting type of clock is one which has moving figures in the arch. On brass dial clocks one occasionally finds a figure of Father Time with his scythe swaying to and fro in the arch. This is basically a simple device, the moving figure being attached to an extension wire from the escapement arbor, so that as the pendulum swings to the right, the figure swings to the left, swaying once a second in other words. The dials which have moving figures are a little more complicated than ordinary ones, because of the construction of the

27　A black japanned dial, perhaps unique, the 'negative' appearance being very impressive. The dialmaker is unknown and this looks as if it may be a brass dial which has been japanned later, dating from c 1770.

purpose-made dial from composite pieces. The backcloth of the arch scene was usually set back from the foreground to allow a space wide enough for the support-piece of the swaying figure. These dials were more costly to buy. (For prices of dials, see Chapter 9.)

I have seen white dials with swaying figures which were made as early as 1790, though the majority seem to be later, about 1820–30. This is consistent, as we shall see later, with the general dial style which by this time has a fully painted scene in the arch. There are all sorts of interesting versions, being generally far more varied than the swaying figures on a brass dial clock. A common theme is a ship rocking on a painted sea, but all kinds of themes are possible. I have seen a swan swimming on a lake; a blacksmith striking his anvil; Eve picking an apple from the tree and then swaying across to hand it to Adam. Sometimes one sees two moving figures, eg two men sawing wood with a two-handled saw. These moving figures, not particularly common on northern clocks, seem to have been most popular in the West Country. Perhaps a rocking ship was more appropriate for a seafaring county such as Devon.

An indication of the variety of rocking figures available can be gathered from the Wilkes price list on page 84, where they do in fact offer to make moving figures to *any* design.

Illustrated is a black white dial—the only one of this type that I have ever come across. I have not examined the clock itself, but it does look as though this may have been a conventional brass dial which was later japanned over, like the one by Hardaker. It is certainly a most unusual and effective treatment.

7

Dial Progression:
Period Two, 1800–1830

The period beginning about 1800 and lasting at most thirty years is one partly of experiment with dial styles. It is a hard period to define clearly and precisely, but there are a few factors which crop up regularly, if not constantly, during this time.

The first dial we show is from a clock by Robert Gillies of Beith, near Glasgow. It was made in 1802. Under the seatboard is written, presumably by Gillies himself, 'Robt. Gillies, Clock Maker, July 1802'. This is not proof, of course, of his having written it. It *could* have been written by anyone at any time. However, it is in a script of this period, and as the dial features suggest the same time, I am inclined to accept it as accurate. Gillies is known to have been working there by 1780.

With this dial we are just entering the new century, and much of the style of it is reminiscent of the old one. Minutes are marked by dots and numbered fully; the arch is not yet filled completely with painting; the corners are not filled but have flowery tracery only. There is no falseplate on this dial, and no dialmaker's name; but painted large on the back of the dial is the number 44, the meaning of which is now lost to us. One quite often sees numbers of this sort painted on dial backs. Perhaps they meant something to the dialpainter: maybe the number of dials he had painted. It could even have been the number of the clock the maker sold, though this is unlikely. It may have had some temporary meaning only. I remember once pointing out the numbering 1140 on the back of a dial which produced the suggestion that perhaps this was the time the dialpainter went for lunch!

What is new about this dial then? Just the hands. These are now of matching pattern, though still in steel, of course. Hour and minute hands match each other; seconds and date hands also

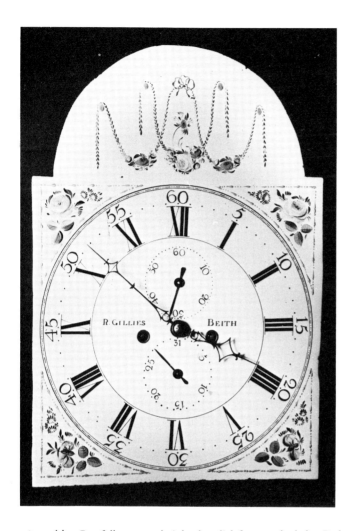

28a and b Carefully-restored eight-day dial from a clock by Robert Gillies of Beith made in 1802. The underside view of the seatboard shows the maker's signature and date and also shows well the two thumbscrews which attach the board to the lower two movement pillars. The matching steel hands appear to be original.

match each other, but not the two larger ones. This is an arrangement which is normal from now on. Naturally, datelines must not be taken too rigidly. It is not impossible for a clock to have matching steel hands by 1795, or even 1790. But one can be reasonably sure that they would not appear by 1780. A line has to be drawn somewhere, and 1800 is a good clear date after which one would normally expect a clock to have matching steel hands.

Early matching steel hands are usually of the 'diamond' pattern, as here. We are assuming that this dial is an English-made one. It may not be—it could have been made in Scotland (see Chapter 13)—but for the purposes of this discussion it makes no difference whether it was made in England or Scotland, for we are here interested in its stylistic features.

The next dial of this period is one which exhibits several interesting transitional features. Another reason why I have used it is that, in the arch, on the stone against which the gentleman in naval uniform is leaning, 'Horace Nelson' is written. This does not show in the photograph, as the dial is obviously in a very shabby state. However it is reasonable to assume, especially since the dial style is also consistent with that assumption, that it was made about the time of Nelson's death, 1805. Fothergill's were established in Knaresborough, Yorkshire, prior to 1807.

Some of the changes taking place in dial styles as shown by this example are as follows. The minutes are no longer numbered 5, 10, 15, 20, etc, but merely 15, 30, 45, 60, the other numerals being replaced by little star motifs. Minute numbering will soon be dropped completely, and this is a step on the way. The minutes are still marked by dots, but this too is soon to change. One factor which may have a bearing on the dropping of the five-minute numerals is the general increase in education. More people now could read and write, though by no means all, and with the increase in literacy and 'scholarship' of the average person comes a decrease in the need to spell everything out for him. People now knew from infancy that two past eight meant ten minutes past eight. This cannot have been the case when a clock was the possession of the few. The white dial clock was rapidly becoming cheap enough to be bought by the masses. Children growing up in a home with a clock in it soon learned to tell the time, while it can hardly have been as important to them to learn how to do this in a house where there was no clock.

As the minute numbering gradually drops out, along with this

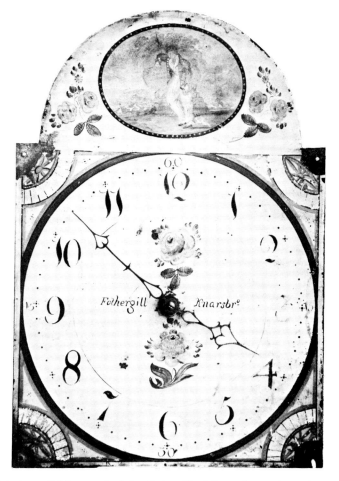

29   Thirty-hour dial from a clock by Fothergill of Knaresborough, made c 1805. The figure in the arch in naval dress leans against a stone on which are the words 'Horace Nelson'. The dial is in very dirty and neglected condition.

comes a switch in the hour numerals. Roman hour numerals, used on all earlier clocks, now begin to be replaced by Arabic numbers, as on this Fothergill dial. There may have been a slight saving in time in that these may have been somewhat quicker to paint than Roman numerals.

The arch painting is spreading. No longer a simple spray of flowers but a whole vignette scene takes up much of the arch, with a spray at either side. The painting of the corner decorations is also spreading. Again, this becomes more than just a spray and begins to fill the whole of each corner. The corner designs now often cease to be floral and become much more geometrical, the quarter circle or fan pat-

30 Unrestored dial (maker unknown) from a clock by Joshua Pannel of Northallerton, made c 1800. The clockmaker died in 1803. The portrait in the arch would appear to be Nelson and the naval battle below presumably represents one of his victories. The very high quality of the painting contrasts strongly with the feeble efforts on many late dials. An odd feature is that the Roman numerals are all set vertically, instead of radiating from the centre.

31 Dial from an eight-day clock by Tate of Winterton, c 1815, the dial by William Francis of Birmingham. Wellington's name is lettered on the trumpet sash and the names of his victories are lettered on the drapes, terminating in Waterloo.

tern, as illustrated here, being much favoured. The hands, as with the last example, are in matching pairs, still made of blued steel.

The nineteenth century is getting under way: things are moving. The changes mentioned above mostly arise from a saving of work. An increase in the *painted* area perhaps arose from a desire for a more colourful, showy dial; but the extra painting time is offset by a saving in lettering time. The features of this Fothergill dial are typical of the time, though of course some dials still follow the traditional pattern more closely (as with the Gillies one) or depart from it in more gradual stages, with a mixture of old and new styles in this change-over period.

A clock by Joshua Pannel of Northallerton also has Nelson as the theme. The dialmaker in this instance is not known, but the painting is obviously of a far superior quality to the rather feeble effort of the Fothergill Nelson dial. The Pannel dial retains dotted minutes, drops the 5, 10, 20, 25, etc, numbering, but retains Roman hour numerals, in this instance rather unusually set in a vertical position. I would date this dial about 1800 to 1810, but as Joshua Pannel died in 1803, we have to assume that it would be limited to the 1800–3 period. We have, however, to bear in mind that it was not unusual for a clockmaker's widow to carry on trading after the death of her husband, especially if she employed a journeyman clockmaker, and it is therefore possible theoretically to have a clock made in 1805 bearing the name of a clockmaker who had died in 1803.

The clock by Tate of Winterton, Lincolnshire, can again be closely dated to about 1815–16, because the name of Wellington is written in the trumpet sash and his many victories are named on the drapes, terminating with Waterloo (1815). The only real progression from the Pannel dial is that a full minute band has returned. This dial was made by William Francis of Birmingham, working c 1810–31.

In Period Two, the hour numerals alternate between Roman and Arabic, probably depending on the whim of the dialmaker. The minutes are marked by dots or a band or sometimes by a single line with markers through it, again probably depending on the dial-maker's own choice. Any of these permutations may appear at this time.

The next dial illustrated is by John Palliser of Thirsk, Yorkshire, and was made in 1817. There is no guesswork about this. We know exactly, as the movement is also engraved with his name and the date '8th March 1817'. Why it has the precise date in this way, I

32 Thirty-hour dial from a clock by John Palliser of Thirsk, dialmaker unknown. The clock movement is engraved with the maker's name and the date 8th March 1817. The original hands are of matching pattern in steel. Corner patterns of a semi-geometric nature were popular at the time, especially fan-like motifs.

do not know. I am only thankful to have found that it has, since dated longcase clocks are very uncommon. They are especially valuable for noting changes such as those we are discussing. This dial shows a mixture of features. The arch is filling up, though it is not quite full. The corner decorations are of a semi-geometric nature. The hands are of matching steel pattern. Then—a rather unusual feature—the minutes are marked by dashes, not dots, almost joining the black circles into a minute band, something which will in fact take place regularly before much longer. The minutes are not numbered at all. The hours have retained Roman numerals. This is an early clock of John Palliser's, just as the clock by Fothergill was an early one of his production. The Palliser dial has no falseplate, the movement being fixed direct to the dial.

I shall now show you a later dial by each of these men. Both have matching steel hands still; and the arch part of the dial is now entirely filled with painting. Both have full minute bands with no minute numbering at all; and the corners are completely filled with decorative painting, the dial by Palliser being of a geometric nature still. The Palliser dial retains the Arabic hour numerals of the transitional period; the Fothergill one has gone a stage further in a *return* to Roman numerals for the hours. Incidentally, the Fothergill dial is a 'dished' one, ie the entire centre area bearing numbers is in the form of a raised convex bowl, which is not apparent from the photograph. 'Dished' dials of this type are not uncommon from this time on. The

33 (*left*) Dial from a thirty-hour clock by Palliser of Thirsk, made about 1820. The numbers and name have been restored clumsily. These are tumbling numbers, reversing direction from 4 to 8. Fan corner decorations are typical of the early years of the century.

34 (*right*) Thirty-hour dial of c 1825–30 from a clock by Fothergill's of Knaresborough. The dial was made by Walker & Hughes of Birmingham and is of the dished (convex) centre type. The original hands are of matching steel pattern. The numbers here indicate a return to Roman lettering.

second Fothergill dial has no falseplate, but fits direct to the movement. It has no dialmaker's name, but behind the arch, impressed into the dial sheet, are the initials 'W. H.' This must surely represent the firm of Walker & Hughes which, as we have seen from the list of Birmingham dialmakers, was working from 1811 onwards. The second Palliser dial is about 1820–5; the second Fothergill one about 1825–30. In these dials we see the departure from the early type; experimentation through the early years of the century; and the return with the later Fothergill dial to a more standardised, but new, type. These styles are in *northern* clocks: not quite the same thing applies in the south, as we shall see.

Next we examine the dial (and hood) of a clock by John Farrer of Pontefract, Yorkshire, included partly because of its style and partly because it is a rather attractive clock. It has Arabic hour numerals, no minute numbers, geometric corner patterns, and arch painting enclosed in an unusual octagonal box instead of the more normal oval shape, and matching hands now in brass. It was made about 1815–20. Hands in brass are a new feature which are shortly to become standard in all later clocks (of northern or Midlands areas). Notice that their shape is not unlike those of the first Fothergill clock, and quite different from the later matching ones in brass. The Farrer clock has brass hands but of the normal steel hands shape.

Notice that this dial appears not to have a full minute band, the minutes being marked by dashes. In fact, this is an omission in the relettering, and when one examines the dial closely, it is obvious that it did originally have a full minute band, just like the second Fothergill and second Palliser dials. No factual data can be assembled on this maker, since there was a whole family of this name making clocks in Pontefract and the data on them are too confused to be of assistance.

Now we examine a dial by Woolston Roberts of Derby. It has the traditional and still typical moon dial. By this I mean that where white dial clocks have a moon dial, this is usually the kind they have. Some square dials have a semicircular moon dial set in below the numeral XII, but this type is less common and is largely northern. For dating purposes a moon dial is disappointing since the same type of moon dial is used virtually unchanged over a long period, and it takes up all the arched top area, which would otherwise provide very helpful information from its decorative style.

One gets used to seeing moon dials like this one, as it is the com-

35 Hood and dial of an eight-day clock by John Farrer of Pontefract, Yorkshire, made about 1820. The brass hands appear to be original. Decoration of the corners and arch have bold black borders edged in gold. The corner motifs are based on shell and fan themes.

monest type. But in fact probably no more than 10 per cent of white dial clocks have these moon dials, and since they involved more work and cost in manufacture, presumably we ought to value a clock with a moon dial a little more highly than one without. They appear on thirty-hour clocks less frequently than on eight-day ones.

The two hemispheres below the moon disc are painted here, as normally, to represent terrestrial globes. Of course, they serve no purpose other than that of decoration. Presumably they arose from some dialmaker's idea of how to use up two almost circular spare shapes. They are usually, but not always, mapped out as a globe.

This dial by Roberts has corner decorations which are unique in

36 Unrestored dial from an eight-day clock by Woolston Roberts of Derby, made c 1820. The brass calendar disc is a later replacement. The hands are of matching pattern in brass. Patches can be seen where 'shake' on the dial feet ends has caused chipping, but a good dial restorer could soon put this right.

my experience. The little oval urn decorations are half-round (convex) beads actually stuck on, and the painting is applied on them and around them in the usual way. The owner of the clock told me that at one time one of the beads fell off and was lost, and he replaced it with an imitation one, repainting it to match the others.

The dial has suffered a little with time. In particular, the date disc which shows through the aperture above the maker's name is an incorrect replacement. Originally it was made for a brass dial clock and is of course made of brass. The seconds hand is a modern replacement. The main hands are apparently original, being of matching brass pattern.

There is a similarity in numbering on this dial to that of the first Fothergill clock, ie the 5 and 10 minutes numbers are replaced by a decorative motif. It also has Arabic hour numbers. A difference, however, is the full minute band: the Fothergill dial had dots. There is no dialmaker's name. The reference books immortalise Roberts, like so many other makers of white dial clocks, by failing to mention him at all. So here you will have to rely purely on my dating—about 1820. Why not nearer 1800? Well, the use of the full minute band and the brass instead of steel hands suggest to me no earlier than 1815. (Since the first edition of this book was published, Woolston Roberts has been recorded in *Watchmakers and Clockmakers of the World*, Volume Two. Latest information puts his working dates as 1818–49.)

The next dial to be discussed (see page 51) is by Juler of North Walsham, Norfolk, and it is a little unusual. All the painting on the dial is in gold with black outlines—different and very effective.

There is no corner decoration; in fact there is no decoration at all, apart from the gold scrollwork around the name. The dial is 12in wide. The use of just the name in the arch is reminiscent of the Nicholas clock. The steel hour and minute hands are probably replacements and can be disregarded for dating purposes. The steel seconds and date hands are probably original.

On the reverse of the dial there are a few items scratched on by a clock cleaner or repairer who must have serviced the clock in the past. This is an interesting feature which many clocks have, and of course you will see this sort of thing only if you look specially for it. Such things add to the interest of a clock, but you have to know what to expect in order to be able to watch out for them. The repairer's name could not be deciphered. Following it are these dates scratched into the black backing paint: February 72; February 74; January 77; April 83.

If we look at G. H. Baillie's *Watchmakers and Clockmakers of the World* we find: 'Juler, John, N. Walsham 1753–73'. With this to guide us we might arrive at a date of pre-1772, say 1770. If so we would be quite wrong.

The original hands would almost certainly have been matching steel ones, though you have only my word for that. The largely white dial is misleading, looking superficially like the Nicholas type, but not when you examine it properly. Arabic hour numbers, full minute band without numbering of minutes—these together ought to date the clock about 1810 or 1820, no earlier. The date pointer instead of the aperture date is often a late sign. An important clue is that the dial has a falseplate stamped 'Finnemore—Birmingham', and Finnemores worked there after 1812. The cleaners' dates of '72', etc, must be 1872 not 1772. The clock was made about 1820.

But what about Baillie's dates? Well, I say again: judge for yourself on evidence, then turn to a reference book for confirmation if you wish. But don't change your ideas because of a date given in a book. I am not saying that Baillie is wrong about John Juler, who may well have been working at the dates he quotes. But if so, he did not make this clock. This must have been sold by a later man of the same name, perhaps a son, unless John was still selling clocks in his nineties. The fact that Baillie does not show a John Juler working about 1820 does not mean that there was no such person.

Since these words were written for the first edition a second volume to Baillie has been published, compiled by myself. This is known as Volume Two and includes several other members of the Juler family, amongst them George Juler, working 1830–58, who may have been the maker of this clock. However this principle still holds good. Learn to judge for yourself, then you can form an opinion whether or not the standard reference books can assist you. By all means use Baillie, Volumes One and Two, but you ought to *know* the age of a clock just by looking at it.

Dials of this almost-all-white style seem to have been popular in East Anglia rather than throughout the country as a whole.

Finally, in this same period still, I illustrate a southern clock by Joseph Keys of Exeter. This dial, as is obvious, is in rather poor condition, the white background being crazed. This is a fault which affects some clocks as they age, though fortunately not too many of them.

37　Unrestored thirty-hour dial in very poor condition from a clock by Joseph Keys of
Exeter, the dial by Walker & Hughes of Birmingham. The clock was actually dated
15 April 1825. The matching steel hands are original. Though in a very worn state, this
dial is basically sound and could be restored to its original condition by a good dial restorer.

The top right-hand corner has been cleaned and relettered to show
clearly the original numbering, and also to illustrate how dirty and
faded the rest of the dial is. It is 11 in square and has an aperture date.
At first sight this may seem to be an early clock. But southern dial
styles tend to be conservative and lag behind northern ones in some
respects. Therefore we get used to adding a few years on to the *painting* style of a similar northern clock, with which we might compare
it. The numbering style should give the main clue: full minute band,
Arabic hour numbers, no minute numbering. These suggest a date
of post-1815. The matching steel (original) hands suggest a date of
post-1800. By 1830 we shall see that further changes have developed.
We are reasonably certain by these features to be in the period 1815–
30. There is no falseplate on this clock, but careful examination
showed 'Walker & Hughes' stamped into the rear of the date wheel.
On the reverse of the dial is an unclear impressed mark reading 'W.
& ?', which must have been 'W. & H.' Walker & Hughes we

already know were Birmingham dialmakers working from 1811 to 1835, being consistent with the period we have already estimated. We said 1815 as an 'at least' date. A fair assessment would be, say, 1820–30. The case, in solid mahogany, has *branded* into the backboard and into the back of the door, 'J. Keys'; and penned alongside the name is 'April 15 1825', unquestionably the year in which the clock was made. Since I wrote this, the clock has been cleaned, and the same date and name were found engraved *inside* the movement. When the first edition was published Joseph Keys appeared in no reference book. Not because he was not a clockmaker, but just because reference books are not 100 per cent complete. I therefore tried to look him up through local directories. He was a watchmaker at West Street, Exeter, from 1830 to 1837. By 1852 he was at James Street, and was still listed there in 1857. If therefore he did appear in a reference book, the book could well give his dates as 1830–57; rather misleading. However, while I was unable to locate a pre-1830 directory, we know from his thoughtfulness in dating this clock, that he was working prior to 1825. And, most important, we know from the dial style that the clock was made before 1830 and could not possibly have been made anywhere near as late as 1857.

I let this last paragraph stand from the first edition to show the principle, but research has also caught up with Joseph Keys in recent years. He appears in Baillie, Volume Two, now, but the latest research on him is in Clive Ponsford's book *Time in Exeter*, which shows him working there by 1822 till his death in 1865 aged 76.

As an interesting oddity in Period Two dials, we next have a dial from a clock by Stonehouse of Leeds. A whole family of this name worked there and information on the makers will not help pin down the age of this clock, but by now we know that this dial must date from about 1820–30. It has a most unusual black band with white (negative) numbering. The dial has been restored, but not altered. It has no falseplate or dialmaker's marks and may perhaps be a locally made dial. I have not seen this style before. The corner paintings illustrate Faith, Hope, Charity and Justice. In the arch are The Three Nuns. The quality of painting is not superb, but neither is it of the appalling quality of some religious dials of the 1840s. The hands on the two subdials are modern replacements. The main hands of matching brass pattern are original.

38 Unusual, restored arched dial, maker unknown, from an eight-day clock by the Stonehouse family of clockmakers in Leeds, made c 1820–30. It has the Four Virtues in the corners, the Three Nuns in the arch. The hours band is painted in negative with white lettering on a black ground, an extremely uncommon treatment. It may be a locally made dial.

8

Dial Progression: Period Three, 1830–1870

Having begun the previous chapter with a Scottish clock, it seems only right to begin this one with a Welsh clock, though perhaps it is slightly out of sequence here. I illustrate a clock by Stephens & Davies of Neath, Glamorgan. This has a falseplate dial, the falseplate being stamped 'Finnemore—Birmingham'. We know that this puts the date as post-1812, but as this concern worked through a long period, this is as far as the dialmaker's name helps in dating.

The dial is not unlike the one shown a little later by Richard Snow of Pateley Bridge, Yorkshire, though an eight-day one. When we compare the cases of each later, it is only fair to point out that Snow put considerably better cases on to his eight-day clocks than on to his thirty-hour ones. The arch area is entirely filled with painting, joining up to the corner paintings, which run into each other. Actually, this clock has five oil paintings which run into each other around the dial. A romanticised scene of a shepherd with his dog fills the arch. This liberal use of paint dates the dial as post-1830. So too do the brass hands, full minute band, Roman hour numerals, and the absence of minute numbering. I would put this clock at 1840, but 1830–40 would be an acceptable estimate.

The dial is fairly typical. One might normally expect a date pointer at this period; but, as here, an aperture date is not impossible. The black numbering seems unduly heavy on this dial, but that is how it was originally. It has not been relettered.

The dial by William Hooker of Lewes, Sussex, is of course a southern clock. At first sight one might be deceived into thinking that the date of it is earlier than it really is. The dial is 11in square. Fortunately it bears an additional name, 'C. Waldrett', and the date '1833'. Dated clocks are very unusual, though of course I have tried to show a number of them in this book, one with a known date being by

39 Dial from an eight-day clock c 1835 by Stephens & Davies of Neath. Bold painted scenes joining together around the dial centre and heavy Roman numerals without minutes become increasingly typical from now on.

far the best for reference purposes. Don't expect to come across many dated clocks in the normal way of things, however, as I should think you would find a date on less than one in a hundred.

We can only assume that C. Waldrett was the clock owner who wished to have his name on the dial, and the date was perhaps to mark some special event. Clocks were quite often made as wedding presents, and of those that do bear the names of owners they often have the name of both the bride and bridegroom, as well as the wedding date. This clock was probably made in 1833 to mark a special occasion for the owner. An alternative explanation of the second name and date is given a little later on in this book. It is just possible

40 Thirty-hour dial from a clock by William Hooker of Lewes, Sussex. This one is dated 1833, though one normally expects fan-pattern corners to be a little earlier. The name 'C. Waldrett' may be the owner the clock was made for, or perhaps a journeyman working for Hooker's widow.

that 'C. Waldrett 1833' could have been painted on the dial at a later date, but the dial-numbering style is consistent with this post-1830 period. I keep trying to anticipate possible objections on the grounds of something being a later modification or alteration, but in reality it is the exception which has been tampered with and one does not expect this to apply to the general run of white dial clocks one meets with. On the other hand it is best to approach a clock suspiciously and critically if you are thinking of buying it or even simply of studying it. If you are looking for faults you are perhaps more likely to spot them, but some people may look so searchingly as to find faults that are not really there. It is I think true that of all antique objects which may suffer from alteration, modification and sheer faking, white dial longcase clocks are among those *least* subject to such practices, probably because their value until quite recently has been low. A man with the talents of faking would not waste them on a thirty-hour clock by William Hooker, when he could be faking much more valuable stuff. The more modest the clock, the more likely it is that no one has ever thought of tampering with it.

In the north in 1833 they were generally using much bigger dials, and even a square one by then would measure 12in or 13in. The 'north' in this context and throughout most of this book means any-where which is not the south: in other words, Wales, the Midlands and all central England would come under the heading 'the north'. East Anglia and any counties to the south of London, I would regard as 'the south'. Square dials seem to be less common in the north by this time, and an arched dial of 1833 in the north would usually be 13in or 14in wide, and even 15in is not unusual. White dial clocks were always more popular and therefore more numerous in the north than in the south, and southern clocks therefore are more likely to lag behind in fashion. There was not the same enthusiastic demand for them in the south, and I think it would be very uncommon to find southern clocks as large or as late as the northern ones. Clocks such as the J. C. Elliott one illustrated later would be totally unknown in the south, which is why some of the old-fashioned clock books refer to any big clock as a 'Yorkshire clock', regardless of where it was made.

The Hooker clock is evidence of this fashion lag. The corner decorations of the fan type would be far more likely to occur on a northern or Midlands clock about 1810; and by 1830 they are defi-nitely out of favour in those areas, as will be seen in the examples I show. What reveals the age, apart from the date on the dial, is the full minute band and the lack of minute numbering; also the return to Roman hour numerals which we saw in the Welsh clock. The case of this clock I cannot comment on, as the clock had lost its case. The hands too were lost. There was no falseplate; the long dial feet fitted direct to the movement. Nor was there any dialmaker's name.

I have learnt from a gentleman who owns an eight-day Hooker of Lewes clock, of the all-white-dial type, that William Hooker first appears in Lewes records in 1803 when his shop was at 12 High Street. This eight-day clock is not unlike the Juler dial, but it has Roman hour numerals, a full minute band, and in the arch just a strike/silent lever—no coloured decoration at all. Hooker of Lewes is probably the same man listed by Baillie as being apprenticed in London in 1794. He would then have been about fifteen years old, serving a seven-year apprenticeship, and so would be 'out of his time' about 1801. It seems that he was making his presence felt at Lewes shortly afterwards. He appears in various directories up to 1832. In the next directory, of 1839, a Mrs Mary Hooker, clockmaker, is recorded at that address. Evidently William died before 1839 and not long after making the clock illustrated. It is even possible that C. Waldrett was a journeyman clockmaker working for Mrs Hooker after her husband's death and that he was given 'second billing' on the dial.

The strike/silent lever I mention is a simple lever device which allows one to have the clock running without striking if one so wishes. It seems to be much more a southern feature than a northern one. I don't know why, but it is very uncommon on northern white dial clocks. A possible reason might be that northern clocks tend to have the arch fully used up by a painted scene, thereby leaving no space for such a lever which, when present, is almost always found in the arched area.

Another southern clock illustrated (see page 44) is by a Dawlish, Devonshire, maker, whose name unfortunately is so worn away as to be illegible. The 10½in square dial, aperture date, flower corner decorations—all these we would expect to be early features on a northern clock; but we know to expect them slightly later on southern clocks. The hands are of brass and matching pattern, as will apply to virtually all white dial clocks from now on. The hour hand of course has partly broken away. It has a full minute band without minute numbering: the minute band has been partly touched in to show the style. The hour numerals are Roman. All these later features give us a clue that the dial was almost certainly made after 1825, even later than 1830. If the maker's name had been legible we might have been able to look up some working dates to help. In this instance, however, we are lucky since the dial, though not a false-plate one, is stamped with the dialmaker's name. In the top left-hand corner (from behind) is stamped 'Wright—Birm.', and the same wording is also stamped into the reverse of the date wheel, ie the numbered date disc which shows through the aperture. We know that Christopher Wright of Birmingham does not appear in the records until the directory of 1835–6, and his name disappears after having been entered in the directory of 1845. We can therefore set the date of this dial as after 1830 to before 1849, and probably in the 1835–45 period. It is very satisfying to be able to pin it down to a short period in this way. There is no guesswork about it: we *know* when the clock was made. The case, we shall see, also *appears* at first sight to date considerably earlier than it is. More recent research dates B. Wright of Birmingham as c 1805–20, so this dial need not necessarily be post-1830. I stick to my 1835 dating.

To those of us who are familiar with the established horological reference books, these last two clocks might come as a surprise. Almost without exception we are told that London led the field, and in dating a provincial clock we could expect to add twenty years or so to the date of that style in London. This may even be true in the pre-1750 period of longcase clockmaking. From the latter half of the eighteenth century onwards, however, the longcase clock was not really a popular form of clock in London, and it never became so firmly established there or elsewhere in the south as it did in the north. So far does this apply that, rather than being twenty years behind the southern fashions, the north was in fact twenty years ahead of them where the development of the longcase white dial clock was concerned. William Hooker, being London-trained, presumably was as familiar with the fashions of the capital in clocks as anyone else in the southern provinces.

Clockmakers like the Snow family of Pateley Bridge, Yorkshire, were ahead of their southern contemporaries in catering for the demand for the newer styles of white dial clocks; and clocksellers in the Midlands and north were prompt to anticipate the demand for clocks of ever increasing novelty, size, and colourfulness, to the extent of their being leaders in the field.

The reason probably stems from the fact that, in the early nineteenth century, the Industrial Revolution centred around the coalfields of the north and Midlands, drawing other industries into those areas. Iron, steel, cotton, textiles, shipbuilding, engineering—these were the boom industries. The population migration was northwards, not to the south as it is today. The north was where the jobs, the prosperity, the clock market, and most other markets, were. This new affluence created a demand for larger, more extravagant clocks for the larger, more ostentatious homes of the newly rich of these industrial areas. But these clocks were not just for the rich. The newly not-so-poor-any-longer could also now afford longcase clocks as they too prospered with rising standards of living.

To say that the Midlands and north were at the forefront of the new fashions in no way implies that these fashionable products were good. On the contrary, it could be argued that the more conservative styles of the south were an attempt at retaining pleasant and proven forms, while in pursuing novelty the Midlands and northern clockmakers sacrificed good taste and balanced design. I do not say that it is so, simply that it could be said to be so. I would be the last person to decry northern clocks, which developed into a style of their own. What view we take will depend on what type of clock we like personally, and this in turn probably depends on what type we have grown up with and become used to.

What I am showing you is typical, not exceptional. These clocks represent what was then considered desirable and fashionable in the respective regions. Clockmakers, dialmakers and casemakers all made what was wanted, and they certainly knew the difference between northern and southern tastes. Part of our difficulty in forming an attitude to an antique clock today is that we judge it in the only way we can, that is by *our* standards of design and taste. We expect the clock not only to have survived intact and to function accurately, but also to conform to our tastes of a century or two later. This is really asking a lot! Yet we are unable to judge the clock in the same way as the contemporary customer did. How much of the furniture we make today will be considered tasteful a century or two from now, if it survives that long?

Whatever our own initial reaction to some of these clocks may be, one thing we can be sure of is that at the time these clocks were made they represented the height of fashion, each in its own way and in its own area. A family did not invest in a clock unless it was exactly the type they wanted. There were plenty of clockmakers, and customers had a wide choice. The typical clocks I illustrate represent those that the majority of people at that time considered not just acceptable but highly desirable.

The next dial to be discussed (see page 67) is by Thomas Snow of Knaresborough, Yorkshire. It is considerably different from the Dawlish dial, yet I use it purposely since it is made by the same dialmakers, having a falseplate stamped with the name of Wright's of Birmingham, and also since it was made about the same time as the Dawlish clock. Snow's shop was in the High Street in Knaresborough between 1834 and 1844; Wright's appear in Birmingham from 1835 to 1845. This clock must have been made about 1835–40, and this should be apparent from the dial style alone. The full minute band is worn away, but it had one originally: I know this as the clock belonged to me at one time. Roman numerals mark the hours; the minutes by this time are no longer numbered. The corners are filled with painting. The arch is filled with a complete scene. Hands are of matching brass pattern. What a totally different clock in regard to the painting, yet the basic features of numbering are similar to those of the Dawlish dial. This dial is much bigger, of course, being about 14in wide. The small pointer is a date hand, the date numbering being entirely worn off: if restored, the dial could look truly immaculate again.

There is an odd feature about this dial that may not be obvious at first sight. It looks like an eight-day clock with winding holes and winding squares protruding. It is in fact a thirty-hour clock with *dummy* winding holes, the squares blanked off behind the dial. This is a feature by no means rare on clocks. You bought your thirty-hour clock at the thirty-hour price, which was considerably less than the eight-day price. But your neighbours and visitors were deceived into thinking you had bought the more costly eight-day clock. Several such deceptions were practised. For instance, an eight-day clock would generally have a seconds dial while a thirty-hour clock very rarely did. On some thirty-hour clocks, however, you do find a dummy seconds dial with a hand pinned to the dial. It never moved, it just completed the resemblance to an eight-day clock. Sometimes, too, one gets dummy date hands, which were never connected, but were there just for show. They are far less trouble mechanically, of course, than a real date hand, where if the mechanism is a bit worn or out of true it can often jam the clock. It seems to have been very common practice in the past to remove the operating pin and/or wheel connecting the date hand, and to leave the clock with the date feature not working, rather than run the risk of an incorrectly set date mechanism stopping the clock occasionally. On many clocks I buy this is an item which needs replacing because of shoddy repair in the past.

These dummy features are unusual. If you do come across a clock with them, be rather careful. Sometimes one finds an eight-day dial which now has a thirty-hour movement attached to it; but it was never made that way. On such a converted clock the seconds and date pointers would probably not work, as there would be no linking wheelwork behind the dial. While a converted clock might still have winding holes, it probably would not have the dummy winding squares. The Snow clock is quite original, and so were many others with these dummy features.

I mentioned that thirty-hour clocks very rarely have true working seconds dials, and this is on account of the layout of the wheelwork (called the 'trains') of the clock. If a seconds hand were fitted on to a conventionally laid out thirty-hour clock, then the seconds hand would rotate in an anticlockwise direction, ie backwards. To reverse this, ie to make a seconds hand rotate clockwise on a thirty-hour clock, the maker would need to insert an extra wheel to change this direction of rotation. Some thirty-hour white dial clocks have this extra wheel and therefore a normally-rotating seconds hand. Most of these thirty-hour clocks (white dial ones), with seconds dials, have dummy ones. I do know of one with a seconds hand which rotates anticlockwise. It was made by Joseph Belles of Fixby, near Huddersfield, Yorkshire. This clock, whilst a thirty-hour one, does have a falseplate dial, contrary to my earlier statements. This is because an eight-day dial has been used to give the superficial eight-day appearance.

The direction of rotation of a date hand need not be clockwise and commonly is not. The '*wrong*' direction of rotation is not so obvious with a date hand: one does not see it moving, because of the slowness of the date-change which takes place over a period of several hours usually.

After Thomas Snow we have a dial by Richard Snow of Pateley Bridge. These men were brothers and second-generation clockmakers. Richard's clock is a little later than Thomas's, I would say. This is one of those clocks I mentioned as having a dummy seconds dial: the hand pinned flush to the dial and linked to nothing behind the dial. Richard worked in Pateley Bridge until at least 1837. A few differences indicate that this dial is a little later than the previous one illustrated. Typical corner scenes of churches, houses, etc, actually join up along the sides and run into each other. The arch painting runs down to meet the painting from the corners. Everything is colour and paint except for the white centre. The painting is crude but effective. The hands are of matching brass pattern. Notice the design of them: crowns on the main hands, a pattern normally found only on late clocks. It is not a common pattern but one sees it now and then, perhaps suggesting a date of 1837 or later, with the theme set from Queen Victoria's accession in that year? I would date this clock about 1840. It is a thirty-hour clock, very ordinary, and not costly.

On both these Snow dials we have to accept that the painting is pretty awful, probably because they were cheap dials. The Little-Bo-Peep theme is common in this area, which is sheep country. I have handled dozens of clocks by Richard Snow of Pateley Bridge and without exception they have all had these cheap dials, to the point

41 Thirty-hour dial from a clock of c 1840 by Richard Snow of Pateley Bridge, probably Birmingham-made though dialmaker unknown. Crude artwork is not too obvious in the scenery but shows up in the painting of the shepherdess. The matching brass hands are original, here in crown pattern.

where I know what to expect of one of his clocks before I see it even. I am not intending to praise these dials, just to explain them.

There is something strange about this dial, something wrong, something that anyone who knows Yorkshire should spot instantly. The romanticised shepherdess is acceptable in this sheepfarming area. The bridges are quite pretty and appropriate to a place of that name, though, like the paintings on most dials, they are fictitious bridges and are not supposed to represent the bridge at Pateley. It is the cottages which are wrong. Presumably it is a Birmingham dial painted by a Birmingham man whose ideas of country cottages were based on the half-timbered, thatched-roof cottages of Warwickshire— quite out of place in Yorkshire. Cottages in Pateley Bridge bear no resemblance to these, which are not at all typical of Yorkshire buildings. There is no falseplate on this dial and no dialmaker's name to guide us; but it must be Birmingham made. This clockmaker sometimes used dials by Jukes of Birmingham (post-1839), whose name I have seen impressed into the reverse of such dials.

This paragraph explains why most dials have scenes which are *not* supposed to represent the places where the clocks were sold. An owner of a Leeds-made (or, more correctly, Leeds-sold) clock which might depict ruined abbeys in the dial corners, usually assumes that these are renderings of Kirkstall Abbey. They are not at all, of course, having been more than likely painted in Birmingham by a man who may not even have known that there was an abbey in Leeds. Ruined churches were typically favourite themes, and that is the reason for their being on clock dials, not because they represent the actual buildings of the locality. Very occasionally one may find a dial with a scene painted on and the placename painted on below it as a title, but these are very exceptional.

Now we come to a late dial of a clock by John Catcheside Elliott of Leeds, made about 1855. Elliott came to Leeds in about 1840 and worked there for at least twenty-five years. It is a superbly extravagant and exotic dial, beautifully painted. The paint completely fills the arch and the four corners run into each other. The corners depict Victorian ruins seen through luxuriant foliage. It is an unusual subject for an arch painting, and it may have been intended as some biblical scene. This dial and the next are two of a whole series of dials of this type which suddenly flourish about this time. They show very bold, colourful and vigorous painting styles, a kind of wild last fling at decorative dials, often with much use of gold and silver paints

42   Ornate eight-day dial from a clock by John Catcheside Elliott of Leeds c 1855. This
has not been restored but is preserved in good condition. The brass matching hands are
all original. The dialmaker is unknown, but the style is typical of late dials with an exuber-
ant and exotic character and in this case pleasantly painted.

and luminous paints. One sees them especially on Yorkshire-made clocks, but this may be partly because this was one of the few counties still producing them at this late date. This dial by Elliott has flowers in the corners, but they are totally different from the flower sprays of those more delicate early dials of the 1780s and 1790s.

Not a falseplate dial, this one: very few of them are at this time. It has the long dial feet fitting direct to the movement frontplate, probably indicating that Elliott bought in the whole clock ready-made, perhaps just assembling it himself. On the back of this dial is painted 'Pascoe No 2'. Was Pascoe the dialpainter or dialmaker? I cannot tell. One often sees painted numbers or 'hieroglyphics' on the reverse of a dial, but the meaning of them is lost to us today. Quite possibly they may refer to the style of dial or the number done by that particular artist.

A point about this dial which may not be obvious in the photograph is that the background to the painted areas is coloured entirely in gold, like a gold backcloth to the scenes. This is a feature of many mid-nineteenth-century dials, with gold and silver and luminous paints highlighting certain details.

By this time the painting has progressed so far that the dial is almost one large, coloured panel of paint with a white circle within to show the numerals. The earliest dials were of course just the opposite, being almost all-white with just a little colour. Notice that we have no minute numbering at all; a full minute band; and large Roman numerals for the hours. Roman numerals never seem to have been used for seconds or date dials, perhaps because they are not so easily understood when they run higher than XX.

Matching brass hands are there, of course, at this period, with the seconds and date pointers also matching in brass. Once you have really looked at a dial of this sort, you cannot possibly confuse it with one of an earlier period, say of fifty years earlier. The two are totally different. It would be like confusing a car of 1920 design with one of 1970!

Another dial, of a similar type to the Elliott one, is that by Joseph Jefferies & Son of Leeds. In the arch is an attractively painted scene of the battle of Waterloo, the title 'Waterloo' being written just above the XII hour-number. Don't let the subject mislead you into thinking that the clock was made in 1815, the year of the battle. It was probably made in 1865, marking the fiftieth anniversary of that battle. Jefferies worked in Leeds from about 1850 into the 1870s. The

43 Handsome late dial from an eight-day clock by Joseph Jefferies and Son of Leeds. This dial has not been restored but is preserved in good condition. The arch scene shows the battle of Waterloo and may have been chosen to mark the fiftieth anniversary in 1865. Luminous gold and silver paints are used for the highlights. The dialmaker is not known.

background to this painting, like the Elliott one, is all gold; and very effective use is made of luminous silver and gold paints for the uniforms and to highlight the church in the bottom right-hand corner. It has long dial feet fitting direct to the movement.

There is now no further progression beyond the Elliott clock. All the signs tell us that this clock is a late one, after 1840 certainly, maybe even after 1850, but there seems to be no further development later than that in the dial *style*. The Jefferies clock might have been made in the year of Wellington's death: 1852. I was more inclined to favour

44 Three dreadful cheap dials of the 1840–60 period, dialmakers unknown. The clock on the left was by Blakeborough of Otley, the two on the right by John Waite of Brad-ford. The left-hand two illustrate the Four Continents theme, showing here America and Europe. All three have religious themes in the arch. The right-hand dial is a dished one (convex centre). It was appalling, crude 'art' such as this that put collectors off white dials for a hundred years. Whilst such crude work is not too obvious in the 'landscapes-with-ruins' scenes, it shows up in its true light in the cardboard figures and translucent flesh of heavy ladies and the misshapen animals.

1865, after seeing the clockcase, which unfortunately has not been photographed. It was a large case, even larger than the Elliott one, and of the 'dartboard base' type. The dial was most attractive, but the clock was hard to sell on account of its size. Like many others of its kind, it is now in the Netherlands.

Many of the Period Three dials are of cheaper quality, in the artistry and also probably in the japanning quality, as they seem to have survived the years less well than those of the eighteenth century, often despite being only half the age. Some of the attempts at paint-ing, especially the people, are very feeble. It is this lowering of quality and the high survival rate of late clocks which helped to give white dial clocks a bad name generally. The three overlapping dials show further examples of these poor-quality late dials of the 1840s and 1850s.

Up to a point one can get away with poor artwork on country

cottages, ruins, etc, because they have a warm folk-art quality, but on these cheap dials the people and animals are usually pathetic. Add to this the religious themes which were very common on these dials (the Garden of Eden as in the top centre dial, characters from the Bible complete with haloes, etc) and it is small wonder that these dials have come to be regarded as 'death' in the trade, for they have remained the least-wanted of all. Combine these dreadful paintings with their enormous cases which would not fit into a modern house at all, and we realise why the only buyers for these clocks in recent years have been the bulk shippers, who will buy virtually anything if cheap enough.

Some people must like them, and if you are one that is fine, as long as you recognise that from the investment point of view it is what the wider public likes that matters, but we will deal with that in another chapter.

9

Dial Development and What It Cost

In this chapter I shall try to summarise briefly the main features in the progression of dial styles, which we have examined in the preceding chapters. On page 136 these features are shown for quick reference in chart form.

Period One   Dials begin basically with an all-white background. Numbering initially shows hours in Roman numerals and minutes in Arabic numerals. Each minute is marked by a dot. I describe the minutes as 'fully numbered', by which I mean that each five-minute period is marked in Arabic numbers—5, 10, 15, 20, etc. The painting at this time is usually sparingly applied. It can be simply in gold, showing gold corner 'spandrel' decorations, or it can be more colourful showing such typical themes in the arch and/or corners as a spray of flowers, a single flower (often a rose), a fruit (often a strawberry), a bird (usually one of the artists's invention rather than a portrayal of a real bird). Birds as a theme are usually colourful ones, and can sometimes be taken for eg a jay, or a bullfinch, or a bird of paradise, but they are usually not intended to represent an actual species. The painting is usually of objects rather than patterns. Hands are of steel and do not match. If a calendar date is indicated on a dial it is usually by means of a disc showing from behind an aperture.

Period Two   Experiment is the main feature of this period. Dial styles are gradually developing towards Period Three, but erratically. In the lettering the minute numbering is gradually reduced. The 5- and 10-minute markers begin to be replaced by a dash or symbol and minute numbering is often limited, still in Arabic numerals, to 15, 30, 45, 60. Hour numbers begin to change from Roman to Arabic. The marking of minutes by dots now gives way gradually to a full double band, each minute's portion being marked off along this band.

In painting the coloured area begins to take up more of the dial. The corners and arch begin to be more 'full', though perhaps not completely so. Fan patterns are popular as corner decorations, and so are various types of semigeometrical patterns such as sun-rays. Shells too have become a corner theme. The corner paintings are now more often patterns rather than representations of objects. The arch begins to fill, often with an oval vignette scene, or the beginnings of a landscape or seascape. The arch begins to carry a picture rather than a pattern though this does not usually fill the arch panel completely. People appear both as individuals (eg Nelson) and as allegorical figures (eg Britannia; Justice; the Harvest, represented by a female figure holding a sheaf of corn; etc).

In the south and east of England, dial styles lag behind the north and Midlands in all except numbering. Dial sizes grow larger in the north, remain small in the south. Moon dials in the arch are not uncommon. Hands are still of steel but now match. Dates may be indicated by aperture dials or pointers; the former earlier, the latter later, as a general rule.

Period Three Numbering has now developed fully to a revival of Roman figures to mark the hours. Minutes, shown by a full minute band, cease to be numbered at all, as the 15-30-45-60 numbers of Period Two disappear completely. The Roman hour numerals now used are of course larger in size than in Period One, since they extend in length to cover the area previously taken up by minute numerals. This can mean, though not always, that Period Three hour numerals are heavy and clumsy.

The painted area continues to increase, particularly on northern-style dials The arch is filled completely with coloured paint; so are the corners. Eventually, painting in the arch and corners joins up, forming a painted area within which a white circle remains. Religious scenes now often fill the arch, and landscapes and seascapes, rather than patterns. Hunting scenes are popular. Luminous colours are sometimes included. Favourite themes for the corners are ruins, churches, ivy-clad buildings, castles; also animals and hunting scenes. People appear both as specific heroes and as figures in a landscape. Ships are not uncommon. Southern dials lag way behind northern ones in style of painting, and do not seem to develop much beyond Period One and the beginnings of Period Two. Few clocks were made in the south at all in Period Three, relative to northern production. While southern clocks lag behind in *painting* styles, the number-

CLOCK DIAL FEATURES

solid line = normal
dotted line = unusual

1770   1780   1790   1800   1810   1820   1830   1840   1850   1860   1870

NUMBERING
dotted minutes
mins numbered 5, 10, 15, 20, etc
mins numbered 15, 30, 45, 60 only
mins not numbered
hours in Roman numbers
hours in Arabic numbers
full minute band
single-handed clocks (almost entirely Southern)

FALSEPLATE (eight-day clocks)
with
without

PAINTING OF CORNERS
spray of flowers or fruit
shells/fans/semi-geometrics
ruins, churches, landscapes
all-white, no corner painting (largely Midlands and North)
gold 'spandrel' corners

PAINTING OF ARCH
name only
birds/flowers on white ground
vignette inset on white ground
filled with painted scene
gold or silver background
luminous paints
swaying figures
moon dial (largely Southern)
strike/silent feature

SHAPE/SIZE
arched
square
circular
width 10½in-13in
width 13in-15in

DATE INDICATOR
none
pointer, steel
pointer, brass (unusual)
aperture, square box
aperture, curved

HANDS
non-matching steel (date and
second hands may match)
matching steel
matching brass (rarely copper)
non-matching brass (exist only as incorrect replacements)

(largely East Anglian)

45   Clock dial features.

ing pattern on them is similar to that on northern dials. Moon dials in the arch are now less common. Hands match, but they are now normally made of brass and usually have much punched surface decoration to them, which the steel hands did not have. A date dial is often included, usually shown by a pointer, matching the seconds hand.

H. L. Honeyman began a most interesting examination of white dials as described in the *Proceedings of the Society of Antiquaries of New-castle upon Tyne*, 28 November 1946. He classified the painting subjects into religious 10 per cent, patriotic $6\frac{1}{2}$ per cent, romantic 16 per cent, sporting 10 per cent, landscapes $19\frac{1}{2}$ per cent, flowers/birds 14 per cent, and so on. He is one of the very few people I know of who has even attempted to look analytically at white dials. However, by analysing them into subject matter, he was unable to arrive at any conclusions, but has presented an interesting list of 113 dial descriptions. What such an analysis did, without realising it, was to begin to break down the clocks into periods. The religious subjects would mostly be painted after 1820, the birds/flowers mostly before 1800, and so on. What a pity that Honeyman did not research the dates of the makers whose clock-dial subjects he analysed; he would then have realised the importance of his recordings. The subject matter tends to be illustrative far more of the period of the clock than of the whims of the artist. It seems likely that clock dialpainters were painting the subjects which they were asked to produce by their employer, rather than being allowed to paint any subject they found appealing.

The notes given above may help to elucidate what is meant by the brief captions used in the chart.

In concluding the section on dial development I would like to mention prices, as very little has ever been published concerning original prices, either of dials, movements, cases or complete clocks.

I have recently come across a fascinating document concerned with the transfer of stock in the year 1800 from a retiring northern clockmaker (Jonas Barber of Winster, Westmorland) to his successor. We can assume that the successor is taking over existing stock at cost (or maybe fractionally less) but the most interesting aspect is the price structure of white dials, published for the first time below. By this date, of course, brass dials were very much a thing of the past, and while some were still being made in the south, they were regarded as old-fashioned and out of favour throughout the

Midlands and north. The white dial prices were, in 1800 (words in brackets are mine):

Double Moon Clock Faces, 13in [arched moon dials]	£1 2s 0d
Land Skip 13in [landscape painted in arch]	16s 0d
30 hours, 13in with arches [arched dial]	14s 0d
13in square	12s 0d
12in with arches	14s 0d
12in square	10s 0d
11in square	8s 0d

It is interesting to note that the 'Double Moon' type (Bancroft type) cost nearly three times as much as the 11in square (Terry) type. Also of interest in this same document is the price of hands per pair (steel at this date) as too is the terminology used: 'Seven pair of Pointers at 7d per pair'.

There were sixteen dials altogether. Also in the transfer were four eight-day and seven thirty-hour movements, an interesting indication of the kind of stock carried by a full-time clockmaker, though one at the age of retirement. (This particular clockmaker was close on eighty years old.) However, there is another most interesting point in this. He had sixteen dials but only eleven movements. This is supporting evidence for my view that the movements were made to fit on to dials, not the dials purchased to fit pre-made movements. It may also indicate that the maker could show his potential customers his 'range' of sixteen dials available, and make up the movement for whichever of them they selected, thereby eliminating the need to carry a large range of completed clocks.

When the first edition was published (1974), Jonas Barber's stocklist was the first price list of white dials ever published. Now that we are able to include the list of Wilkes's dial prices (page 84) it is interesting to be able to compare the two, despite the twenty-year time lag between them.

Some very interesting records have been preserved concerning the clockmaker John Manby, who set up shop in Skipton, Yorkshire, about 1815. Many invoices are preserved concerning the goods he bought, with sales ledgers of goods he sold, and these go back to about 1822. The family business still continues in Skipton under the same name, though nowadays as ironmongers. I am very much obliged to the Manby family for allowing me to examine some of these accounts, some extracts from which are published for the first time below.

John Manby, who would be typical of thousands of country clockmakers and hardwaremen of this period, bought in his dials from Birmingham, from Joseph May of St Paul's Square (from 1832 onwards), Messrs Mabson, Labron & Mabson, 'gunmakers' (from 1833 onwards), and also from John Balleny of 50 St Paul's Square (from 1837 onwards) ... and no doubt from others too. These suppliers were mainly merchants supplying the hardware and clock trades with all kinds of wares. The dials from May's seem to have been almost half the usual price, but perhaps of poorer quality, as Manby bought from the other two suppliers at the same time despite having to pay them the full prices. It is interesting to compare these prices with those of Jonas Barber thirty years previously; Barber, incidentally, also bought at least some of his dials from Birmingham (from Osborne & Wilson and from Wilson alone later).

Mabson's charged for '14 inch (ie wide) arch 30 hour dials, assorted patterns, no seconds dials, open month (ie aperture month dials) and named (ie with seller's name painted on)' ... 15s 0d each. The explanations in brackets are mine. This was in 1833 and 1835.

Balleny charged in 1837 for:

14inch arch 8 day dials, solid months, & seconds	16s 0d
14inch ditto, 30 hour	15s 0d
14inch ditto with convex★ centres	16s 0d

However, May's much cheaper dials were in 1832 and 1835:

14inch arch 30 hour	7s 6d
14inch 8 day	8s 0d
14inch 30 hr. single figures	7s 0d [? hour numbering only]
14inch 30 hr. ship to move	12s 6d [rocking ship in arch]
14inch 30 hr. Adam & Eve	14s 6d [moving figures in arch]

Manby bought other clock fittings from these suppliers, some of the prices being (descriptions as used in accounts, my words in brackets):

spire clock balls [set of three]	1s 5d [spire finials]
eagle clock balls [set of three]	1s 7d [eagle finials]
clock hands [per pair]	8d
seconds hands [each]	2½d
clock case hinges [each]	4d
2in clock roses [paterae] approx.	½d each

★ See, for example, the dial by Fothergill illustrated on page 109.

Notice how much cheaper are these stamped brass items compared with the cost of cast ones as detailed on the Nicholas clock case of fifty years earlier. (The costs are given in Chapter 10.)

The English dials of Period One are generally speaking amongst the finest ever made. They tend to have survived the years well (unless abused), often better than cheap examples of Period Three, although sometimes being a century older. As far as artistry is concerned, and the themes displayed, these are usually restrained and refined. Few could take offence at them. Background colours are frequently duck-egg blue or green. In general perhaps those by Wilson were the best, followed a close second by the Osborne ones, with those made during the 1772-9 partnership also high on the list and perhaps having the extra attraction of being the first of their kind.

Where a dial was ordered specially to portray a particular scene or event, then the standard of artistry is usually very high in Period One, particularly if compared to the appalling work of some of the later dials—eg the crude religious scenes on some northern dials of the 1840s and some of the luminous schoolboy portraits of cluttered folklore characters on late Scottish dials. Period One often includes some particularly fine ship paintings and superb landscapes. Where moon dials are present, the scenes on these and the moon faces themselves are often very pleasingly executed.

Only a very few years ago (in the 1960s), when we used to sell these clocks at the ridiculously underpriced levels of £30 and £40 each, it seemed to me that a comparable landscape painting of the type and age found on these dials would *on its own* fetch more than the whole clock, movement and case together. I am sure that if dial arches had been of rectangular shape they would have been sawn up by the thousand, framed and sold as 'painting on iron panel, unsigned, late eighteenth century'.

We must remember that these dials were very costly to the original buyer, and if he paid the extra 4s od for a landscape in the arch, then that represented perhaps two days' wages on top of the basic dial cost. In today's terms that might equate to £50 extra for the landscape. The buyer expected, and usually obtained, value for his very high outlay. With the later half-price dials, you got half-price quality too.

Moon dials are not too common on English dials, perhaps only 10–20 per cent of those produced. There seems to be a very much higher proportion of moon dials on those used in America, whether ordered from England or made locally (see Chapter 14).

Centre-seconds features are very unusual on English white dials, but much more commonly found on those used in America. Centre-calendar work again is not common in England, though it is more common than centre-seconds work. In particular one finds centre-calendar work was popular amongst certain individual makers in parts of northern England.

Automated scenes are not common in Period One, but are increasingly met with from about 1800. The earliest examples tend to be of the rocking ship type.

Calendar work in Period One is usually of the open mouth type, which was no more difficult for the dialmaker to produce than the pointer type and saved the clockmaker the cost of making the extra wheel (known as the twenty-four-hour wheel, because it received the twelve-hourly push from the hour-hand pipe and converted it by means of a pin projecting from the wheel into a once-in-twenty-four-hours push to drive the calendar pointer).

Manby bought his movements from Greaves & Newton, 'knife-makers', Portobello Works, Sheffield, not as complete ones but in ready-to-assemble form. This supports my view that falseplates were sold with the dials, and not with the movements. Falseplates often have 'Birmingham' stamped into them—none is recorded with 'Sheffield' stamped into it! Movements seem to have been bought by the weight of worked materials at so much per pound weight:

> 3 sets of 8 d(ay) clock, brass at 1s lb.
> 3 sets of forg'd work & pinions at 1s 2d

There are a number of such entries, some more explicit, costing the brass parts and steel parts separately. Jonas Barber too had sold his (presumably already assembled) movements by the pound weight: 'Seven 30 hours movements 39½ pound @ 1s 4d lb = £2 12s 8d'. This system of selling worked materials by weight may have been the standard method used in the trade, though I do not know of any reference book which mentions this practice.

Manby sold a 'new clock & balls' to a Mr Lister of Grassington, a joiner, for £4 2s 0d. We can assume that this clock was without a case, which Lister would no doubt make himself. Manby's charge for cleaning a clock, by the way, was a very reasonable 1s 6d! Gillow's, the Lancaster cabinetmakers, sometimes sold cases complete with clocks. One such clock they sold in 1771 for £4 4s 0d, plus a case for £3 13s 6d, presumably a brass dial eight-day clock. In 1799 they paid £2 11s 0d for a thirty-hour clock with 'china' dial from Newby's of Kendal. This would be a painted dial, of course, which Newby's probably got direct from Birmingham and fitted their own movement on to. This was to be sold by Gillow's in a case of their make. A Gillow case cost the customer from as little as £2 5s 0d in 1771 to perhaps as much as £10.

Not many clocks have the original bill of sale preserved with them. One that does was brought to my attention recently, an eight-day solid-arch white dial by Benjamin Cope of Franch(e) near Kidderminster. It reads:

clock	£4 10s 0od	
case	£4 0s 0od	
glass	4s 2d	Sept. 2nd 1808.
£8 14s 2d		

On 4 March 1795 a group of about twenty clockmakers gathered together at the Admiral Rodney Inn in Leicester to set up a price-fixing ring, which they named the Society of Watch and Clock Makers in Leicestershire. John Deacon (the son of Samuel mentioned in Chapter 5) was secretary and treasurer. They resolved to set a minimum price list below which no member would sell his clocks (and watches). If anyone broke the agreement and undercut his 'competitors' in price, then the others agreed to subsidise work in order to underprice the offender and run him out of business. As with every monopoly, the only loser was the customer! These were the agreed minimum prices *without* cases:

30 hours

square or round dial 12inch	£3	0s 0d
ditto ditto 13inch	£3	3s 0d
arch ditto 12inch	£3	7s 0d
ditto ditto 13inch	£3	10s 0d

8 day

square or round with or without seconds 12inch	£4 12s 0d
ditto 13inch	£4 14s 6d
solid arch 12inch	£4 17s 0d
ditto 13inch	£5 0s 0d

landscape or figure 12inch		£5 0s 0d
ditto ditto 13inch		£5 5s 0d
ditto ditto 14inch		£5 10s 0d
Moon 12inch		£5 10s 0d
ditto 13inch		£5 15s 6d
ditto 14inch		£6 0s 0d

NB. the above with common steel hands. If gilt ones they must be charged extra

For extra painting 25% on the Birmingham prices		
Cases oak/deal plain	10% on joiner's wholesale	
ornamented ditto	15%	ditto
plain mahogany	20%	ditto
ornamental mahogany	25%	ditto

Whilst round dials were popular in the area, they were actually a little cheaper (about a shilling each) from the japanners. But no price distinction is made between square or round on the above list, so on any round dial clock sold the clockmaker made an extra shilling before he began work.

It is interesting to note that gilt hands were available this early, as we are not accustomed to seeing them in common use until after 1800.

10

Cases:
Period One, 1770–1800

On first looking at a longcase clock most people ask: 'Is it the original case?' This is a question to which one can very seldom give a definite 'Yes' in answer, as in most instances there is no certain way of knowing whether the clock has been recased at some time in the past, unless it has been put into a case of an obviously wrong period. It takes great experience to decide such things unless a replacement is obvious.

Very rarely one may find a casemaker's label somewhere on the case, perhaps at the back of it, or inside the door. I know a clock by Agar of York (a brass dial one in fact) with a paper pasted on to the back which reads: 'To Mr. Agar, York (?with) 2 clock cases'— the word I have put in brackets would appear to be 'with'. Another case by Woolston Roberts of Derby also has a delivery label on the back, the wording of which is given fully under the detailed description of the case. Neither of these labels, however, gives the name of the casemaker, being apparently just delivery instructions.

When we get into Victorian times a printed cabinetmaker's label pasted behind the door or on the backboard becomes less of a rarity, though they are always sufficiently unusual to add considerably to the interest of any clock. In his book *Stamford Clocks and Watches*, Laurence Tebbutt illustrates two such; one reads 'J. Wilcox, clock-case maker, Dyke' (near Bourne), the other 'Oliver, Clock-Case Maker, Spalding'. Both date from the 1860s.

Few clocks retain the clockmaker's own trade label, but when they do this adds a seal of authenticity to the original partnership of case and clock. A label adds an interesting touch of history, even a repairer's label, and whenever I sell a clock myself today I always attach my own trade label, as indeed many other dealers do, to mark a stage in the clock's life. Original case labels are very unusual and for the most part all we can say is that the case is apparently or probably original. All the cases shown in this book are believed to be original to their clocks, otherwise I would not illustrate them.

It is a fact that, in the past, clocks were often recased. If the original case became badly infected with woodworm or rot or suffered any one of the hundreds of mishaps which could happen to it, or even if the owner simply decided on a case of newer fashion, then a new case might be acquired, either a brand new one or a second-hand one. This replacement case could be of the same age and style as the previous one, older or newer, and usually it would be newer. A clock of 1770 recased in 1810 would most likely have been put into a new (1810) case. Cases were far more subject to deterioration than were clocks. Any dealer knows that it is fairly commonplace to come across a clock without a case, but the reverse (a case without a clock) is hard to find.

In this situation it is instantly obvious what is bound to happen. Suppose you are an antiques dealer and come across a fine clock, say an early eighteenth-century one, with a case beyond repair. You then see an insignificant country clock with a 'suitable' case. You buy the country clock and rehouse your early clock in that case. The merits of such an action are debatable but, all the same, this was done in the past and is still done today. The biggest query, of course, is: 'What is a *suitable* case?' Ideally, a suitable case would be one of the same age, dial size and type as the clock you are rehousing, but some dealers may have been prepared to accept a compromise or may not have had sufficient knowledge to determine what sort of case would be 'correct'.

Potential clock buyers may now be wondering how, in the final analysis, they can know what they are buying. There is only one answer to that, and that is to know for yourself the various case styles and types, so that your own knowledge of the subject equals or surpasses that of the dealer you are buying from. I will try to give some hints to help with this, but first I must relate what happened some years ago concerning a clock by Caleb Nicholas of Birmingham.

I was showing the clock to a man who was a clock enthusiast and a collector with considerable experience, but who said quite openly that he had never looked seriously at white dial clocks. He had been influenced by certain writers into thinking that white dial clocks were somehow not clocks at all. He did not look much at the dial, since with his preconceived idea there was no way in which he could

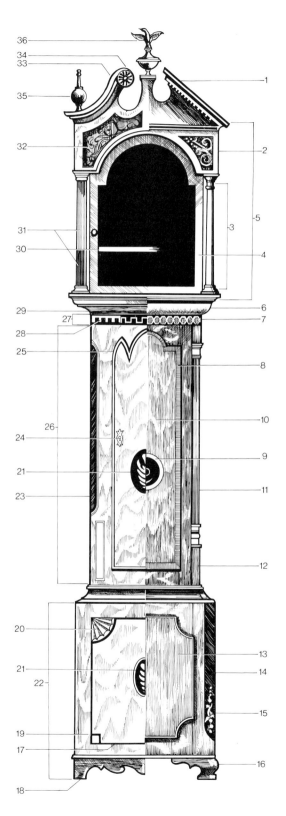

46 Casework terminology. This drawing illustrates various casework features which may be met with in widely varying regions and periods. *1*, pitched pediment with dentil moulding beneath; *2*, spandrel area on case, here containing a fret; *3*, pillar caps and bases; *4*, hood door; *5*, hood (or head); *6*, convex (early) moulding; *7*, fret in the impost; *8*, crossbanding on door; *9*, lenticle glass; *10*, counter-matched veneers on door; *11*, reeded quarter column; *12*, pedestal under quarter column; *13*, base panel; *14*, canted corner; *15*, applied carving; *16*, ogee bracket foot; *17*, stringing line; *18*, semi-French foot; *19*, broad crossbanding; *20*, fan inlay; *21*, shell inlay; *22*, base (or pedestal, in old terminology); *23*, canted corner with stringing; *24*, escutcheon; *25*, gothic top; *26*, trunk; *27*, impost; *28*, dentil moulds (*left*, plain; *right*, key-pattern); *29*, concave moulding; *30*, seatboard; *31*, pillar, reeded and double-reeded; *32* inset painted glass panel; *33*, swan-neck or scrolled pediment; *34*, carved rosette; *35*, finial—spire type; *36*, finial—eagle type.

begin actually to like it. But he looked at the case, and expressed a measure of satisfaction with that. He then found that the attractiveness of the case conflicted with his ideas about white dial clocks. How could he find himself beginning to like a white dial clock, when all his reading had taught him that they were merely tasteless degenerations of the brass dial ones? The answer was not long in coming. 'Of course,' he said, 'a case as attractive as this one must have been made for a brass dial clock, and someone has later put this white dial clock into it.'

Before going further, I may say that there is nothing magnificent about this case. It is mainly oak, with mahogany bandings and trimmings here and there. The brass fittings are of exceptional quality, and the proportions are good. It is a well-balanced and very nice case of its kind, but there is nothing really outstanding about it.

I disagreed with the man politely and took off the hood to let him see that there were no obvious alterations to the seatboard and fixing of the clock.

He next looked at the movement. 'What sort of date would you put on that?' he asked. 'About 1820?' I said that I would date it about forty years earlier, and this quite took his breath away. This was probably because most antique objects tend to arouse in us a greater reverence the older they are. Now he was quite convinced that he was right and I was wrong. Then I mentioned that Baillie (G. H. Baillie, *Watchmakers and Clockmakers of the World*) gave details for this maker as 1787–1808, not so far away from my own estimate of the clock's age. (I shall explain later why one does not take dates such as Baillie's as being precise limits.) The fact that Baillie gave a date similar to mine must have impressed this man, though one could not hope to convert him in the course of a few minutes' conversation.

This story is important in illustrating several points, mainly that the man was conditioned to the view that the white dial clock was a poor relation to the brass dial one and therefore, by his reasoning, would have had only a poor case. The fact alone that some white dial clocks are in splendid cases, despite many of the best ones having been taken to be put around brass dial movements over the years, tends to disprove his view. As to the dating of the clock, it was obvious that having never troubled to look at them, he could hardly expect to be able to date one.

The suggestion he made that someone had taken this case from a brass dial clock to put around the white dial one was ludicrous. In 99 per cent of instances of case-swapping, precisely the *reverse* is done, ie a good case is stolen from a white dial clock to be put around any old brass one. That is where the financial gain lies and any dabbler in clocks who started to swap cases in the way this man suggested would find he was on the shortest road to bankruptcy.

In this instance under discussion I was convinced that the case was the correct one. I bought the clock in a very dirty and shabby condition from having lain in a cellar, where it had not been touched or tampered with in many years: one had only to see the state it was in to appreciate this. Forty or fifty years ago there was not the present heavy demand for clocks, and it could hardly have benefited anyone to have swapped this case. Most important of all, the style of the case was right for the period of the clock.

A couple of other little hints might be worth mentioning to help you spot a swapped case. Firstly, the seatboard arrangement often has been altered and will betray more modern signs of sawing and chiselling than other parts of the case (though with little trouble new cuts can be made to look old with a touch of stain). Secondly, in most cases on the inside of the backboard there will be some sort of scratch-line caused by the pendulum-adjusting nut, below the bob, having rubbed against the back when leaning slightly back from the vertical. If one puts a different clock into that case, its pendulum will not usually swing on quite the same level, and a second and newer scratch-mark might begin to appear. For more complicated reasons which I will not go into here, neither of these pointers is *proof* of a case change, but they are helpful indications if taken in conjunction with other factors.

Another point is worth mentioning in this connection. On many cases there is some sort of sign of wear caused by the descending weight(s) rubbing against the interior framing below the case door, sometimes to the extent that a couple of hollows are worn into the wood. If the descending weight(s) touch the interior framing (or fail to touch it) in different positions from these worn spots, this can be another indication of the movement's having initially belonged to a different case. On the other hand, repositioning of the attachment of the gutlines to the seatboard, as when new guts are fitted, can also affect the positioning of the falling weight(s). Similarly, if replacement weights are fitted, they could be of a different shape from the former ones and thereby hang differently as they come down.

This pointer, then, is by no means an infallible guide, but it helps. When one sees a seatboard that has been tampered with, a pendulum that rubs in the wrong place, weights that descend in the wrong positions, all on the same clock ... one ought to begin to feel suspicious about the clock's authenticity.

One thing more I ought to mention, obvious though it may seem. A check should be made that the dial fits the case. Not infrequently I have seen the larger white dial clocks, say with 14in- or 15in-wide dials, in cases that were obviously designed to take 12in or 13in dials. A correct dial usually fits in such a way that the numbering, corner and arch decorations all show fully, and there are no gaps around the edge. When too large a dial is put into a case, the corner decorations are cut off by the door and part of the arch painting is obscured too. Dials were made larger as time went on, and what such a switch usually means is that a dealer has come by a good 12in to 13in case (with or without a poor clock in it) and come by a good *later* clock of the 14in or 15in size (with or without a poor case). When this happens not only is it apparent that the dial does not fit, but also that dial and case are of different periods. And so we come back to the advice I offered you initially—get to know for yourself the styles of different periods. Then you are in a stronger position to make your own decision.

Let us now look closely at the first two cases, those of the William Terry and the Caleb Nicholas clocks. Both of these I believe to be original. The Terry case is made of oak: plain straight-grain oak with a pine backboard. This was a farmer's clock, made in 1787 for a farmhouse or cottage, not for the lord of the manor. Made by a local joiner, it is simple but well balanced in outline. Neat and plain, it is just over 7ft in height. It has the original bracket-type feet (no plinths on north-country clocks as a rule) with two front feet only, no back feet. This is intentional, since it saves carpentry and the clock is far easier to stabilise on an uneven flagged floor when it has just the two feet, and not four. The back simply leaned against the wall; frequently the clocks were screwed or nailed to the wall, and many cases have numerous holes and splits in the backboard as a result of being fixed to the walls of the many homes they have seen over the years. The hood pillars are simple wooden rods with turned capitals and the bases painted gilt to look like brass fittings. Turning was cheaper than brass and the joiner could no doubt do this himself and have the job completed before the fancy brass cappings could

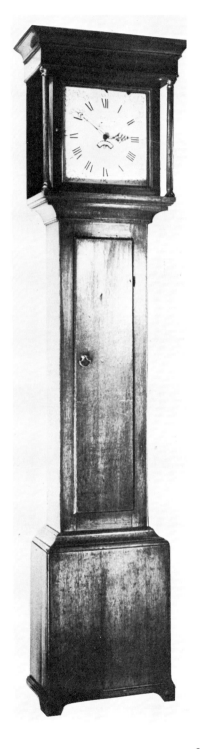

be ordered, let alone delivered, from the brassware merchants.

The case door is long and slender. Doors are made shorter as the years go by. Generally speaking, the longer the door (proportionate to the case), the earlier the clock. This case is strictly traditional in style, just the same as that made for a brass dial clock and typical of a simple country style made for twenty or thirty years either side of that date—1787 in fact. It is as small as the smallest London clocks (rare museum pieces excepted) and several feet smaller than many of them. This Terry case is typical of many thousands of provincial country cases.

'The Yorkshire clocks stand in a class by themselves. The cases, hardly without exception, are gigantic—almost elephantine...', so say H. Cescinsky and M. R. Webster in *English Domestic Clocks* in 1913. In making this totally incorrect statement, the writers go on to illustrate the point by showing photographs of three *Lancashire* clocks, which they misdate. We are forced to the conclusion that they had never seen a Yorkshire clock! Well, the Terry clock *is* a Yorkshire one, and as neat a little clock as you could wish for. It is absolutely typical of this style and period.

I get hot under the collar when so-called experts pronounce about things of which they clearly have no knowledge and, as here, write off at a stroke a whole category of clocks. The amazing thing is that people still buy this book today and learn about clocks from books which are not only almost a century old themselves but which were written without knowledge.

The Nicholas case is entirely different. It was made about the same time but for a quite different customer: a town customer with larger, taller rooms in his house. Such town clocks were made taller and grander for the larger houses—not mansions, not stately homes, but the ordinary town houses of more prosperous citizens.

This clock stands 7ft 8in to the top of the highest finial, or 7ft 2in without finials.

Look at the brassware on this case. All of it is original and in my

47 (*opposite left*) Simple oak cottage or farmhouse style of case housing the clock by William Terry of Bedale and made in 1787. This plain yet handsome style could house either a country brass dial or white dial at this period. Height about 7 ft.

48 (*opposite right*) Ornate and elaborate case housing the clock by Caleb Nicholas of Birmingham made c 1785. Made of oak with mahogany crossbandings and trim, this case shows lavish use of costly brass fittings, all original. It stands about 7 ft 8 in including finial.

experience quite exceptional. The brass caps and bases for the hood pillars at this period cost the casemakers between 5s 0d and 7s 0d a set; the quarter caps for tops and bottoms of the trunk quarter pillars cost perhaps 3s 0d to 4s 0d a set (as against 1s 0d or so for wooden ones). Add on about 7s 0d to 10s 0d for finials, 2s 0d or so for paterae (the brass discs on the faces of the horns), add about 8s 6d for gilding all these, and you arrive at a cost for brassware alone (without counting hinges, locks, fastenings, etc) of over £1 10s 0d. This was to add to a total cost for such a case of about £4 10s 0d to £5 10s 0d. In other words brass fittings such as on this clock would add about one-third to the cost of the case—the cost of *manufacture*, that is. Then the cabinetmaker adds his profit, and the clockseller too presumably adds his profit on the case as well as the clock. The clockmaker's profit on cases is illustrated on page 143.

I base these figures on those shown in the business records of the cabinetmaking firm of Gillow's of Lancaster, whose records include detailed costings of clock cases with sketches in some instances. (See *Gillow's Clock Cases* by Nicholas Goodison, published by the Antiquarian Horological Society, 1968; and also *Complete British Clocks*.)

The brass fittings, then, add about a third to the original price of the Nicholas case. The price of this case would in any event be considerably higher than the Terry case as it has much more work in the shapings and bandings. The Nicholas case is by far the better in the sense of being a better-quality piece: better woods, better design, better workmanship, nicely proportioned. Today, however, with somewhat smaller rooms, the Terry clock would fit more comfortably into more homes and therefore might appeal to a wider market. The two, while contemporary, had a quite different appeal at the time they were made and still have today. You cannot compare one with the other except to illustrate their differences rather than their similarities.

The hood top of the Nicholas clock is finished with swan-necked pediments, sometimes referred to as *horns*. This method of finishing the hood top continues right through the white dial period and is perhaps the most popular style of all, especially on arched dials, though it is also used on square dials occasionally. It was especially popular in the north and Midlands.

The door, like the Terry one, is as long as it could be, filling the entire length of the slim trunk. The figuring of the oak stands out well on this door. These figurings are called medullary rays and occur only in oak. I have read books which decry this medullary figuring as spoiling the look of the wood, but I personally quite like it. Whether people today like it or not, there can be little doubt that at the time this clock was made this sort of ray figuring was considered very desirable. You will see this figuring on the door, base panel and hood of the Nicholas clock. On the sides, however, there is not a single ray, the wood being absolutely plain and far less interesting. This happens on very many oak clock cases: the sides, which do not show up so importantly, are often quite plain; yet the front faces have rich ray lines. This is not by accident but by design. A similar thing happens with mahogany cases, the fine figurings being used for the faces and plain straight-grain for the sides. Sawing logs straight across produced straight-grained oak. One had to *quarter-cut* the wood to get the medullary rays to show, and this was a more wasteful, more time-consuming, and therefore most costly process, and also not quite as simple as it may sound. The Terry case is all straight sawn: easier, cheaper, less spectacular but functional.

The purpose of quarter-sawing was to prevent warping, which was more likely to occur in wood sawn straight across. The medullary rays came as a bonus in so far as the finer-marked planks were selected from the sawn-up results. Oak is a sound, hard wood virtually immune to woodworm unless rotted, such as from contact with damp floors. In quarter-cutting the sawyer did not use the very dense heartwood from the core of the tree or the paler sapwood from the outer edge near the bark. A slice of a tree incorporating these extremes of very different density would warp and perhaps snap in use.

Sometimes one does see oak with woodworm, though usually they have made only a half-hearted attempt at inhabiting the wood. This is often in a situation where a sliver of sapwood has been used, perhaps escaping notice at the time the wood was newly sawn. On old oak the pale sapwood usually shows up as being much paler (yellow) in colour and if one sees worm in oak at all, it is usually in these pale sapwood streaks. A trace of sapwood streak can just be made out down the door of the Terry case, and a more obvious one down the door of the Donisthorpe case (page 160).

Sapwood naturally occurs at the edges of the wood, not in the middle. In this case the streaks appear in the middle because the clock doors consist of joined panels. It was often thought preferable to join small panels together to avoid the far greater risk of warping in a larger panel. This was particularly a problem of clock doors, which at this time were very long and slender and of course had no surrounding support to help keep them flat, except for the hinges. It is very common to see clock doors warped, especially those in solid mahogany.

A few other features of this Nicholas case are worth mentioning since they are typical. Notice the mahogany banding around the edge of the trunk door, hood door and base—a feature often found in the 1770–1800 period. It begins before 1770 really, but in this book we are not concerned with pre-1770 clocks. Sometimes the banding is set in about 1in from the edge, which is perhaps a slightly later sign. This crossbanding is not done just for effect. Its real purpose is to present a crossgrain all round the outer edges for strength. Crossgrain wood is less likely to chip away or chafe in use than long-grain. Sometimes, but not often, long-grain banding is used. Of course long-banding is for nothing but show. It frequently chafes away at the exposed edge.

The shaped top to the door is another feature to notice. The flat-topped Terry door is the traditional shape, though sometimes an arched door top echoes the shape of an arched dial. By the 1770s door shapes start to develop. The Nicholas door shape is typical of this time; but watch for the exotic developments to come in the next century, when cabinetmakers begin to strain after novelty in shape.

The pillars of the hood are reeded, as are the quarter pillars of the trunk. Strictly speaking, these should be called pilasters. More work is involved in making these than with those of the Terry clock. Reeded pillars again are typical of the 1770–1800 period. Watch what happens to these slender reeded pillars in the next century, as casemakers continue with extravagant experimenting.

The bracket feet on this clock do not show up too well in the illustration, but notice that they *are* bracket feet, miniature versions of those on a chest of drawers of the same period. Some strange things happen to feet in the next century, that is when owners of clocks have refrained from sawing them off to get a tall clock into a low-ceilinged room.

These few pointers, I hope, will help you to fix this case in your mind. It is an excellent example of this type of clock because so many things about it are just right as typical features of the period. Fix those Corinthian brass capitals in your mind too, as you will seldom see their like again in the next century.

These first two cases exhibit the two quite distinct types of clock: country clocks and town clocks. As time goes by, this distinction becomes blurred and eventually even the village clocksellers were putting their clocks into more imposing *town* styles of case, as we shall see.

I shall enlarge on the point I touched on above when I mentioned sawing off the feet of a clock. On most clock cases the feet were the first thing to deteriorate. Many floors in the past were stone-flagged. People washed these by swilling water across them and brushing out the water and dirt together through the doorway. A few decades of that sort of treatment can soften up even tough English oak and make it an inviting home for woodworm, against which it would normally be almost immune. The damp wood starts to rot, the worm starts breeding, and before long the feet collapse under the strain; or they are sawn off and the process starts all over again, this time a little higher up the case.

If a clock has banding like that on the Nicholas one all around the hood and the door, but only on the top and sides of the base panel, then something is wrong. No designer in his right mind would do that intentionally. What has happened is that the case feet or plinth have been sawn off for some reason, and perhaps a new plinth or new feet have been put on too high up. No bottom row to the banding is an almost certain sign of an altered base.

If you wish to shorten a long clock, there are two ways in which to approach the problem, from the top and from the bottom. One thing to watch for is the sawing-off of the 'horns' from a Nicholas-type case. The man who did this left a flat top right across from side to side and added a new moulding across this top: and the result was a clock a good 6in or more shorter. Shortening the hood and base can bring a 7ft 8in clock down 12in or more in height. This was often done, to get a tall clock into a low-ceilinged cottage.

There was another answer to the problem and this I have heard of as an occasional practice until quite recent times, by which I mean within the last twenty years or so. I have talked to numerous people who recall this happening in the homes of their parents. The trick was to cut a hole in the floorboards and to sink the base of the clock into this hole to whatever depth was needed to get the top clear of the ceiling. With a stone floor of course you had to remove one flagstone and dig a hole in the soil beneath. Another version of the same trick was to cut a hole in the ceiling to let the 'horns' through and, ridiculous as it may sound, I once did buy a clock that had been in that very position.

Now for the Lomax case. One is tempted to think that this would have been made by the famous cabinetmakers, Gillow's of Lancaster. It does have several features which one sees on cases by Gillow and it *could* have come from that firm. There were, however, many other cabinetmakers who could produce work just as excellent as that from the Gillow workshops, provided the customer would pay for the cost of the workmanship and materials. After all, Gillow's were only working to designs that were already fashionable.

Personally I rather object to the attitude whereby a chair, which for instance happens to have features that Chippendale copied, is called a *Chippendale* chair, implying not that it was made by the man but that it was based on his designs. Such a term also imparts a suggestion of the Chippendale fame to that particular chair. In fact Chippendale was merely translating existing tastes and designs of his time into 'published' form and relating them to furniture, and in some instances, as with his designs for tall clock cases, quite impractically. In this instance this Lomax clock case has no need of the Gillow name to enhance its standing; its excellence is there for all to see, regardless of who made it. But perhaps we could say that it is a case of a style which Gillow's *also* made. (All the clock case designs preserved in the Gillow's records are illustrated in my book *Complete British Clocks*.)

It is obviously a beautiful piece of work. It is made of solid mahogany with the front veneered in choice pieces. Its shape is typical of its period for a northern clock with the exception of the hood pediments, which are in a less common design. I have had clocks with this type of pediment, though not many, and mostly they were in the 1770–90 period. The oval opening to the hood door is forced on the cabinetmaker by the shape of the dial, and this oval dial shape is extremely unusual.

What a fine case this is, standing exactly 7ft 8in high. It is a clock that was up-to-the-minute for fashion: the newest white dial, probably made in this special shape for an owner who wanted and could afford the best; a case of superb craftsmanship, in the finest woods that money could buy; reeding on the trunk pilasters and hood pillars, which are capped by Corinthian brass capitals; ogee bracket feet; all these would mean extra time and cost in the making. The shape of the door top on this case is most unusual, and indeed the

49 Fine mahogany case from the clock by Lomax of Blackburn, Lancashire. The oval dial shape forces a long hood-pillar on the casemaker, resembling the west-of-Scotland style. The architectural pediment, sometimes called a pitched pediment, is an unusual variation for a hood top. This is an excellent example of Lancashire casework.

oval dial and enforced longer-than-normal pillar style give this clock a very untypical appearance. I am not pointing it out as a model of design, but rather as a model of execution. Its date is about 1785–90, about the same time as the next case, that of the John Bancroft clock.

The Bancroft case is a country cousin to the Nicholas and Lomax ones. It lacks much of the fancy brassware, having just simple brass caps and bases to plain columns. Its trunk sides are square—no quartered and reeded pilasters here. The square trunk sides are an earlier feature retained by the casemaker for simplicity. The wood is straight-grain oak. The case would originally have had bracket feet, though these are now missing. The door takes up the whole trunk length, the top of the door being arched in imitation of the dial shape. This is a quite common shape for a door top in this period, again carried through from earlier times.

The door and base panel are crossbanded in mahogany. Swan-necked pediments to the hood complete a very pleasantly proportioned and neat case, standing exactly 7ft high. Small decorative features which barely show in the illustration are an oval stringing of light wood in the centre of the base panel and quarter-circle (fan) inlays of light wood in the corners of the base panel. While the Bancroft door top follows the dial in shape, clocks with square dials naturally tend to retain the flat door top for a longer period, and then eventually these too adopt experimental shapes. Square-dial clocks tend to be less common, and especially by about 1820–30 they are dying out.

The mouldings between trunk and base on the Bancroft clock are simple in style and contrast strongly with the heavily-indented one on the Lomax case, which with its canted corners is very typical of the Lancashire style.

I am unable to illustrate the cases of the Day and Rowlands clocks.

50 (*opposite left*) Oak case with mahogany trim from the clock by John Bancroft of Scarborough, c 1785. The case has a simplicity of line and construction, simple and reasonably cheap to make, yet handsome in a quiet way. Height 7 ft.

51 (*opposite right*) Solid mahogany case c 1790 in the plain dome top often found in the south-east corner of England, this particular one housing the clock by Forster of Sheerness, Kent. Attitudes may vary about the suitability of finials on this type of hood. It is a neat little case standing only about 6 ft 8 in. Canted and reeded trunk corners are found in the late eighteenth century, whilst flat canted corners are usually from the nineteenth.

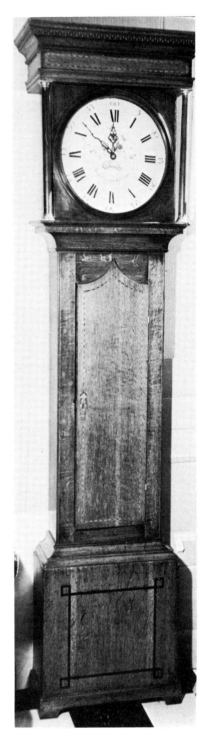

The Forster case is made entirely of solid mahogany except for the softwood backboard. The design is pleasing though plain. There is nothing fussy or fancy, but the case is in the best wood, which in the solid is virtually immune to woodworm. The pillars are reeded, as are the chamfered trunk corners. The plinth shaped into bracket feet is typical. Shaped back splats to the hood are an interesting variation. This design of hood top, while not rare, is a little unusual and more common in the south than in the north. The total height is only 6ft 8in, which is smaller than normal, making it very acceptable in a present-day home. Notice that there is none of the spectacular veining of the Lomax clock in this wood: the grain is relatively straight. Ornate grains are usually sliced into veneers and solid mahogany cases made of wood with a less exciting grain.

A word of warning may be useful about the plain dome style of hood top of this clock. It is not unusual for a tallish clock of the pagoda-top style to have been shortened over the years, whether through damage or otherwise, and to have had its 'pagoda' removed, which can leave a case very similar to the Forster one in appearance. It would not work with the Woolston Roberts case, but it would with the Husband and the Tate clocks shown later—block off the top with your finger and you will see what I mean. So if you are buying a dome-top clock, look carefully to see that it was not once a pagoda top. Often such alteration throws out the whole balance of the case and makes it look pin-headed. You can soon spot a cut-down bell-top with a little practice.

The Samuel Deacon case shows how much more important is elegance of design than fancy woods. This is a very pleasant case, yet simple, made of oak. The hood pattern on this one is sometimes known as a break-arch top or a broken-arch top, because the arch is interrupted. (This term is also wrongly used sometimes to refer to an arch, eg an arched dial is termed a break-arch dial, but this use of the word only makes life more complicated.) The break-arch

51a (*opposite left*) A neat oak case housing Samuel Deacon clock No 224 dated 1783. The lines are simple and elegant. This style of hood is often called a break-arch or broken-arch pediment.

52 (*opposite right*) Neat case of a round-dial Leicestershire thirty-hour clock of c 1785 by Donisthorpe of Loughborough. Though housing a simple clock, the case has much chequered stringing to the door and hood top, inlaywork to the base and key-pattern moulding round the hood top, making a very attractive case.

53 (left) A superb example of a pagoda-top case dating from c 1790 housing the clock by Thomas Husband of Hull. This case of the finest mahogany veneers on a basically solid mahogany construction is one of the best white dial cases, preserved in immaculate condition.

54 (below) Trunk of the Thomas Husband case. Note the very careful choice of veneers, here applied onto an oak base. Such selected woods are always used as veneer, as solid wood would have been too wasteful. Even the three-sided quarter columns are crossgrain veneered (in rosewood) with stringing between each flat. The crossbanding within the stringing lines on door and base is in rosewood. A magnificent example of a 'Yorkshire' clock.

55 High-quality case of solid mahogany, c 1780, housing the clock by Robert Swan of Bridlington. A fairly tall example this, standing about 8 ft, obviously made for a gentleman's house with high ceilings. The sound-frets in the hood sides show up clearly, as does the dog-tooth (or dentil) moulding below the hood. This is another example of a case with front feet only.

163

top was popular in certain localities, for instance in the Darlington area many clocks have it. It is interesting to note from Deacon's records that his father used to make him oak clock cases at £1 each. It is impossible to say whether this might be one such.

The case of the Donisthorpe clock is a neat example of a round-dial clock case in quartered oak with ornamental stringing lines in a chequered pattern, alternate yellow and black. When seen close up such chequered stringing looks like a sandwich with the top and bottom layers of 'bread' holding a filling of alternate yellow and black pieces. Of course, the clock casemaker did not stick thousands of bits together jigsaw-like, but he bought the fancy stringing ready-made, literally by the yard. Then he cut to length such sections as he needed for inlaying.

The case of the Husband clock is a magnificent example; in fact I have never seen a finer one. It is very ornate, very costly, required great skill in the making and yet, most important, retains slender elegant lines, and furthermore is preserved in very good condition. The Swan case is also grand in a different way. This one uses solid mahogany with no inlay or veneer work at all and so must necessarily present a quieter appearance, but at the same time it is a well-proportioned case, well built, with no skimping or corner-cutting. Both these clocks were obviously built for wealthier than average customers and both are excellent examples of their respective types.

11

Cases:
Period Two, 1800–1830

The next case is one in solid mahogany, housing the clock by Robert Gillies of Beith, near Glasgow. A solid mahogany case, by the way, is always much scarcer than one in veneer. There is no debate about the age of this clock, because Gillies wrote his name in ink underneath the seatboard: 'Robt. Gillies, Clock Maker, July 1802'. This is not proof of the case's being original, but it is convincing circumstantial evidence, especially as everything fits as being in period. There are several unusual features about the clock. When I first saw it I thought it had a Scottish look about it. I bought it and, on my showing it to a friend who is a clock enthusiast, he immediately said the same thing. At this time we had not seen the name on the dial, which was very worn away and has been repainted since.

It is Scottish then, but why? The Scots casemakers seem to have been keen to do things in their own way, following the fashion of the period, but somehow doing it rather differently. For instance, the hood pillars and quarter pilasters of the trunk have twisted *fluting*—the quarter pilasters of an English clock would tend to have reeding there. The English version would be convex, while the Scots version here is concave. Not an important feature, but a noticeable and unusual difference. I had never seen fluted reeding on a clock before I saw this one.

Notice how the hood pillars are attached—onto projections above the hood door. This is a most unusual method which I have seen used on other Scottish clocks. The feature is none too practical, since it prevents the hood door from opening more than 90°. Then again many hood doors (not having this feature) will not open further than 90° because of the case design. It is not that one has reason to open a hood door further than this. It is simply that in opening it carelessly one might cause some damage by the sudden and unexpected contact.

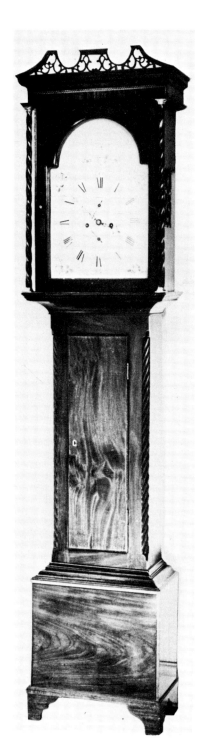

56 A good west-of-Scotland case in the
long-hood style. This one in solid mahogany dates from 1802 and houses the clock
by Robert Gillies of Beith. The twisted,
fluted columns are an interesting feature.
The fretted pediment may originally have
been of swan-neck pattern later cut down.
Height just over 7 ft.

The fretted pediments would have been of the swan-necked type, which are not a common feature. It seems that someone may have cut down the tops at some time in the past, and they have been replaced with straight moulded capping. The total height of the case is 7ft 1in.

The bracket feet are replacements, and since the base panel has crossbanding around the top and sides only, this suggests that the base has been shortened, perhaps when the new feet were fitted, though probably not by more than an inch or two. The most unusual thing of all is the proportion, the height of the hood taking up a far greater part of the total height than one would normally expect. Whether this aspect may be said to help the overall design or not is a matter of personal taste.

I show this clock as an example not of the typical, but of the design of the period as modified by the Scottish casemaker exercising his own independent whims and tastes. Don't misunderstand Gillies' casemaker. He knew how to make clock cases well enough, and he did not skimp the work he put into them. He knew how the English made their clocks, which may be the very reason why he did it *his* way. The measure of how far the design succeeds is for you to judge for yourself.

I must mention the frets in the sides of the hood, backed by (new) velvet. These are for the same purpose that we put frets in a radio set: to let out the sound. Here the sound would be that of the bell. Such frets are rather unusual in English longcase clocks of the white dial period, but they occur regularly on Scottish clocks. Occasionally one sees a clock with glass panels in the position where the frets are on this clock. The popular view is that such glass panels are replacements where original frets may have been broken in the past. Personally I feel that one sees too many hoods with glass side windows to assume that they are all replacements, and a great many show no signs of being tampered with. Many probably had glass panels originally. One finds glass panels were popular in certain regions only, notably Scotland and London (and the south-eastern corner of England).

Glass panels in the sides of hoods may perhaps have been provided so that one could see by glancing inside whether the clock needed winding, as this would be evident from the amount of gut left on the winding barrels. It would save unlocking the trunk door to see how far the weights had descended. If my suggestion is correct, it would preclude the existence of glass side panels in the hoods of thirty-hour clocks, as these would not show the need to rewind this type of clock.

The cases of the clocks by Tate and Robert Rowntree of York (page 24) are both superb examples and obviously are developments from the Thomas Husband style of pagoda-top case. Both are in very fine rich mahogany and in superb condition. Clocks in cases of this quality were costly when they were new, which would mean they were going into a wealthy household. The chances are that these are the kinds of households which did not have to sell off everything at the first spell of bad weather and such clocks have often been cared for far better than have cheaper ones in farmhouses where the dogs chewed the feet off. For this reason clocks of this calibre usually come down to us today in good condition. They have always been well cared for, and hopefully always will be. The Tate case dates from about 1815, and that by Rowntree from about the same time.

The Tate case has front feet only (so did the cases by Husband and Swan). This was not done for economy but for stability on uneven floors, where the case rested against the wall. The feet on the Rowntree case may not be original; they are a little old-fashioned for its period.

The case of the first Palliser clock was made in 1817. It is neat, about 7ft tall, basically an oak case with mahogany bandings and occasional inlays of fancy woods. It has swan-necked pediments ('horns', if you must), a feature very popular right through the white dial period. The case proportions are quite reasonable and well balanced. The pillars are simple, plain rods with plain brass caps and bases—nothing like the Nicholas case. The door is slightly shorter, but still a long door taking up much of the trunk. The proportion of trunk above the door is greater than on the earlier cases illustrated. Notice the pointed door top. Flat door tops are now developing into more interesting shapes, not necessarily more attractive, more exciting, or more difficult to make, but really less sensible, as slender points

57 (*opposite left*) A fine mahogany pagoda-top case dating from c 1815 housing a clock by Tate of Winterton, Lincolnshire. The use of fine veneers and much stringing and inlay work is typical of better examples of this type of case, which often has front feet only.

58 (*opposite right*) A neat case of reasonable proportions and size (about 7 ft tall). It was made in 1817 to house the clock by John Palliser of Thirsk. It is largely of oak, the cross-bandings and trim of mahogany. Canted corners to the trunk are not normally found prior to 1800.

like these are prone to damage, and often one sees the tips broken off. Notice too the lock and ivory escutcheon as an inlaid diamond shape. This ivory diamond came in about 1800 or so and was amazingly popular. One sees it very often on chests of drawers of Regency and early Victorian period. On clock cases it survives right through to about 1860–70, and is quite common.

A point about locks on clock cases may be worth making. There would seem to be more sense in fitting a lock on the case of an eight-day clock rather than on a thirty-hour one, as one would hardly take the trouble to lock and unlock the door every day when winding. Yet one does see locks on thirty-hour cases quite often, and frequently, as here, on cases which seem quite original to the clock. It is a possibility that the clockmaker had a steady order with a cabinetmaker to supply cases at regular intervals, may be one a week, or one a fortnight, according to his needs. It seems that the clock production of an average clockmaker working single-handed was about one clock every two weeks, roughly between twenty and twenty-five clocks a year. It is possible that he may have put his clock into whatever case suited the customer from the stock he had available at the time, and hence would arrive at a thirty-hour clock in a locking (eight-day?) case.

The Palliser case has two front feet only, no back feet. The feet are of an intermediate type, halfway in style between the earlier bracket feet and the later splayed feet, often known as 'French' feet, which we shall see on later clocks.

Notice the chamfered corners on this case, and also on the second Palliser case and the one by Fothergill. These are a compromise, a little fancier than the square (Bancroft) corners, but easier to make than the reeded quarter pilasters of the Nicholas clock. Chamfered corners are quite a common feature in the first half of the nineteenth century.

The case of the first Fothergill clock was probably original but it was in very poor condition when I bought the clock. Having spent some years in a hayloft it was very shabby and badly infested with woodworm. We have no photograph of it but it was a typical case of the period (1805). The interesting point about it was that it had shell inlays. I don't know the reason for it, but shell inlays became very popular on furniture about the turn of the century. There was a fashion lasting about twenty years or so for shells. Shell-like decorations appear in the corner paintings of dials and often on cases, where there is frequently an inlaid shell in the centre of the door, with sometimes another one in the centre of the base. Shell decorations usually appear about 1790–1810, and they continue for some years. An alternative popular theme for these door-panel inlays was a motif of Britannia with a lion, and sometimes a simpler rosette or wheel motif.

The second Palliser case (see page 41) is perhaps a slight reversion in style: height about 7ft, flat door top, bracket feet (front feet only, again), plain pillars—largely oak with a mahogany hood door and a band above the trunk, also of mahogany. The trunk door does not quite fill the whole trunk length, but it almost does. Chamfered corners to the trunk are also in mahogany. A very simple clock, it is not quite so well balanced, as the base is a little out of proportion. The interesting point about the case is the hood top, which is of a break-arch pattern. This was an alternative to the swan-necked pediment and a design which I happen to like, though one sees it less often than the 'horned' top. The implication is that the 'horned' versions were more popular at the time. This, by the way, is another clock which is now in the Netherlands.

The second Fothergill case has progressed further. It is still a pleasant enough clock and reasonably proportioned, standing 7ft 4in—almost a small one by London standards! There are swan-necked pediments, straight pillars, and front feet only again. The case is basically oak inlaid with mahogany banding, and the hood face and the trunk are veneered in mahogany with some rosewood. Notice, however, how the door has shrunk in length, leaving almost a square area beneath it, for what purpose I cannot imagine. This shortening of the door in many cases can often spoil the whole look of a clock, and there is no practical gain or economy in having done this. If anything, a short door makes it harder to get the pendulum in when setting up the clock. One possible reason may have been to prevent the warping which was very prevalent with those slender long thin clock doors of the later eighteenth century. I have seen one or two clocks which were built (around 1800) with long doors and later had the doors shortened and a small inset panel set in below the now much shorter door. I have seen this particularly on clocks from Cumberland and from Lancashire. Obviously someone somewhere thought it was an improvement, though clearly not a visual one.

This Fothergill case (about 1825–30) still has the flat door top and chamfered trunk corners retained from a slightly earlier period. It is important always with case styles to remember that each feature is subject to change independently of any other feature, and variations will occur according to the whim of each individual cabinet-maker. A point also to be borne in mind with styles of both cases and dials is that a feature of a past style can be reintroduced by any designer who may wish to revert to that earlier feature. The opposite, however, does not apply, ie a designer will very seldom incorporate a feature that has not yet been tried out and 'accepted'. For example, a casemaker of 1860 could if he wished revert to the plain round pillars as on the second Fothergill case. A casemaker of 1790, however, could not possibly use pillars of the reeded twisted type on the J. C. Elliott case. They would have been utterly out of proportion and, more importantly, they had not yet been designed for use on a clock: no cabinetmaker would dare jeopardise the sales potential of his goods by experimenting so boldly. Experimentation tends to be a slow and gentle process.

Some conservative clockmakers may have stuck to traditional case styles long after others had begun using newer designs. A clock of, say, 1820 could conceivably have been housed originally in a case of a style more appropriate to twenty or thirty years earlier, though in fact this is unlikely to have happened. I am thinking here of different casemakers in the same areas, rather than variations between regions. Again the reverse is not true: an 1820 clock could not have been housed originally in a case of 1850 style. Fortunately when it comes to spotting swapped cases they are often easy to detect, as the case style is usually later than the clock style: almost an impossibility for an original clock-with-case. A case which has been changed with care and knowledge is almost impossible to spot.

The whole question of whether or not one should change cases is very much open to debate. There are times when it can be a desirable improvement—if, for instance, a case of the wrong period can

59 (*opposite left*) Oak and mahogany case c 1830 housing the clock by Fothergill of Knaresborough. The swan-neck pediment was probably the most popular of all hood patterns. The trunk door is noticeably short, leaving a large unused section below it. Height about 7 ft 4 in.

60 (*opposite right*) Good-quality mahogany case housing the clock by Woolston Roberts of Derby. This case style is sometimes called a pagoda top, a bell top, or a tea-caddy top, and is one of the most elegant of white dial case styles. This one dates from c 1820.

be replaced by one of the right period. It would all rather depend on the ability to discriminate of the person doing the substituting. In view of the fallible human factor, cases are probably best left alone. In instances where the existing case appears to be original to the clock, it seems a great pity to switch it for another, whatever the motive. I know dealers who switch cases regularly. I have done it myself on infrequent occasions when, I tell myself, I felt justified in doing so. I must also on occasions have bought clocks which were not in their original cases without ever knowing this; and so must most dealers and, even more so, private buyers.

As far as possible I am trying to give positive dates for each item I illustrate, but of course changes were not as sudden or as precise as may sometimes be implied. Obviously, a style did not end in 1820 and a new one start in 1821.

The case of the Roberts clock was made about 1820. It stands exactly 7ft high, a neat example of a north-country clock. In size it is typical of most northern clocks of this period. The very large provincial cases were mostly made after 1830, as we shall see later; but this Roberts case is still reasonably proportioned and small enough to go into any modern home. The size and proportions are typical of northern clocks, but the style is unusual in so far as the hood shape is concerned. This pagoda-top style is more usual on southern cases, though not rare on northern ones.

The case is original. On the back is pasted the original delivery label, but unfortunately it does not tell us the name of the casemaker. It reads:

> Mr. Wolster Roberts watch and clock maker Derby
> two clock cases to be forwarded
> direct with A Derby Boat
> with great care and kept Dry
> By the Nottingham Steem
> Packet to Gainsbro.

Notice that the label miswrites the name, which on the dial is Woolston Roberts.

The case is in solid mahogany, the front veneered with selected figurings. Cases of solid mahogany made (in this example indisputably) for white dial clocks—in this instance, too, brought some considerable distance—show that there can have been no feeling at that time of white dial clocks being 'second-class' clocks. Apart from this illustration of the trouble taken over such a clock, at this period if you wanted a longcase clock, this is what you had. Brass dial clocks, while still being produced here and there, were very largely out of date by this time.

The white lines are inlaid *stringing* with paler woods. Notice the double-arrow stringing line on the chamfered trunk corners. These chamfered corners very commonly carry fancy inlay decoration from this time. The ivory keyhole escutcheon is also a typical feature from now on. The hood pillars are still reeded with brass Corinthian capitals which, however, are not commonly used as late as this. A wavy-topped trunk door is typical. The base tapers off into feet which are now an extension of the base itself, not separate as were the bracket-type feet of a few years earlier. It is in absolute contrast to the next case, though of the same period. Many a case of this Roberts style is now seen housing a late eighteenth-century brass dial clock, because a dealer thought he could make more out of it that way; also collectors wanted good cases, but not if they had white dial clocks in them. A few misinformed writers produced a misinformed market of 'collectors', and to meet their needs dealers destroyed many original white dial clocks by robbing them of their cases. The finer the case, the less the chance of its being allowed to remain with its white dial clock.

The case of the J. Keys clock is undoubtedly original. Inside the door is *branded* 'J. Keys' and written in pen alongside this is 'April 15 1825'. The same wording is on the backboard inside. On the inside of the movement frontplate is scratched 'Made by Joseph Keys April 15th 1825' (also: 'cleand February 15th 1832' and cleand by ditto August 13th 1834'). Maybe Keys was farsighted enough to do this on purpose, to prevent the case of his clock from being swapped.

It could be argued that this is not proof. However, when taken with the details of the clock and its maker, it is consistent. The question of faking hardly arises, as no one could possibly have gained financially by putting a better case on such a clock than the one it was made with. Any tampering with or faking is almost always done for financial gain.

The case is made entirely of solid mahogany, except for the backboard which is oak. The plinth is a replacement: probably the case originally had a bracket-foot type of plinth, ie a plinth shaped into a foot at each side. It stands exactly 6ft 3½in high. It is a very neat and simple case: nothing fancy. Two things are remarkable about it. To begin with, it is a simple thirty-hour clock, yet obviously in the opinion of the purchaser or maker it merited a solid mahogany case. Not that the case itself is very special. However, it would have been cheaper to make one in oak or deal. The fact that this clock was thought at the time to deserve mahogany may indicate that a thirty-hour clock was perhaps not looked upon as the poor relation to the eight-day one in the way that is sometimes suggested. Evidently it was considered more important to spend extra on a mahogany case, rather than have an eight-day clock in an oak case. All I am saying is that the standards or values by which we judge today are perhaps not the same standards as those of the time. It is often true of a country clockmaker that his normal production was a thirty-hour clock and that an eight-day one was the exception, not the rule. This is not the place to go into a detailed argument of that point. However, I have a record of over 100 clocks made by an above-average late eighteenth-century clockmaker and of these only fifteen are eight-day ones.

Records I have of another clockmaker's output at the same time show that, out of a total of almost 300 clocks he made over a twenty-year period, only six were eight-day ones. Six eight-day clocks in twenty years is an extreme example, but I mention it simply to clarify that for most people a clock meant a thirty-hour clock. Those who were prepared to pay twice the price to get an eight-day one were in the minority in the eighteenth century. In the nineteenth century, however, the trend changed and increasingly more customers preferred to pay for the costlier eight-day rather than accept the daily duty of winding a thirty-hour one.

The other point about this case is its style, which has barely changed from that of fifty years earlier. Notice the long door, the three-quarter pillars attached to the hood door, and the quarter pillars at the back of the hood. That is really all the style there is to it. The door, you will notice, has the best piece of mahogany with the finer figuring. The sides and base are plainer straight-grain. As we shall see shortly, the case of the clock by another Devon maker (of Dawlish) is also in this similarly archaic style. These examples teach us, if anything, how hard it is to draw firm conclusions about case styles. There is no reason why a particular maker should not have kept to the styles he personally liked, and of course a clockmaker aged sixty could still retain a fondness for, or even be hidebound by, the styles of the days of his apprenticeship. The same thing can happen in a whole district. A quiet country area like Devonshire need in no way feel the need to imitate up-to-the-minute fashions prevalent in industrial centres such as the Midlands or north of England.

It takes a lot of practice to be able to say with any certainty that a case is right or wrong just by looking at it.

One point I have not mentioned could be argued. Suppose the case were older than the clock, and that J. Keys sold the clock in a second-hand case? That could explain the old-fashioned style, admittedly. However, one must remember that Keys was selling a *new* clock, not an antique. Could he have got away with an older case? I doubt it. And then when we think that Keys was proud enough of the work to put his name on the movement, the dial, and twice on the case ... That was a new case all right, and it is original.

Unfortunately the archaic nature of the case style which Keys used was its downfall. I sold this clock some time ago. Recently I was surprised to run into the case again in an antique shop, but now containing a thirty-hour *brass* dial clock by Abraham Fell of Ulverston, made about 1760–70. I could recognise it as unquestionably the same case because of various minor repairs to it, which I had personally carried out. On account of the older-than-period style of case it is unlikely that anyone will now know that it was made about sixty years later than the clock it now houses—unless they read this and can spot the marks where Keys had once written his name inside the case. Incidentally, the price of the clock had multiplied almost by three in a period of less than a year because of the switched movement and dial.

Since a conservative clockmaker, if he so wishes, can retain features of earlier traditional styles, we can find other examples similar to this Keys case, and we grow to accept the possibility of what is termed a 'throwback' to earlier styles. What no clockmaker could do, of course, is to use case styles which have not yet been conceived. While we might find an 1825 clock in a 1795 type of case we could hardly find a 1775 clock in an 1825 type of case, that is in areas where such styles have changed during this period.

In attempting to assess the originality of a case, it is always as well, if you begin to doubt, to look for the motive that might have led to a case being changed. Remember, the older the case, the harder it is for a dealer to come by a spare one to fit a caseless movement. Sometimes he will have to make do with one less old than he would like. Hence if a clock seems to have a case *newer* in style than one might expect, you might sensibly regard it with caution. If a clock seems to have a case *older* than one might expect, here a little more tolerance is needed, because of the possible *throwback* of case styles we have been discussing. In thinking along these lines we have to credit the dealer with the ability to recognise cases of varying ages, and there will be occasions where we may be giving credit where it is not due. Anyway, I still feel that it is as well always to bear in mind the motive for a change you think might have taken place. Has there been a financial gain to the dealer by such a change, either now or in the past?

Recently, at a very highly esteemed Antiques Fair, I saw a provincial clock of about 1730, a brass dial one of course, in a solid mahogany case of quite obviously late eighteenth-century style. The description ticket gave details of the maker's known dates. A solid mahogany case as early as this would be very exceptional anyway, as the wood was not imported in any great quantity until 1750 or so. However, the case was typically 1780 or 1790. The price was several hundred pounds. It is as well to look carefully, not just appreciatively.

Also illustrated is the case of a clock by Peter Penman of Dunfermline, Scotland, made about 1840. The dial is circular, plain, with Roman numerals only, matching brass hands of crown pattern, and no falseplate. The case, while at first sight of an unusual shape, is a style met with occasionally on Scottish clocks. The pointed hood top lacks finials above each pillar; it did have them once as the holes are still there. The door is a circular brass one, an attractive though impractical feature, since these heavy brass doors wear out their hinges by their own weight. The trunk door is convex, a frequent feature of Scottish casework. The carved decorative piece, which looks like the door top, in fact is attached to the trunk, and the door top is flat. This is a sensible idea as over-elaborate door tops

61 (*opposite left*) Mahogany case from the thirty-hour clock by Joseph Keys of Exeter, made in 1825. The simple, slender style, with pillars attached to the door, is not a great deal different from the style of fifty years earlier. Height 6 ft 3 in.

62 (*opposite right*) Interesting mahogany longcase clock by Peter Penman of Dunfermline, c 1840. Whilst made of beautiful woods, this is a strange design by English standards. The circular dial is here not of the all-white type, but has a gold band, chapter-ring fashion, around the numbers. Sometimes these dials are all gold.

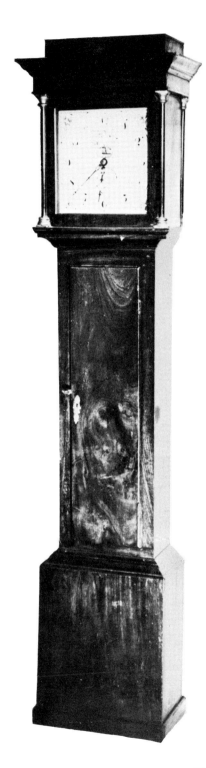

are very prone to damage. This point is worth mentioning again, as it is apparent that casemakers eventually began to recognise this factor themselves, as in this example. Full-length trunk pillars are an interesting feature of this fine case, which stands exactly 7ft 2in to the top of the centre finial. The case has solid mahogany sides and superbly figured mahogany veneers to the front. Scottish cases are often of high quality in both woods and construction.

12

Cases:
Period Three, 1830–1870

The first case we examine is that of the Stephens & Davies of Neath (Glamorgan) clock, and a very pleasant case it is too for this period. It is made of solid mahogany with veneers on the front. Not too large, it stands about 7ft 6in high. The proportions are good, well balanced, traditional. There is still a long door, which by now is an unusual feature except with conservative casemakers who, as here, retain the earlier type. Notice that the hood door has scalloped (wavy) edges, this also being a feature more usual on clocks of a slightly earlier period. The pillars are turned, generally a late sign, and the splats at the back of the hood are shaped, which latter feature can occur at any period on white dial cases. The swan-neck scrolls have very exaggerated curls, though I find these attractive. The hood pillars have brass Corinthian capitals—rather a late use of these, for one normally associates them with the late eighteenth century. When compared with the cases by the Snows, of almost exactly the same period, this one certainly has the better lines and proportions. I show it as an interesting example, not as typical of most Welsh cases of this time which would perhaps tend more towards the style of the Snow cases.

The case of the Dawlish clock is most interesting because of its apparently early style. It stands 6ft 6in high, and is mainly of straight-grain oak with mahogany-veneered hood door, mahogany bandings to the trunk door, and the same to the base panel. Pillars are still, even at this late date, attached to the hood door, where one would normally expect free-standing pillars by now. Bracket feet are also carried on here into a considerably later period than one would expect. The brass escutcheon is a modern replacement. I bought this clock in a very dirty condition, and it could not have been working for many years. In view of this and also in view of the unusually

 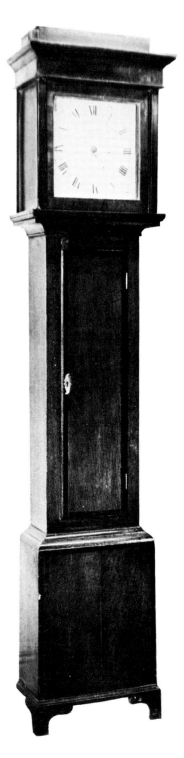

small dial aperture of 10½in square, it seems unlikely that it was a replacement case. I cannot be certain that the case is original to the clock, but it seems very likely. It is interesting to find, as with the Keys clock, a case of such early traditional style being made as late as this: 1835 or even later. Such a case one might expect in the 1780–1810 period, but 1835 is unusually late for this style. The dial also had several features which were reversions to a style of twenty or more years earlier.

We cannot show a case for the Hooker of Lewes clock. It had no case when I bought it, nor when I sold it. However, I did see a photograph of the case of the second, arched-dial clock I have mentioned by that maker, and its style too was vastly earlier than one might expect for 1835 or so, being very similar to the case of the clock by Forster of Sheerness, Kent (c 1790)—in other words unchanged in almost fifty years.

The next two cases are by the Snow brothers, Thomas of Knaresborough and Richard of Pateley Bridge (Yorkshire). In many ways they are typical of the less-handsome north-country cases of this period, 1835–40. They are relatively tall, measuring about 7ft 6in. A clock of this type standing much over 8ft high is quite exceptional and usually confined to very late cases of after 1850. They have high bases and therefore shorter trunks with short doors set into these trunks, so that quite a wide expanse of case surrounds the door. This is the type of high-based, short-door case which, while typical of Yorkshire clocks after about 1820–30, is frequently mistakenly cited in reference books as being a normal feature of Yorkshire clocks from about 1770 onwards. Clocks with this type of short door, as in the two Snow cases, were made in Yorkshire and most other counties too of the north and Midlands from about 1820 or 1830. Earlier than that they would be extremely unusual.

These cases have swan-neck pediments, ivory keyplates, 'French' feet (at the front only)—the Knaresborough case feet have been cut

63 (*opposite left*) Solid mahogany case c 1835 from the clock by Stephens & Davies of Neath. Here the wood is used largely in the solid with applied beadings to give the impression of panels. The scalloped edge to the hood is a feature found in the south-west corner of Britain. The swan-neck is here more exaggerated than usual. Height 7 ft 6 in.

64 (*opposite right*) Oak case with mahogany crossbanding from the Dawlish clock of c 1835. The simple lines are reminiscent of earlier periods. The pillars attached to the hood door are square in cross-section, a most unusual feature. Height 6 ft 6 in.

off—turned hood pillars and wavy-topped doors. All these points are typical of *this* period. The Knaresborough case is in solid mahogany with a veneered front in handsomely veined pieces, and it carries much inlaid stringing of lighter woods. It has flat canted corners to the trunk, which flats are inlaid with stringing lines, and it has criss-cross stringing above and below these canted corners.

The Pateley Bridge case is in oak with mahogany and rosewood veneers on much of the front, but is still largely oak. Notice the sapwood streak in the door centre. This is more a country case, but by this time very much imitating the style of a town case. The pillar turnings are heavier, and the general build is slightly heavier. This is the case of a thirty-hour clock and Richard Snow could and did frequently supply better cases with his eight-day clocks. The latter tended to be all-mahogany versions of his thirty-hour cases; better in materials, but of the same overall shape and style, which was *the* fashionable style. Thomas's cases were generally a little more graceful, perhaps that bit sleeker and more slender. Richard's case also has twist-turned quarter pilasters to the trunk, a feature which crops up quite often from this time on: one sees it also on chests of drawers in this area.

The oak of this case has a yellowish look and contrasts strongly with the mahogany. Early oak cases tend to be darker in colour, the original (usually stained) oak having darkened further after years of having been polished with wax, and through dirt being polished in rather than cleaned off. Cases of the Snow period, however, were often treated when new with a thin French polish type of finish, and this tends to preserve the original colours by preventing wax from seeping into the wood. The strongly contrasting yellow and dark brown of these cases must have been popular at the time, though personally I cannot say that I care for it.

Finally we come to the case of J. C. Elliott's clock (page 187, left).

---

65 (*opposite left*) Large, heavy, fussy case of c 1840 housing the clock by Richard Snow of Pateley Bridge. Basically of oak construction with such a jigsaw of other woods (principally mahogany) in the trim that oak is the least visible wood. This case is well made and in good condition. Height about 7 ft 6 in.

66 (*opposite right*) Mahogany case with much crossbanding, stringing and inlay work, housing the clock by Thomas Snow of Knaresborough c 1835. Made of superb woods, it is often in proportion that these clocks fail. In particular they lack the slim waist of earlier examples. Height about 7 ft 6 in.

Elliott worked at Blyth in Northumberland early in his career, I discovered recently, and moved to Leeds probably not long before
1840, when his shop was in Leighton Lane. This clock was made
about 1865. It stands exactly 8ft high, yet looks very much bigger
than this. Some people would find this clock repulsively ugly—over-
fussy, tasteless, disproportioned, yet fascinating. When I first saw this
clock in a gloomy attic, it very nearly frightened me to death, but
I bought it. Carrying it single-handed down three flights of stairs
did little to help me recover from the shock.

A few people might find this case beautiful, though they would
be in the minority. While not exactly typical in every detail, it does
represent a certain type of late case to be found in the north. When
it was made it was one of the best examples of its kind—whether
or not we happen to like this type of clock today. Many hours of
the most skilled work went into its making, as did the choicest woods
available. It is solid mahogany with the front veneered with rosewood, mahogany, and with marquetry inlay in lighter woods. The
feet are very shortened, stumpy feet of the 'French' type: front feet
only, again. Notice the enormous reeded, twisted pillars to the hood
and similar though larger ones in the trunk corners. Full pillars on
the trunk and even on the base corners were very fashionable at this
time. Look at the very elaborate shape of the door top.

The biggest fault really is the proportion, the trunk now being
much shorter in relation to the hood and base. The clock is too wide
for its height; at least, this is what we may feel today. It is interesting
to wonder what opinion might be in 100 years' time. This clock,
like so many others, is now in the Netherlands.

The men who made this case are long dead, and with them died
craftsmanship of the highest quality. The design of this case may be
criticised, but the execution, the workmanship, are such that we shall
probably never see the like of again. Anything involving the
materials, skill and time that this case involved would today be
thought far too expensive to be undertaken. How many cabinetmakers are there today who could make a case like this?

In the photograph this Elliott case is shown alongside one of

67 A large 'Yorkshire' case of 1865 alongside a smaller one of c 1800. They are from
clocks by John Catcheside Elliott of Leeds and Richard Morland of Kirkby Malzeard.
Notice how the long waist and door have been both shortened and widened to produce
a much stockier line. Height 8 ft and about 7 ft 8 in.

c 1800–10 containing a clock by Richard Morland of Kirkby Malzeard, Yorkshire. It is useful to contrast the two, especially in regard to the proportions. The Morland case was of oak with mahogany bandings, a shell inlay in the door and reeded quarter-trunk columns of mahogany. The real difference is not so much in the extra height of the Elliott case, but mostly in its extra width and its much higher base with consequently shortened trunk length and squat door. The Elliott case must have been far more costly to make, but today most of us would prefer the Morland case.

Cases of the Elliott type are exceptional and not typical. However, if we take the essential features of the Stephens & Davies and Snow cases, these set the pattern for most casework of the period. Longcase clocks after 1840 are less common. In the south they are relatively infrequent; in the Midlands and Wales they persist; the stronghold after 1840, however, is mainly in the north with Yorkshire and Lancashire by far the most prolific areas at this time.

Illustrated is the trunk of a late clock of about 1840 which housed the clock by Moorehouse of Wetherby. This close-up reveals the beautiful woods used, here entirely mahogany of varying types all inlaid with yellow stringing lines. This particular case was in reasonably good condition and had a fine patina. The workmanship is superb; it is the design which is not popular today, largely because such clocks are very bulky. I sold this clock (about 1978) for less money than a cabinetmaker would have charged at the time even to make the door—and he could not have got woods of this quality to make it from anyway!

The clock base illustrated is an extremely late form found in the 1850 to 1870 period in the north, this particular case being from another Leeds clock by J. C. Elliott. Once more the materials and workmanship can be seen to be superb, but very few people today can accommodate a clock of this size. Twenty years ago there was no market at all for this type of clock; I used to buy them for £5 a time to use for spares. The clock movement went straight into the stockroom to break up for spare parts, for its value as spares was higher than when complete. The cases went straight to the cabinetmaker to break up so that the woods could be used for repairing other, more desirable, clocks. At £6 I would refuse to buy them, because they were so numerous that I could find another one the next day for £5. Those were the prices for eight-day clocks. Similar thirty-hour clocks cost £3. This was all within the last fifteen years.

68 Trunk of a mahogany-veneered case of the clock by Moorehouse of Wetherby, c 1835. This short-door, wide-bodied style is not popular with everybody, but the woods and workmanship are of the highest calibre. Details of the matching panels and stringing-work show up well.

69 Base panel of a clock of c 1860 by John Catcheside Elliott. This pattern has a sunken circular panel, veneered in counter-matched sections, referred to, perhaps unkindly, as a 'dartboard base'. The wood and workmanship are fine but the design is not popular today.

CLOCK CASE FEATURES

	1770	1780	1790	1800	1810	1820	1830	1840	1850	1860	1870

solid line = normal
dotted line = unusual

WOODS
oak, plain
oak, carved
deal
mahogany, solid
use of veneer
use of rosewood

DOORS
full length of trunk
half length of trunk
arched top
flat top
wavy top
multi-pointed top

PILLARS
attached to hood door
plain round, wooden caps
plain round, brass caps
square pillars, usually reeded
round reeded
turned (increasingly heavily)
twin front pillars
on clock base

FEET
front two only
four
bracket (two or four)
french (splay)
turned bobbin
none (ie plinth)

PEDIMENTS
swan-necked
break-arch
flat top (with arch dial)
architectural
bell-shaped
southern traditional

TRUNK CORNERS
square
quarter pillars, reeded
quarter pillars, plain
chamfered
quarter round turned pillars
full pillars

(post-1810, mainly in South)

(post-1810, mainly in South)

(mainly Lancashire and Cheshire)

(mainly in South)

70 Clock case features.

It seemed a pity at the time and seems even more so looking back, but we just could not sell them. The only chance was the overseas dealers, and if we could get £8 for one of these clocks in running order from the Dutch buyers we thought we were doing well. Many a time I have loaded these clocks literally by the dozen on to roof racks, two or three tiers high. Our museums could have had them at these giveaway prices, but most museums laughed at the idea.

This last fling at lavish casework was perhaps the only answer that British clockmakers had in the face of the competition which now threatened them and finally crushed them in the form of imported clocks. The American shelf and wall clocks, the imported 'Vienna' wall clocks, were pouring into the country. Against these 'miniature' mass-produced clocks, the British product could not hope to compete either in size or price. Perhaps the only hope was deliberately not to try to compete, but to go to the other extreme in making the longcase more lavish than ever. Cases like the Elliott one illustrate how far the clockmakers went in this attempt. But the attempt failed.

I have bought these large cases of the Elliott type on many occasions purely to break them up for the veneers, and tragic as this may seem, it is true just the same that only a very few years ago there was no market at all for clocks of this extreme width. No doubt we shall be criticised in the future for this, just as we now criticise those who weighed in brass dial longcase clocks for their value as scrap brass fifty years ago.

> My grandfather's clock was too tall for the shelf,
> So it stood ninety years on the floor.

The well-known song by the American, Henry Clay Work, was first published in 1876 (E. L. Edwardes records in his excellent book, *The Grandfather Clock*). Perhaps the first line of the song sums up the problem. Ironically, the song that gave these clocks their lasting name also sounded their death-knell.

Space will not allow illustration and detailed description of every variation in case design, but the principal aspects have been covered. The reference table opposite attempts to summarise in brief form the major aspects involved in the dating of case design.

13
Scotland

The white dial, initially Birmingham-made, very soon spread into Scotland. Indeed Birmingham-made dials are found on Scottish clocks right through their timespan. By a Scottish clock I mean one bearing the name of a maker (or retailer) in Scotland, regardless of where the dial originated, but it was not long before the Scots had their own local dialmakers.

The first dialmaker in Edinburgh, and probably the first in Scotland, was William Dallaway, a japanner known to be working there as early as 1775. When he first made clock dials is not known but it is thought to have been about 1780–5. An advertisement of his in the *Edinburgh Evening Courant* for 1793 points out that 'He has taken in partnership his son, who has been in London and Birmingham for the improvement of that art' (ie japanning) and 'has procured the secret of inlaying stove fronts, dressing-cases, candlesticks, etc, which is a thing never attempted here before. . . .'

Whether the son had been learning the art of clock dial japanning we do not know. Indeed it is difficult to see what he could have learned of that skill in London, as the London contribution to the subject was so slight that we have so far not met any example of it. It is interesting to note that the same advert mentioned that Dallaway 'still continues to teach drawing in all its branches as usual'.

In 1797 another Dallaway advertisement reads:

H. Dallaway & Son, Japan Manufactory, North Back of Canongate, Edinburgh.

H. D. & Son return their grateful acknowledgements for past favours. They beg leave to inform their friends and the public that they have on hand a complete assortment of the following articles which they continue to sell Wholesale, Retail and for Exportation:-

Japanned Fire Screens of black iron, a capital invention, and for elegance and neatness nothing can excel them; *Clock Dials a fine collection*; Tea Trays, Waiters, Candlesticks, Snuffer Stands, Knife Slips, Bread Baskets.

H. D. & Son cannot let slip this opportunity of particularly recommending their Tea Trays, Waiters, etc. as they have now brought them to that perfection as would do honour to an English Manufactory. They flatter themselves that from their perseverance and attention they still will merit a continuance of past favours. Commissions from the country in the Japanning line or for any of the above articles will be carefully attended to.

So Dallaway's supplied dials singly to private customers or in quantity wholesale to clockmakers and even for export, which must mean essentially to America, for it is difficult to see where else they might be wanted. I do not imagine they regarded selling to England as exporting. Their claim that they have brought their quality up to that of the English manufacturers shows that the English were regarded as the best japanners.

Patrick Dallaway, a son of William's, was in dispute with the local trade guild for clockmakers, the Incorporation of Hammermen, about 1809 for allegedly infringing their rights. He was essentially an ironmonger and tinsmith but obviously traded in Dallaway dials too. It seems that it was his tinsmithing activities to which they objected (presumably japanning came outside their scope) and during the wrangle the following interesting information came to light in a letter from the Hammermen:

> ... yet as the father of Mr. Dallaway had introduced the Art of Japanning into this quarter, which had turned out to be beneficial to the trade of the country, they therefore recommend that out of respect to his memory his son should be allowed to carry on the tinsmith trade within the city (for the sum of forty pounds, etc) ...

Whether this means that William Dallaway was the first in Edinburgh or in Scotland generally is not too certain, but it looks as if he was the first in the whole country. In 1811 Patrick Dallaway wrote that:

> ... from the death of my father, I find that I cannot carry on the ironmongery business and follow the japanning also; therefore I must relinquish one of them. I have now come to the resolution of giving up the said ironmongery and mean to devote my attention to my (japan) manufactory.

But it seems that in 1812 Patrick did go back to tinsmith work, though whether the production of dials then ceased altogether is not known.

There are several intriguing aspects of white dial clocks in Scotland. Firstly the trade seems to have concentrated almost entirely on eight-day clocks. There must have been some thirty-hour ones, but they are few and very far between and I have never personally come across one. Another odd feature is that the Scots seem to have preferred the arched dial; square dials are quite uncommon. This may have been, in the later period, because the popular taste was for very 'busy' colourful dials and there was obviously more colour to an arched dial than to a square one, but early Scottish dials are very similar to English ones in being largely white with a little delicate colour—indeed many *are* English ones.

Like English dials, some have falseplates and some do not, and falseplates generally fall out of use by about 1830. Falseplates on Scottish clocks often seem to be unmarked, but at least some dialmakers stamped them. Known examples of impressed falseplates are recorded marked 'Dallaway & Sons, Edinr.', 'H. Dallaway & Son, Edinr.', 'Paterson—Perth' and 'T. Smith & Stevenson, Edinr.'. All the Scottish dialmakers known to me are listed on page 57.

Some Scottish dials are marked on the back with painted lettering, and examples are known 'signed' on the back: 'Bell & Meudell, Edinr.', 'Russell & Clark, Edinr.', 'Peter Bell, Edinr.' and 'D. Sinclair, Japr. Edinr.'. Some of these dialmakers also added the words 'Best Fancy' or 'Finest Fancy', apparently indicating a style or quality of dial—we will come back to these terms later.

Unfortunately a lot of dials on Scottish clocks cannot be attributed to a maker, and with pre-1800 dials we cannot often be certain whether they were made in Scotland or England. Those prior to 1800 were either English or in the English style. That by Robert Gillies (page 103) could be English or Scottish, but it is certainly English in style.

Not many dials of known Scottish manufacture date prior to 1800, so by the time we can be sure that we are into the native dialmaking period, the style has already usually reached the stage of fully painted corner decoration with corners of a geometric or semi-geometric patterned type—fans, hatchings, etc, sometimes incorporating flowers into the patterns and often with the corner enclosed by a solid line (two straight-edged and one curved). Sometimes the four corner decorations join up to each other, a feature which becomes increasingly common as time passes and by the 1840s has become the rule.

By about 1815–20 we find the corners sometimes contain painted pictures, perhaps of famous people (eg Nelson, with whose portrait this habit may almost be said to have begun), sometimes—especially later—just of an allegorical nature such as the four virtues, the four continents, the four seasons, etc. These are just the same trends really as in English dials, and of course some still kept the flower corner patterns into the 1820s and '30s.

The dial arches in the 1815–30 period often kept the bowl-of-flowers type of unbordered decoration, sometimes a vignette style of bordered oval picture, sometimes a hero's portrait. Increasingly, however, starting from about 1815–20, one finds the whole arch filled as a complete picture, not just a pattern but an actual scene. At this time the arch tends to become more of a complete semicircle, perhaps to allow for more colourfulness, whereas the arches of earlier clocks tend to be shallower.

Some arch pictures follow the English fondness for a country scene, with perhaps a castle, romantic landscape, church, ruins, windmill, cottages—often a pretty scene of romanticised type, the kind of thing categorised by the six-year-old child of a friend as being 'like Hansel and Gretel's cottage'. That is what they are, fairy-tale scenes in tremendous contrast to the true country-cottage life of the period and region, where people lived knee-deep in mud, poverty and squalor, often sharing their cottages with the pigs and poultry. They take one's mind away from reality and into the countryside as we like to think of it, beautiful when the sun shines and the crops ripen.

Oddly enough the use of the moon dial in the arch seems to have been considerably less frequent in Scotland than in England, perhaps because the Scots liked more paint and less frippery along the lines of the typical Scottish dials in the major category we consider next.

Whilst some dial arches followed the English country landscape pattern, another very different type became increasingly popular, starting about 1820 and running on in ever-increasing strength of execution and popularity until the longcase clock died about 1870–80. This type is what became the typical Scottish dial, so characteristic that it can be recognised across the street as very different to the English type. The fully painted arch often shows a painted scene from Scottish literature (Robert Burns and Sir Walter Scott being favourites). Some of the scenes bear a title—'Burns at the Plough', 'Auld Robin Gray', 'Patie and Peggie', etc. Many show Scottish heroes of literature or factual heroes from the past; perhaps this great hero revival may have been inspired by Sir Walter Scott's works. Many arches contain scenes with people playing a prominent role in the picture, figures from history, legend or literature.

By the 1830s, along with the popular 'folk hero' themes were others of a more allegorical nature. Corner decorations included popularly the Four Continents, the Four Seasons (often actually named, one by one), the Four Elements (again often named—Earth, Air, Fire, Water), the Four Countries (England, Scotland, Wales, Ireland), almost always personified as ladies of ample proportions hampered by the essential accoutrements of their calling, usually sitting self-consciously and wearing crowns or bonnets and holding a variety of symbols of office (having more objects than hands available to hold them), ranging from a harp or spear to a parasol or hayrake. They put one in mind of how the newly crowned Miss World might have looked on the night of her victory a hundred years ago.

The tone of these later Scottish painted scenes is usually that of folk art and reminiscent of the type of painting one sees on fairground stalls or canal boats. There is a compulsion to cram as much as possible into the pictures, so that the effect is so busy as to make one feel dizzy. A sensitive friend of mine describes them as 'migraine dials'! A great fondness for the use of luminous paints, both as highlights and under some of the colours for greater brilliance, makes them even more eye-catching. The figures are often heavily outlined and everything is so boldly painted that there tends to be little or no depth to the pictures, which are flat and unrealistic despite the fact that much of the painting is carefully done and with great detail.

There were some bad English dials of this type, but some of these Scottish ones are truly appalling. In fairness it is difficult to find dials, English or Scottish, of this later period (c 1850–70) which bear any sort of comparison in artistry or taste of composition to the better ones of the earlier periods.

The terms 'Best Fancy' and 'Finest Fancy' were apparently used to distinguish different grades or qualities of this type of dial, though the numbers recorded as yet are inadequate to enable us to draw precise conclusions. It looks as if these highly luminous multi-coloured dials came into the 'Fancy' category. Anyone not familiar with these typically Scottish 'Fancy' dials should consult Felix Hudson's publication, *Scottish Longcase Clocks*, where a good number are illustrated.

The transition from the more restrained, earlier Scottish styles at

71 A dial of the typical 'Fancy' type very popular in Scotland during the 1840–70 period.
This one, by John Golder of Alloa, dates from c 1845. The corners show (clockwise
from bottom left) Fire, Earth, Air, Water; the arch has 'Auld Robin Gray'. Whilst a busy,
fussy dial style, the painting of this one is considerably better than many.

the beginning of the nineteenth century to these full-blown 'fairground' dials of the 1850s took place more slowly in the eastern part
of the country. The eastern taste, centred on Edinburgh, followed
more along the lines of the English style at first, both in dials and
cases. The dial sizes tended to remain smaller, 12 inch, 13 inch and
14 inch following on slowly over the years. The western taste,
centred on Glasgow, seems to have been eager to progress into larger,
bolder dials more quickly, and here the 14 inch dial had arrived

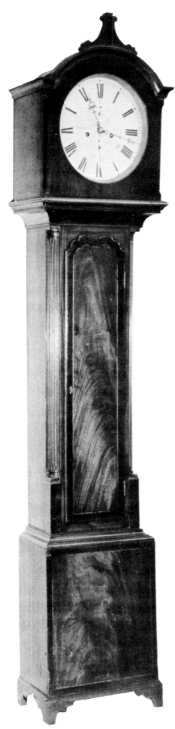

72 (*above*) Plain circular white dial, dialmaker unknown, from an eight-day longcase clock by James Breakenrig of Edinburgh, c 1830. This plain white dial could be used for longcase or spring-driven wall clocks. Its longcase use continued on semi-regulators, especially in London and Scotland, but it did not find widespread acceptance.

73 (*left*) Case of the James Breakenrig of Edinburgh clock, c 1830. Some of these circular white dial Scottish clocks can be extremely neat and handsome. This one stands only about 6 ft 10 in and is in very fine mahogany with crossbanding and stringing.

by 1800 with its full semicircular arch as opposed to the shallower arch of the smaller dials.

Not a great deal of progression is obvious in these 'Fancy' dials once the style began in the late 1830s. A possible exception is that the painted scenes blend ever closer together, leaving less space for the numbered dial centre, and also the white borders to the corner paintings and around and below the arch eventually disappear so that corner and arch pictures come edge to edge, occasionally with a wavy scroll-line to separate the arch scene.

Perhaps the gloomy candle-lit interiors in a more northerly country with its shorter daylight hours, longer winters and colder, wetter and more dreary climate, produced in Scotland a longing for more colourful, more brightly painted dials. At any rate that was the result, for Scottish dials after about 1830 are highly distinctive and usually easily recognised. So much so that it seems readily obvious that, whilst the Scottish dialmakers such as Dallaways may have been willing to offer dials 'for exportation', few seem to have been taken up on the offer, for the dial styles found in America and Ireland follow the English patterns much more closely.

However there was yet another type of Scottish dial which became popular from about 1820, and that was the round dial. As we know, this was the cheapest of all to buy, but it cannot have been for economy reasons that it was so popular, when the square form was almost totally unknown though its price was only a fraction more. Rather it may have been that the round dial filled a more traditional, sober-minded market, just as the London-made round dial had done. Many of these round dials are plain white with Roman hour numbers and the retailer's name—no decoration at all, just like the round spring-driven wallclock dial.

Sometimes a round white dial may have a gold-painted band in the position of a chapter ring on a brass-dial clock; sometimes the whole of the round dial is gold-coloured with the usual black lettering. Some of these round-dial clocks are what we call semi-regulators and are constructed with a dead-beat escapement for accuracy, or with a near-dead-beat if we can coin such a phrase—there is scarcely any recoil visible on the seconds hand, but the escape-wheel teeth are not cut quite as delicately as those of a true dead-beat. These clocks usually have strike-work (which a true regulator does not), and have conventional dial layout (whilst a true regulator may have its hour, minute and seconds hands all centred on different points and reading on three separate sub-dials). To continue this regulator-like approach to accuracy, some of them have wooden pendulum rods which help counter the effects of temperature changes on time-keeping.

One feature on many of these Scottish round-dial longcase clocks is that the hood door may be of the brass bezel type, just like that of a wall dial clock. It may have been thought that this was a more durable type of door, as wooden bezels tend to crack and split over the years. On the other hand, glazed brass bezel doors tend to be so heavy that they destroy their hinge fastenings with their own weight.

The clock by Peter Penman on page 179 shows one example of this round-dial type of Scottish longcase clock. Some are more severe, even austere, in case styles. One variation is shaped like a large key-hole with a circular drum-head and tapering sides, often without a separate base. Another, perhaps less common, version has a similar top and keyhole-shaped outline but the case is semicircular in cross-section and fluted in multiple flutes down its length, the overall effect being like a fluted tree-trunk, sometimes with no visible door but with access through a hinged panel at the sides. Despite unusual designs these round-dial cases are often of superb mahogany and fine craftsmanship, but not in a style that is universally popular.

If some of these case descriptions sound strange, then that is because Scottish cases do appear in a great variety of forms. The cases of the arched-dial clocks made in eastern Scotland, especially those before about 1830, are based on English models. This is what might be called the Edinburgh school, although the trend spread over into central and north-eastern Scotland.

The case by J. Bryson of Dalkeith, near Edinburgh, is an example. It is entirely of oak, simple, reasonably slender and of good proportions with slender reeded pillars and reeded quarter-columns. The low swan-neck pediment is not a fussy one and the whole case is very similar to an English case of the 1800–20 period. This is a modest type of case but many Scottish clocks are in superb mahogany and a slender east-of-Scotland example can be very pleasing.

74 and 75   Two east-of-Scotland cases, simple and restrained, echoing the English style. That on the left in plain oak houses a clock by Bryson of Dalkeith; that on the right in solid mahogany with stringing is from a clock by Stewart of Dunbar. Both are clean, crisp examples of their kind, from c 1820.

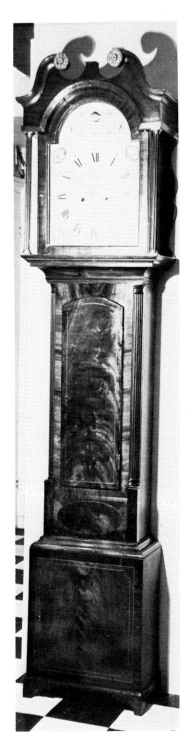

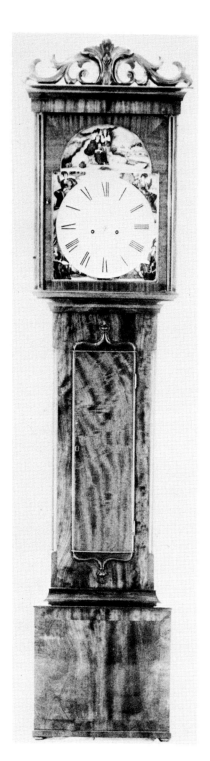

76 A handsome west-of-Scotland case of c 1850 housing a clock by A. Breckenridge & Son of Kilmarnock (south of Glasgow). The case is of beautiful mahogany and skillfully made, but of a highly distinctive, long-hood style. Some cases of this style are without the top cresting-piece. This is as fine an example of this case style as I have ever seen.

The west-of-Scotland case, centred on Glasgow, but also spreading to the north, east and south, had two noticeable peculiarities (not always used, of course, but frequently). The hood pillars often reach full length to meet the hood top, not—as with most other cases— around the break of the arch, but at a point slightly higher than the topmost point of the arch. In other words the pillars are about a third as long again as normal. The hood may then finish flat across its top, or may have a swan-necked pediment sitting atop the flat, almost as an afterthought. The hood door therefore will not have the usual arched top, but comes right up as high as the pillars and has a flat top with an unused blank zone of wood at each side of the door top, which can look very ungainly.

The second peculiarity is that because of this long-pillar hood style, the hood usually does, and in any case appears to, take up a larger than normal proportion of the clock's length. To an eye accustomed to the normal case proportions, these Glasgow-school clocks can look top-heavy. They are very often made of fine mahogany and some of them are very high-quality cases and handsome specimens— once you get used to the proportions.

14

America

The development of the white dial clock in America demands considerably more research than I can undertake from this side of the Atlantic. British writers on horology have been accused in the past—not without some justification—of having scarcely glanced at American clockmaking. Our only defence can be that while British clocks were and still are exported wholesale, the reverse is not true, and consequently we seldom have the opportunity to examine American clocks in detail. I am speaking here of grandfather clocks only. In America these are sometimes known as 'tall clocks'. For much of the information that follows, I am indebted to keen American researchers Chris Bailey, Stacy Wood and Ed La Fond.

Very many British-made grandfather clocks were taken to America among the household possessions of emigrant families, the majority of them being of the white dial type. Far greater numbers have been exported by antiques dealers in more recent times, and vast numbers of these British clocks still are shipped to America every year. Americans interested in white dial clocks in their own country must therefore pay considerable attention to the development of British-made examples, which may constitute a high percentage of those they will meet with. In the absence of knowledge about the maker whose name appears on the dial, the American who is not experienced in clocks might well be unable to decide whether the clock was made in Britain or America.

When we come to white dial clocks sold by American clockmakers, we must remember that some of the clockmakers were trained in this country, and went out to America fully experienced, with a knowledge of trade suppliers in Britain of whatever parts they might wish to purchase. Such trade contacts in Britain would be most useful should there be any problems in obtaining the required materials in America, as at times there undoubtedly were. The practice of some British clockmakers buying in finished or part-finished goods from others in the trade was already well established long before the white dial came on the scene about 1770.

What all this adds up to in the early period of the white dial clock in America, is that there may not always be an easy solution to the problem of which clocks or parts of clocks were made in which country. To add to this difficulty, white dials were an English innovation and Osborne & Wilson, and no doubt other dialmakers, shipped out to America ready-painted dials on to which the local clockmaker might build his own movements or fit British bought-in movements. The falseplate sold with many such dials was designed specifically for just such situations. P. R. Hoopes in his article in *Antiques*, 1931, suggests that white dials were not manufactured in America until after 1800; and he quotes interesting evidence of white dials 'newly arrived from England' being sold by local wholesalers in 1784 in Baltimore, and in 1785 in Philadelphia.

We know that American-made clocks do carry dials by British dialmakers, particularly in the earlier period c 1770–1800, notably the dials by Wilson and by Osborne, less often by Keeling and by Walker & Hughes, but seldom by any other British makers. These are perhaps the bigger dialmaking concerns anyway, Keeling excepted, and Keeling's dials are far from common anywhere.

From quite an early date it seems that native Americans tried to imitate the Wilson and Osborne types of dial but the results, when judged today, have not withstood the test of time as well as the English dials. Perhaps this was because the method of japanning was not so well understood. These very early (pre-1800) American dialmakers and dialpainters are mostly still unidentified, though this problem is currently receiving considerable attention amongst American researchers.

British-made dials are said to have been more popular in the urban areas (New York, Philadelphia, Baltimore) until the end of the century, and of course the locally made dials were probably not readily available until about 1800, or perhaps were not considered as good as the British ones. Locally made dials were used even in the eighteenth century by the more rural clockmakers.

Whilst these very early American-made white dials cannot usually be traced to a particular dialmaker by name, it is often possible to identify an unmarked (American-retailed) dial as being definitely of British origin, or otherwise, by its distinctive style. This is a skill which often requires great experience and it is not always possible even for experts to be certain. It is therefore difficult to give advice to a beginner on how to spot features which the experts have not yet themselves agreed upon. Nevertheless one has to try, and the following are pointers which occur to me and which may help.

Firstly moon dials in the arch were apparently more popular in America than in Britain, and the comments on the moon dial maps in Chapter 15 may help identify an American-made dial.

Quite popular on American clocks were centre-calendar and centre-seconds features—this is where an extra hand from the centre of the dial will register one, or both, of these features. Both these features were very unusual on British white dials, centre-seconds work being particularly rare, and the two features together rarer still. It seems likely therefore that (unless the British were making dials to special order for America) many of these centre-calendar and centre-seconds dials will prove to be American-made. Indeed some evidence towards this will be found later in this chapter. Having said that, we do know that some English-made dials used in America did have these features!

Another feature sometimes claimed for American white dials is that they were supplied undrilled, and the winding-holes were drilled by the clockmaker to suit his needs, any ragged edges being covered by the brass eyelets normally found on eight-day clocks and called in English terminology dial collets and in American terminology dial grommets. Evidence of this late drilling is sometimes allegedly demonstrated by winding-holes which are eccentrically situated relative to the hands hole or at unequal distances from it. It is an almost invariable rule that English dials used in England were drilled *before* japanning—the white base-paint is often visible spilling through to the dial back. (English eight-day dials usually have brass collets/ grommets but not always.) Hence dials late-drilled by American clockmakers must have been supplied as blanks, probably by American dialmakers, but perhaps to special order by British dialmakers. Then again, I have seen (though rarely) original British-made and British-used dials with eccentric winding-holes, and I am at a loss to explain these. It is a fascinating field, where every answer raises several new questions.

An English-made dial has normally four (but sometimes three, especially on thirty-hour clocks) *round* dial feet. Some American-retailed dials have *square* feet which seems to indicate American make. I have never seen a British square-footed dial.

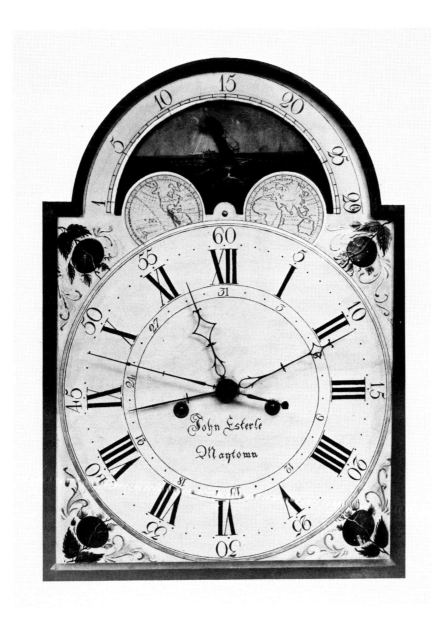

77 Eight-day dial from a clock by John Esterle of Maytown, Lancaster County, Pennsylvania. The clockmaker worked from c 1813 to 1818. This is believed to be an American-made dial (un-named falseplate). Centre-calendar and centre-seconds features were popular in America, sometimes used together, as here. Note the style of the moon globes with degree-numbered borders.

On moon dial clocks of British make the clickspring, which steadies the moon disc, is often attached to a top dial foot, or sometimes attached to the dialsheet itself on the arch above the moon disc or at the side of it. On American-made dials it is often attached to the edge of the falseplate, a little awkwardly I always feel. This is not an infallible guide, however, and I have seen British dials with the moon disc clickspring attached to the falseplate edge in this same manner.

American falseplates seem often to be of thinner sheet iron, and some seem much larger with a bigger metal area than British ones. Some American-made dialsheets too are very much thinner than the British ones; it is said you can even bend them back with your hands. In view of the more frequent handling through suppliers that the American dials would suffer, on account of distances involved, especially with British-made dials, there is a much greater possibility of a falseplate finding its way onto a dial other than its own. Therefore I should think it especially dangerous to draw conclusions about these matters if based purely on the name on a falseplate without any other identifying feature on the dialsheet proper.

The above guidelines are not infallible, but they are the best I can come up with. If you see a dial with degree-marked globes, centre-calendar work, centre-seconds feature, square dial feet, eccentrically placed late-drilled winding-holes *and* moonclick on the falseplate edge, then you can bet your cotton-picking socks it is American!

Of course, it may not really matter to the owner whether his American-sold clock has a dial that was made in Boston or Birmingham. But it seems to me that half the pleasure of owning an antique comes from knowing exactly what you have got, and we owe it to those who do care to try to find out.

By the 1780s white dials were on offer in America through specialist trade suppliers and also in some areas through the local general store or hardware store. What is hard to determine is whether the dials they offered were British-made or American-made. In 1785 John and Daniel Carrell of Philadelphia advertised:

Watch and Clock-Makers, Goldsmiths and Jewellers, In Front Street, seven doors below the Coffee-house; have for sale ... eight-day and twenty-four hour clocks; *clock dials, neatly japann'd, with or without moon-plates*; cast clock work in setts; clock bells; clock pinions, ready slit

208

and all manner of other trade supplies. The italics are mine by the way, as they are in all the following extracts.

In 1791 clockmaker Timothy Chandler of Concord, New Hampshire, advertised amongst other things 'warranted eight day Clocks, *with enamelled moon or plain faces*'. In 1798 H. & B. Penhallow, hardware dealers of Portsmouth, New Hampshire, offered clock dials for sale in their advertisement. In 1811 J. Pond of Portsmouth advertised in the *New Hampshire Gazette* that he 'expects by the first arrival from Boston, *a handsome assortment of Clock Dials of every size*, which will be sold by the dozen or singly at the factory price'.

Clockmaker Abel Hutchins of Concord, New Hampshire, offered in the *New Hampshire Patriot* of 23 November 1812 'warranted eight-day clocks of the newest fashion' but also all types of clock parts and case fittings including:

clock balls—various prices (=finials); clock case capitals; quarter capitals; hinges; clock hands; clock pinions; clock bells and glasses; and *clock faces with moon, plain and ship arches*.

In Hamburg, Pa, merchants Oglesby and Poole were dial distributors in the 1800–40 period.

So the evidence exists both in the surviving clocks and in advertisements that these dials were available; but which dials, American-made or imported British ones? Well, probably both. British dials seem to have been favoured until about 1800–10, perhaps because they were better made. In the rural areas especially the clockmakers may have been of a more independent nature and may have preferred locally made dials. The work of several local dialmakers is recognised as early as the 1780s but in most instances the names of the makers are not known.

One of the few known early makers was clockmaker Christian Eby of Mannheim, Pa, who also was a dialpainter in the last fifteen years of the century. Benjamin Whitman of Reading, Pa, advertised in 1799 that he was giving up clockmaking to 'carry on the clock dial manufactory in all its various branches'.

Perhaps the best-known firm of American dialmakers was the Curtis Manufactory at Boston, believed to have supplied most New England dials once it set up business about 1809. It appears to have started as 'Willard and Nolen' (Aaron Willard junior and Spencer Nolen) about 1805, as 'clock dial and sign painters' and dials are known with falseplates marked 'Willard & Nolen'. About 1809 this concern became 'Curtis and Nolen' (Samuel Curtis and Spencer Nolen) and this partnership lasted until about 1820 and also had a branch in Philadelphia.

The other major dialmaking concern was Messrs Patton and Jones (Abraham Patton and Samuel G. Jones) working about 1804–14 in Philadelphia and also at Baltimore. They were ironmongers and distributors of clock parts but also apparently made dials—certainly dials exist with falseplates marked 'Patton & Jones, Phila.'. At least some of their dials were not drilled before despatch—vide a month clock with one of their dials where the winding-holes are placed exceptionally low because of the movement layout. It seems that at one time the Curtis Manufactory actually supplied dials to Patton & Jones, for some dials carry printed labels on the back which read 'Curtis Manufactory for Patton & Jones, Phila.'

An interesting advertisement for Henry Nolen (relationship to Spencer Nolen of the Curtis Manufactory unknown) came to light recently in *The Western Spy*, 1817:

Clock Dial Establishment.
HENRY NOLEN,
CLOCK DIAL MANUFACTURER,
In Wood between Fourth Street and Diamond Alley,
PITTSBURGH,
KEEPS constantly for sale a regular assortment of DIALS, together with an assortment of
Clock Movements and Materials, Patent Time Pieces,
Looking Glasses, &c.
Which he will sell wholesale and retail at Philadelphia prices, including the cost of transportation. All orders from the states of Ohio and Kentucky punctually attended to.

The surviving business papers of Salem Community Store, Salem, North Carolina, include one or two interesting insights into the ordering of clock materials including dials, most of them believed to have been for the use of the only local clockmaker, Ludwig Eberhardt. The letters to the Philadelphia wholesalers include several requests for 'Birmingham goods', including clock movements and dials in the period 1809–12. A note to Messrs Patton and Jones in 1811 stresses: 'be particular in choise of faces, none but clear and round ones will answer' (this does not make sense in view of later notes in the letter and 'round ones' must be a slip for 'sound ones').

'You will please be careful in packing the faces. Memo:
8—13 inch moon clock dials
4—12 inch solid arch—suitable for 8 day clocks
6 sett 8 day clock brass
1 doz sett pinions for 8 day clocks
1 doz brass minute pinions.

Here we see the same problems appearing as we found in the British trade—the danger of damage to the dials in transit—and the stock of dials held seems to have always exceeded that of movements.

Another letter to Patton and Jones in 1811 asks for the faces to be packed in a separate box: '8—13 inch Moon Dials, net 6 dollars'. Another letter, of 1812, calls for '1 doz—13 inch Moon Dials, 4 with sec'd hand & date from the center. ½ doz. 12 inch solid arch, 3 for 30 hour & 3 for 8 day'. Now this is an interesting item in view of my earlier comments about the centre-calendar *plus* centre-seconds features being common in America and rare in England, and it looks as if this was a feature which was anticipated and catered for by American dialmakers.

As a last extract from the Salem Store papers here is a complete letter which highlights the transportation problems—and notice once more the request for the centre-calendar feature:

Messrs Patton & Jones   Salem December 22 1812

Gentlemen

Our last of 30th Ult. trust has reached you safe since we have re-ceived the clock faces lot of you, the wagon however that brot our goods had the bad luck to overset, by which the box containing the clock faces, not being hooped, burst open and whole of faces have thereby been considerable damaged, so as to render them entirely un-saleable, and not to loose the whole of them, have packed them up and shall send them back to you by first good opportunity to have them repaired, which have the confidence you will do, or have done for us on most reasonable terms, meanwhile please send us immediately the same quantity and assortment, *some with the date by a hand from the center*, well packed and hooped, by way of Baltimore & directed to Mr. Joseph Caldwell in Petersburg, not insured, & oblige yours with esteem.

The tall clock in America was gradually replaced by the much cheaper shelf clock (as it was later in Britain), and by the 1830s the flow of production had reduced to a trickle. Therefore one does not come across the very bold Period Three type of dial there which

78 Eight-day dial from a clock by Samuel Breneisen of Reamstown, Pennsylvania, believed made in 1834 (from a date inside). The dial is believed to be American-made and has an unmarked falseplate. The shell corner designs are very different in execution from those seen on English dials. Here the moon globes are more like the English globe styles.

is found in England, or in Scotland as the 'Fancy' dial. Perhaps the majority fall into the 1800–25 period and therefore many dials are typical of this period in style with corner decorations, eg fans, semi-geometrics, shells, sprays of flowers and fruit. Sometimes these corner paintings are heavier and bolder than the English equivalent and to the experienced eye these look very un-English, although in the same style. Oddly enough, square dials seem not to have been very popular in America, nor indeed do round dials.

A list follows of those American dialmakers and dial suppliers known to me—they are not very numerous. Of course not all of them necessarily made longcase dials but may well have made the smaller dials for shelf clocks.

Curtis & Nolen	Boston & Philadelphia	c 1809–20
Eby, Christian	Mannheim, Pa	c 1785–d1803
Nolen, Henry	Pittsburg, Pa	1817
Patton & Jones	Philadelphia & Baltimore	c 1804–14
Whitman, Benjamin	Reading, Pa	c 1799
Willard & Nolen	Boston	c 1805–09

I understand that American-made white dial clocks (with English dials) quite frequently bear no name of the 'clockmaker'. This would seem to be consistent with the English manufacture of these dials, if ordered in quantity by an American wholesaler for individual sale to local clockmakers. At the time the order was placed, the name of the retailer may well have been unknown and the dials would therefore be left nameless. In England with less distance and consequently less delay in order-processing, the individual retailer could order his dials direct and specify the lettering to be painted on them.

The name ultimately to go on the dial could not be known in advance where the dials were to be sold, for example, through a general store. With 'nameless' dials, however, one must always be on guard for those where the name has simply been erased through time or cleaning, and an ultra-violet lamp should be tried before accepting a dial as nameless.

On the subject of falseplates I am advised that these are found on apparently original American clocks with *brass* dials. I am not in a position to dispute this. However, if it is correct that American makers used falseplates in this way, it does not invalidate my view that falseplates were initially made specifically for sale with, and for use with, white dial clocks. See also my remarks about the use and misuse of falseplates on page 61.

By about 1800 the practice had arisen in America of making movements of tall clocks, many of the thirty-hour type, of *wood*. British longcase clocks with wooden gearing would be extremely rare, with the exception of imported German clocks with painted wooden dials and wooden wheels which one sees occasionally bearing an English clockseller's name. These are mostly post-1830 and of course they are not strictly British clocks. The making of American wooden movements soon grew into a mass-producing business with interchangeable standardised parts. Wooden dials were used too, some early attempts having a printed paper face pasted on to the wooden dial proper. Later wooden dials had the decoration and numbering painted directly on to the dial boards. Clocks with wooden wheels had long been known in Holland and Germany and clockmakers from these countries emigrating to America may have been the source of inspiration to use locally available materials.

The name of Eli Terry is normally associated with the beginnings of mass-production of wooden clocks in America. The brass-wheeled clock movement was now more a product for the wealthier few; the cheaper wooden one, usually a thirty-hour clock, was for the majority. It was Terry too who first developed the shelf clock about 1815. Shelf and wall clocks were ultimately and rapidly to dominate the scene both in America and in Britain. American shelf and wall clocks poured into Britain in the late 1840s, rapidly putting an end to the manufacture here of longcase clocks. This may be one reason why this type of clock tends not to be very highly regarded in Britain. Many dealers in Britain today are only too happy to ship them back again.

Casework on American tall clocks begins, as one might imagine, as an attempt to follow the English equivalents. However, factors such as the sheer size of the country, the relative sparseness of the population and the consequently greater distances between clockmaker and customer caused a more rapid, varied and individualistic

79 (*opposite left*) Case housing clock by John Eberman of Lancaster, Pennsylvania, made c 1805. The wood is cherry with fan inlays and stringing of lighter woods. A handsome example of American casework and not very much different from the contemporary English styles.

80 (*opposite right*) Walnut case of clock by John Conrad Heinzelman of Mannheim, Pennsylvania, dating from c 1795–1800. This is in the style described as Lancaster County Chippendale, very different of course from the English 'Chippendale' style.

development of casework in America. This was further varied by the different woods used.

It was not uncommon for tall-clock movements to be sold caseless with the option open to the customer to hang the clock on a wall bracket as a 'wag-on-the-wall' clock. Alternatively, he could order a case for himself from a local cabinetmaker or joiner. Or he might make a case for the clock himself. The result was that some superb traditional cases exist alongside some extremely crude softwood ones, which may present a very strange appearance to an eye accustomed to British casework. While the swan-necked pediment top of the British type was quite popular, the plain arched top of many American clocks was capped with a fretted or crested decorative flourish, the latter sometimes called 'whales'-tails'.

By 1830 the tall clock in America had largely been superseded, as it later was in Britain, by more compact, cheaper, mass-produced wall and shelf clocks. This chapter can do little more than indicate some of the important differences between white dial longcase clocks in Britain and America, yet these differences may help distinguish those clocks imported from Britain from those made in America. While painted dials would be of British make up to about 1790, after that date they could be of either British or American manufacture. The lists of known dialmakers may help decide which. A wooden dial, painted direct or with paper facing, would *not* be of British origin, nor would a wooden movement.

15

Moons, Tides and Pendulums

On clocks with arched moon dials, the dialmaker usually formed his dials in such a shape that a large hump remained at each side below the moon dial space. This hump was needed to permit the rising and declining moon disc to show its crescent shape. A glance at any arched moon dial in the book will instantly show the two humps referred to.

The same humps often appeared on brass dial clocks too for the same reason, when they were usually decorated with some sort of engraved sunbursts, etc. Sometimes these areas on brass dials were engraved with two hemispheres in the form of terrestrial globes showing, perhaps crudely, the outlines of the continents of the eastern and western hemispheres. In practice the minute numbering ring usually cuts into the hemispheres, with the result that they are not full hemispheres but have a segment missing at the base, though some are almost full hemispheres (see Lomax dial) and some show only the top half of each hemisphere, ie a 'semi-hemisphere' (see Elliott dial).

On white dial clocks the two humps are almost always mapped out, originally often in great detail. Occasionally a painted scene may fill the hump instead of a map, especially on highly colourful late dials of Period Three—S. Baker dials seem to have this feature, though perhaps not always, nor exclusively. The oceans are usually named and the continents, and numerous lines of latitude and longitude appear as well as the equator, etc. Originally these were very detailed maps, executed in a very fine script. Today a great many have been partly erased by owners who have tried to wash their dials. Some have been penned in again crudely—see the Bancroft dial. Some have been left blank by restorers who could not attempt to re-pen them—again see the Lomax dial.

It is obvious, however, when one studies a well-preserved example that these original globes could not have been done freehand. They

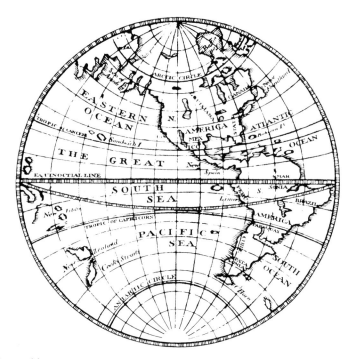

81a and b   Moon globes representing the western and eastern hemispheres.

must have been applied by some kind of printing block in what seems to be black ink and not paint. The maps reveal evidence of having been engraved onto copper as they resemble very closely the style of a contemporary printed map. Wooden printing blocks would not have produced results as fine as this—whether done as woodcut blocks or wood-engraved blocks. It seeems to me that these results were obtained from engraved copper printing plates. (The difference beween engraving and woodcut work is that in engraving it is the hollow areas which are filled with ink and will print under pressure. In woodcutting the principle is to leave the required shape standing proud, which then prints when inked, like the principle of a typewriter key.)

To print an impression onto paper with an engraved copperplate, it is necessary to apply the pressure of a printing press—the plates themselves being engraved in reverse (as in mirror-writing) so as to print an impression with lettering the right way round. This sort of pressure could not possibly have been applied to a japanned dial surface without cracking the surface, as the printing surface is required to 'bend' into the hollow engraved lines to draw out the ink. So how did the dialmakers get what is clearly a copper-engraved design onto a japanned surface? I do not know the answer, but at least I have raised the question.

Perhaps they were printed by a transfer method. This would involve the copperplates being engraved the right way round instead of in mirror-writing. The resulting print, made under pressure from the inked plates (onto paper?), would then emerge the wrong way round (mirror-written). If this wet printed impression were then applied to the japanned dial surface, it would produce the correct-facing image we now see on these dials today. But just what the transfer medium would be I cannot say. Paper? Cloth? If this were the method, then one might expect to see the occasional smudged image, such as happens with pottery, and I cannot recall seeing smudged globes.

A glance at several moon dials will soon show that these hemispheres can be printed on the humps at a variety of angles. Some are set vertically so that both equators are horizontal. Some are set askew so that both equators (or poles, depending on how you view it) tilt inwards, some so that they tilt outwards from each other; some tilt both to the left and some tilt both to the right. Today we usually represent the western hemisphere on the left in an atlas and the eastern hemisphere on the right. On dials they also tend to follow this habit, but not always. It is not rare to see them in the opposite situations—whether intentionally or by mistake we may never know.

Further indication that these were produced by printing blocks is seen in the fact that whilst some globes fit the hump areas exactly, some are clearly too big and run over the edges, and some are too small and leave gaps round the edges.

The globes on most English dials (and Scottish ones) are fringed by a double-line border with hatching. On some dials there is a further circle outside of this hatched one and this outer circle contains a series of numbers showing degrees, 0° at the equator and 90° at the north pole.

I have never yet come across a degree-numbered globe on a dial that can be shown to be English. My own feeling is that dials with this degree numbering are probably American-made. If this is correct then it could be a useful identification feature, because our current expertise in these matters is so lacking that we are often hardpressed to determine whether an unmarked dial is English or American in origin, even though it may bear an American clockseller's name.

A further feature of these degree-numbered globes is that the mapping of Australia is poor. Now I know that mapping of Australia (at the time usually called New Holland) was in its infancy anyway during Period One. Nevertheless in Britain we had a reasonable concept of the northern coastline. This knowledge would be available in America too, but whether because the American mappers knew less or cared less about New Holland, the fact remains that on these degree-numbered globes, Australia is poorly outlined when compared to a contemporary English dial. You have only to see the two alongside each other to appreciate this.

It is an odd fact that the quality of painting on a moon disc is almost always superior to that of the dialsheet proper, and it seems likely that in the English manufactories this work was done by a different and more skilled artist. Perhaps the situation was that almost anyone could paint corner patterns with a little practice, especially simple gold tracery or semi-geometrics and no doubt also flowers and fruit. Indeed some dials reveal precious little talent.

But with a moon dial all attention would tend to be drawn to the moon area and most particularly to the moon face itself when showing at full moon. Hence it must have been thought more important to get a little character into the moon face and it is surprising what

82 Four moon discs shown removed from their dials. The only one to be identified is
that on the bottom right—by Walker & Hughes of Birmingham. The variety in styles
and quality of painting is obvious.

a difference a well-painted moon face makes to a clock when all set
up.

The usual convention was to have two moon faces on the wheel,
so that as one waned away to disappear behind the right-hand hump,
a new moon would begin to appear next day from behind the left-
hand one. The convention developed of having painted scenes
between the moon faces, presumably just for interest. On earlier brass
dial moons these intervening spaces were often painted solid blue
with gold crosses to represent blue sky and stars, but by the 1770s
the 'scenes-between' pattern had become more common.

Usually a landscape alternated with a seascape, but not always. It
is not unknown to have two landscapes or two seascapes. Four moon

discs are shown removed from their dials. On all of them the artistry is considerably better than the dials they belong to. Notice the very different quality of painting between the four discs and the varying treatment of the ship, for example, on each and also the varying manner of blending the faces into the scenes by very different methods of outlining the moon faces with black shadow-effect. The top left disc is by far the crudest in all respects, the top right one highly sophisticated.

A lunar month contains 29½ days. Usually the calibrations are numbered around the arch top and the lunar date is read off by a pointer on top of the moon face.

Occasionally, though not very often with japanned dials, a lunar calendar was incorporated with a tidal dial too, and in those instances the scale of both moon calendar and tidetable would be lettered on the moon disc edge (see Husband dial, frontispiece). Tidal dials are unusual and if such a dial were ordered from the japanners (the Husband dial must have been ordered specially from James Wilson of Birmingham) then local knowledge of tidetimes may well have been sent to the dialmaker at the time of ordering. On the other hand the provision of two adjustable pointers from which moons and tides were to be read may have meant that it was not essential to coincide the two bands of numbers, because the reading pointer for either was capable of adjustment. In fact a clock made in Hull may not necessarily have been destined to be used there and indeed if the owner of a tidal dial clock ever moved house or the clock changed hands, then the indicator pointers could be re-set at will for the new port. If a clock were made purely for tidal times at one place, then the Arabic lunar date numbers could be lettered at the correct coincidence with the Roman tidal numbers, and only a single pointer would be needed to read both times. It is commonly the case, however, that moon-with-tide dials do have double pointers (on brass dial clocks too, where tidal dials are perhaps more common than on japanned dials), and so the inference is that local tidal knowledge would not be essential.

Perhaps I ought to mention at this point the device employed on some arched dials of painting an imitation moon dial in the arch. I have only seen one such dial myself, on an eight-day clock, and it looked surprisingly convincing. All the usual moon dial features were painted on, including the humps and globes, but the whole arch was just a solid one with no moving parts. This could only have been an attempt at producing what looked like a moon dial without the expense of the real thing. In other words it must have been something to impress the neighbours into thinking you had bought the expensive real thing, when you had bought only the cheaper version. This is the sort of snobbery we refer to as 'keeping up with the Joneses' and amusingly enough the name of the clockmaker on the dummy moon dial clock referred to was Jones of Pwllheli!

A moon dial was also available on a square dial (both brass and japanned dials). We usually call this a twelve o'clock moon. Of course, you cannot have a seconds dial on such a clock because both features would require the same area. I suppose you could have a centre-seconds hand on such a dial, though I do not recall ever seeing one.

These square twelve o'clock moon dials seem not to have been very popular, for they are not commonly met with except in certain regions. They are found regularly on clocks from the Lancashire–Cheshire–Lake District area of north-western England, but were not popular nationally. On this type the double humps were often of a shallower cut and tend not to have the globes on them.

The twelve o'clock moon was simplicity itself to drive, because it is usually found in association with the mouth-type calendar feature. A pin or wedge on the hour pipe, often located directly behind the hour hand, will pass the calendar and moon wheels every twelve hours so that it will knock the appropriate wheel forward one tooth every twelve hours, two moves per day.

The motionwork for an arched moon is more complicated and, whilst it usually drives from a pin or wedge on the same principle as the twelve o'clock moon, this pin generally knocks on a pivoted lever which attaches elbow-like to another lever or two to connect ultimately with the moon disc teeth twelve-hourly.

A pendulum is not really an item by which one can positively date a clock, but it can help, and so a few points might be worth mentioning. The pendulum in any eight-day longcase white dial clock you are likely to see will be a 'one-second' pendulum, which means that it beats every second. Its length will be a little over 3ft 3in, which is as technical as I intend to be, and which will serve to en-able you to recognise it when you see it. With thirty-hour clocks there is more variation in the length of pendulum according to the gearing of the wheel trains, and anything between 2ft 5in and 3ft 10in in length would be possible, or even wider variations. Any

83 Dial from an eight-day clock by Barrow of Stockport, the dial by Osborne of Birmingham, made c 1785. This type of moon dial is known as a twelve o'clock moon. The dial has been carefully restored. The hour hand is a later replacement. Notice the cut-out aperture for the moon is not wide enough to allow the full 29½ calibration, but stands at the 4th and ends at the 26th lunar day. During the 'missing' period the moon's shape is seen but not its date.

white dial clock you see with a pendulum considerably different in length from this will be something very unusual and rather than measure it you would be well advised to call in an expert to look at it for you.

On early white dial clocks, up to about 1800, the pendulum is usually made of a length of wire rod terminating with a 'bob' made of lead with a brass (uncommonly, copper) covering on its face side. From the beginning of the nineteenth century the lead bob is gradually replaced by an iron one, its face side painted black, or sometimes faced with a tin covering on the face side and this tin cover painted black. About this time the pendulum wire rod is often replaced by a flat steel rod, $\frac{1}{2}$in wide or so, which form persists right to the end of the white dial period.

Occasionally one comes across a flat brass rod on a pendulum, ie a flat brass strip. These tend to be on late eighteenth-century clocks, often on higher-quality clocks. The reason for the brass rod is not clear to us, because brass reacts more to temperature change and in theory would be less reliable for timekeeping. These flat brass rods are also very difficult to handle without bending them double in the process.

After about 1815 or 1820 it is not unusual to find a wooden pendulum rod instead of a steel one. These occasionally have, in addition to the normal adjusting nut below the bob, a micrometer adjuster fitted at the point where the bob and rod meet: a simple device designed to raise or lower the bob by a very small amount and more precisely than a turn of the rating nut would allow. The reason for the wooden rod-and-micrometer fitting was of course to improve the precision with which the clock's timekeeping could be set. The wooden rod was less liable to contract or expand with changes in temperature. The micrometer fitting is uncommon but by no means rare; nor is it an indication of anything very remarkable about the clock, but rather an interesting variation. The wooden pendulum rod is quite common. It is often found on Scottish clocks of the round dial type—the semi-regulator type—and is not particularly uncommon in northern England generally.

After about 1820 or so one sees not infrequently a pendulum with the bob-face painted in bright coloured patterns (japanned in fact). There seems to be no special reason for this except to make the bob more colourful, in keeping with the dial painting. Such a bob could well have been japanned by the dialmaking concern, and might perhaps be an indication that the dial, movement and pendulum were all bought in direct from the factory by the clockseller. The view is sometimes expressed that such painted pendulums were originally made for lacquer-cased clocks. However, one sees them too often on white dial clocks to accept them all as being replacements. Incidentally, I have *never* seen a white dial clock in a lacquer case, and would feel very suspicious about it if I did. These japanned pendulum bobs are quite common on Scottish clocks, especially those of the fairground dial type.

Another interesting treatment of the pendulum bob-face in this period (post-1820) is the type with a brass-faced bob, the face made from stamped, patterned brass: very ornate and very 'Victorian'-looking, and of course almost impossible to keep clean because of the deep crevices in the stamping.

An interesting type of pendulum, which I see frequently but which seems not to be common everywhere, is one where the bob-piece simply hooks on to the end of the wire rod, which end is formed into a hook. This incredibly simple version is an alternative to the normal attachment where the wire-rod end screws into the bob-stem as a rigid attachment. It is surprising that this idea did not become more widespread, as it very much simplifies the process of setting up a clock by allowing one to slip the pendulum rod into place, and hook on the bob and its stem last of all. This is especially helpful with later northern clocks where shorter door-height can cause the normal pendulum to be bent during insertion. This hook-on bob-piece is usually of the tin-fronted post-1820 type but I have seen it occasionally on brass-faced pendulums and even used on the apparently original pendulums of brass dial clocks as early as 1760.

Pendulums, of course, are frequently *not* original to the clock. It is therefore difficult to determine precise style changes, but those I have given will apply generally. Being a relatively fragile thing, a pendulum is subject to damage and replacement over the years, and no great harm is done if a clock has a replacement one. It is naturally more satisfying if a replacement of the correct type is fitted.

I know one dealer who keeps all his pendulums in a tea-chest and offers his customers the pick of the bunch—steel or wooden, straight or curly, with or without the bob! There is also the true story of one 'horologist' dealer who, after long deliberating the merits of a very ordinary wire pendulum rod on one of my clocks, pronounced that it was made from an old bicycle wheel-spoke. I was quite unable to refute this opinion, and was obliged to admit that I was not well versed in the history of bicycle wheel-spokes, especially of a type made for a wheel which must have had a diameter of 80in or more! However, any reader who happens to have a stock of old 80in-diameter bicycle wheels will be delighted to know that he could find a ready market for their spokes among clock repairers, as their quality is such that I know of only one 'horologist' who can distinguish them from genuine antique pendulum rods!

16

Spring-driven Clocks

At the beginning of the white dial period, say 1770, spring-driven clocks were of two types. One was the table clock, usually today known as a bracket clock although the number which stood on wall brackets was always small and the majority were placed on tables, sideboards, mantelshelves, etc. The second category was that of the wall clock, what we usually call today the English dial clock or the wall dial clock or the spring dial clock. Both categories existed before the coming of the white dial, but they became more numerous from the start of the nineteenth century and are therefore probably best known in white dial form.

The biggest difference between spring-driven clocks and weight-driven ones was that the spring was less reliable as a motive force than the weight. A clock driven by a twelve-pound weight always has the same pull to drive it, whether fully wound or almost run down. A spring pulls strongly when fully wound, weakly when almost run down. Some means was needed to compensate for the alternating strong and weak pull of the spring, and one was indeed found. It was called a fusee and was almost always used in British spring clockwork. The diagram shows the principle of the fusee.

So, the spring clock had to have two items which the weight-driven clock did not have—the spring (contained within a drum) and the fusee. The spring was an item that a clockmaker could *not* make himself, for springmaking was a highly specialised business. Even in the seventeenth century there were specialist springmakers. By the 1770s there might have been one or two concerns here and there who could produce springs, but this was quite outside the scope of the ordinary clockmaker who had to buy his springs from the specialists. To make a fusee one had to have a special piece of equipment, a fusee-cutting machine (they are actually called 'engines'), just as the clockmaker had to have a wheel-cutting engine. Many of these techniques were very highly sophisticated and not,

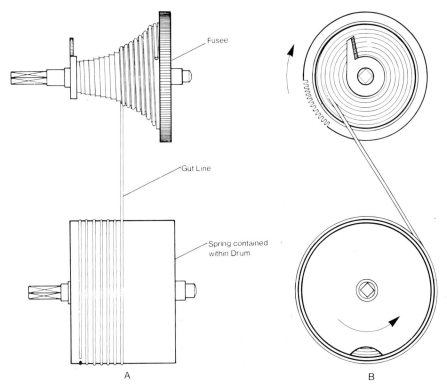

Fusee

Gut Line

Spring contained
within Drum

A B

84 The fusee, seen from the side in A and the end in B. The fusee was a compensating
gear to rectify the variation in the pull of the spring. When fully wound, all the gutline
would be coiled on the fusee so that the spring (then at its strongest) found more resistance
than when almost run down. Arrows indicate direction of winding.

as people sometimes think, done by a hold-it-in-your-left-hand, file-
it-with-your-right, approach.

Add the complications that wheel sizes were considerably smaller
than in the longcase clock; that early examples used the verge escapement rather than the anchor escapement of the longcase clock; that
you needed a tiny, strong drive-chain to transmit the pull of the
spring, and this again was a specialist-made item (you could use gut
line but chains were stronger); that timekeeping was far less accurate
with a spring clock than with a longcase one, principally because
the spring's pulling power still varied despite the use of the fusee;
that you had to have a specialist cabinetmaker to make the case, for
the village joiner could not do this fine work; that together these
factors meant that spring clocks were very costly items, an eight-
day one costing almost twice the price of an eight-day longcase—

85   Bracket clock with circular white dial typical of many such clocks after c 1810. This example by the Arnold family of London dates from c 1815 and is in the distinctive pointed-top style known as a lancet-top. Such ornate casework with stereotyped inlay and frets, etc was quite outside the scope of the provincial cabinetmaker, and even if sold in the provinces such clocks were mostly London-made.

86 Spring-driven bracket clock, timepiece only, made c 1825 by James Smith of London, the dialmaker unknown. In this example the arch is not stepped as it usually was in longcase dials. The dial decoration is restrained. It seldom became as heavy on spring dials as on late longcase ones.

and it is apparent why spring clocks were generally something of a nuisance. Most clockmakers never bothered to attempt to make them, even many of the best-skilled longcase craftsmen.

This meant that the national market was available to those makers who were willing to specialise in this field. One such firm, probably the biggest ever manufacturers of spring-driven clocks, was the London concern started about 1740 by Aynsworth Thwaites, later as John Thwaites, later still as Thwaites and Reed. They supplied a great many makers with spring clocks, both bracket and wall dial types. Many a spring clock with a famous name on the dial has a Thwaites movement, and with spring clocks more than any other types the name on the dial was often that of a retailer. Even though that retailer himself may have been a highly skilled clockmaker, he was not set up for the specialised task of making spring clocks but was simply a retailer of them.

Records of the Thwaites company survive today and many of their movements can be dated from the serial number. Thwaites serial numbers can be found in Ronald Rose's recent book *English Dial Clocks*.

White dials for spring-driven clocks varied in size from about six inches—the Wilkes price list on page 84 gives some examples. For bracket clocks these were available as arched dials or as round ones, but square dials seem not to have been used. Arched ones could be very similar in style to those of longcase clocks in the early period. However, as time went by the fashion turned increasingly towards the circular plain white dial and so by the 1830s the circular type had largely taken over and we seldom find heavily painted longcase-style arched dials on bracket clocks.

Dials for wall clocks are more varied because wall clocks were designed not only for simple domestic use but often for public buildings (such as libraries, churches, prisons, hospitals, railways) and were not always to be hung in an ordinary wall case, but were sometimes actually built into a gallery or wall. Sometimes massive dials were used to suit the particular position, some exceeding two feet in diameter, and these larger dials were often made of wood. Even dials of conventional size (six to twelve inches, probably the commonest always being the twelve-inch size) were sometimes made of wood too. But the commonest dial for spring-driven wall clocks was the ordinary circular japanned white dial, the type we associate today with a school clock, a railway clock, or a waiting-room clock. This

87 A straightforward English wall dial clock, this one with a mahogany surround. Manoah Rhodes and Son traded at Bradford in 1866, and this clock dates from about that time, although in style this kind of clock would look very similar whether made in 1830 or 1890.

reminds me that only a year ago I bought our local police station clock, which was a twelve-inch circular spring dial type and was made in 1880 when the police station was built and had been in daily use ever since until last year, when the police 'went electric'.

Spring clocks were virtually always of eight-day duration, at least British ones were, though some later imported ones were thirty-hour types. Some had strikework, including repeating, whilst others did not. Generally a bracket clock would be a striker and a wall clock would not, and although striking wall clocks are known they are not common. A non-striking clock is called a timepiece.

Spring clock dials, especially the plain white circular type, seldom have makers' marks on them. It is quite possible that the specialist makers of spring clocks made their own dials, though the Thwaites records for instance make occasional mention of a 'Birmingham dial'.

Of the white dial bracket clocks that one sees, by far the majority will have the names of London retailers. After about 1840 there is an increase in the provincial share of the market, but provincial retailers' names on pre-1800 bracket clocks are by no means common. As already pointed out, these names are not very important because, unlike longcase clocks, they were probably *not* the work of the man whose name is on the dial, although the movements may still have been handmade ones, but supplied by a specialist spring-clock firm.

With wall dial clocks the majority of provincial ones seen are post-1820. The real heyday of the spring wall dial was in the 1860–80 period by which time they became very common and after which time they were mostly imported. A great many flooded in from America and Germany and some of them were designed to look very much like the English clocks they were competing with by undercutting in price. It is generally true that if the movement has a fusee it will be English made. American wall clocks, especially of the drop dial type with mother-of-pearl inlay, often look very much like the English ones, but close examination of the dial will often reveal that it is of paper or painted aluminium, that the movement has no fusee, and that it has skeleton plates, or that there is a maker's label inside specifying the origin. The winding-holes on American drop dials can be much lower down than on an English clock.

With German bracket clocks the movements can look very like English ones and their dials will often carry an English retailer's name. Usually there will be some punch mark on the backplate, which will enable one to trace the manufacturer if one consults a book on German clocks (try *Black Forest Clocks* by E. J. Tyler). A common mark is 'W & H Sch', which stands for Winterhalder and Hofmeyer, Schwarzenbach (*not* Walker & Hughes!). Junghans is another well-known German name often seen on these clocks.

In 1791 the Chaplin family of clockmakers of Bury St Edmunds advertised 'exceeding neat new spring dials in mahogany cases at

88 A strange and amusing clock, looking vaguely like a late English bracket clock with
a carved figure on top. The second train is not for strikework but motionwork to activate
the figure who eats plums from his dish every two minutes. His arm rises to his mouth
which opens and appears to swallow the plum, which he chews, rolling his eyes. The
retailer, Dickinson of Preston, is not recorded and it is thought it may have been a show-
piece for the window of a restaurant or coffee-house. It dates from c 1890. To a trained eye
this carved and painted wooden figure is typical of German Black Forest work (the home
of the cuckoo clock), and a glance inside the movement reveals its German manufacturer's
mark. An odd feature is that the winding squares run right through from front to back,
so that the clock may be wound from in front or from behind, a further reason to
suppose it may have sat in a shop window. At first sight it looks like an English white
dial clock but, in fact, it is nothing of the kind.

89 A drop-dial wall clock, this one being a timepiece only as was usual. The maker, T. V. French of Newcastle on Tyne, was listed in the 1848–58 period. This example is in rosewood; more commonly they are in mahogany. The pendulum can be seen through the glass window in front of the box.

£3 13s 6d.' In 1834 Liddall and Sons of Edinburgh offered 'spring timekeepers for shops, counting houses, etc. five guineas and upwards'. In 1843 Thwaites supplied a twelve-inch striking spring wall dial clock to Warley Barracks at £10 10s 0d—a striker was obviously more costly. Some sample prices charged by Thwaites in the 1840s for wall dials were: a twelve-inch circular oak-cased £4; a twelve-inch circular mahogany-cased £5; a fourteen-inch mahogany-cased £6 10s 0d. These were the ordinary circular type, but another type had a boxlike section below the circle within which the pendulum bob swung, and these were known as drop-dials. Thwaites charged £5 12s 0d for a twelve-inch mahogany drop-dial in the 1840s, 12s 0d extra for the drop feature.

17

Buying and Selling

This chapter will not begin to tell you about the price of clocks. That is something you can only find out for yourself by looking and learning. But it may help you to avoid paying far more than the clock is worth. To a certain extent one can expect constantly rising prices to be inevitable, as the supply of antiques on the market gradually shrinks in the face of ever increasing demand. When one buys, the price may seem high; but as the years pass, a good clock can prove to have been a sound investment. On the other hand a clock which has been tampered with, or incorrectly restored, or even plainly faked, will not prove to be the same sound investment. The beginner's problem is to distinguish one from the other.

My aim will be to give you a few hints about *how not* to buy a clock. First of all believe nobody but yourself. There are, of course, dishonest dealers; but there are also those who may mislead a customer quite unintentionally, out of ignorance. As an example of what I mean I will tell you of an experience I had at the time I was doing research into Yorkshire clockmaking. I happened to go into a general antique shop one day in a Yorkshire market town, and there was a brass-faced longcase clock signed with the name only, no town. Suppose the name on the dial was Obadiah Wilson—no town given. It was quite a pleasant country clock, late eighteenth century, but nothing very exceptional. I mentioned casually that it was a nice-looking little clock, or something to that effect. 'Oh, yes,' said the dealer, 'it's a London clock, you know.'

I was speechless. As it happened it was only a few days earlier that I had been looking up some facts about the life of this particular maker who had worked not forty miles from where the clock was then standing. I happened to know about that particular maker, but even if I had never heard of him, everything about that clock indicated that it was a typical country clock, and I was certain that it had never been closer to London than where it stood at that moment.

'Well,' I said, 'there was an Obadiah Wilson who worked at Trumpton on the Wolds. What makes you think this is by a London maker?'

The dealer was quite unruffled. 'Oh, it is', he said. 'He is listed in Baillie's book, you know.' Now I did not doubt for a moment that a man with the same (unusual) name was listed in Baillie, as I believe this dealer was sincere enough. But the London maker of that name most certainly was not the man who made this clock.

It is worth noting, by the way, that a clock signed with the name only, and no town, is very often the work of a maker in a small village, the name of which would not have been recognised even twenty miles away. In any case a maker who was paying the high premium of working in London would be proud of that fact, and would not for one moment forget to make the very best advertising use of it by putting 'London' on his clock dials. Furthermore, he was obliged by law to specify the place as London.

'Well,' I said, 'I would have thought that this was the Obadiah Wilson of Trumpton.' Then followed protests that I was mistaken, that it *was* a London clock, that he knew it was a London clock, that he had bought it as a London clock, and 'Well, it just *is*!' There was no point in pursuing this conversation, and I had no intention of buying that particular clock. The real point of the story was that this person was a dealer of some years' standing, with a reputation for honesty. His sin was ignorance, not dishonesty, and I have no doubt that he genuinely believed that it was a London clock because, 'Well, it just *is*!'

Now this was a year or two ago and somewhere there is a proud owner of a 'London-made' clock by Obadiah Wilson. He cherishes his clock, lives in absolute ignorance of its true origin, and praises the name of the dealer from whom he bought it so reasonably. One day he, or his heirs, will try to sell that clock to a specialist clock dealer, and then will be sadly disillusioned, or else will disbelieve that specialist dealer and sell it to yet another dealer who also is as uninformed as the person in whose shop I saw it.

The conclusion to be drawn from this story is to know your subject for yourself and to buy a clock entirely on your own judgement.

When you look at a clock, ask whether it works properly, and listen carefully to the answer. A frequent reply is: 'Oh, yes, I think it goes all right. At least it was going in the house when I bought it from the lady who had had it for many years, so it should be all right.' With experience you will learn that this means that the clock is a duff one.

If you look at enough clocks you will soon be surprised as to what a large number of them once belonged to elderly ladies who cared for them for many years. Eventually you realise that the story is similar to the one about the second-hand car with incredibly low mileage which once belonged to the elderly vicar's wife and never had been driven at more than forty miles an hour.

The answer you ought to be hoping for is that the clock is guaranteed to be in perfect working order. There are only two possibilities with a clock: either it goes or it doesn't. If the dealer's answer is not an emphatic 'Yes', it can only be because he means 'No'. This is what you must assume until it is proved to you to be otherwise.

There are many sources for buying a clock: from junk shops or sale-rooms, from antiques dealers or specialist clock dealers, or from private collectors who are disposing of an odd one or two. You could buy from any of these, but you ought to understand first which source would be best for you as an individual, and this will depend on your knowledge of the subject.

Forget all about 'picking up bargains' at ridiculously low prices. There are no bargains any more, as far as you are concerned. Thousands of dealers spend their whole lives running from pillar to post looking for bargains, and they have far greater experience in recognising a bargain when they see one than has the average private individual. If you come across a clock in a dirty condition in a little junk shop, that is because that is the best place for it.

Every little junk emporium has its regular throughput of dealers and if the trade has left a clock behind, that ought to be a warning to you. The same thing applies in sale-rooms. If a clock goes for a low price there has to be a reason.

If you go to a general antiques dealer, the clock you get will depend on the class of shop you go to. If you go to a better-class dealer who will guarantee the clock, or to a specialist dealer who will do the same, you will be paying the going price. A dealer sells a clock for what (he thinks) it is worth, or for what he can get, not for what he can get less 10 or 20 per cent. The only way you might get a clock at less than its true market value is if your knowledge exceeds that of the man selling it and you can recognise something special about the clock that the vendor does not appreciate. However, if you pay the going price for a clock from a specialist dealer, you are less likely to be cheated than if you are picking it up for a song in a junk shop.

The same thing applies to sale-rooms. In the top auction houses you can expect high standards to be set, but if you wish to buy a clock at a country-house sale, for instance, you must have the knowledge first to know what you are buying. Otherwise you may get the clock home and find too late that it can never be put into proper working order.

If you are innocent in these matters you may not know that a great many country 'private house' auctions are heavily loaded with goods taken there for the purpose of making them look like 'house contents' and that much of this stock has come straight from antiques dealers. I have seen clocks that dealers have had for months without being able to find a buyer eventually sold in little country sales at more than the price they could not get in the shop. And of course this way they have to give no warranty of any sort. In fact many auction houses disclaim responsibility for any statements they make in describing the goods they offer for sale. If the public are foolish enough to buy this way, you can hardly blame the dealers for obliging them.

Beware of the kind of advertisement one sees quite often in the 'Items for Sale' columns of local newspapers: 'Private collector has grandfather clock for sale. Phone ... after six. No dealers'. Sometimes the advertiser is anonymous; sometimes he is the well-known 'private collector'. Not very often does he give an address. The biggest give-away is the term 'No dealers', an expression calculated to excite the private buyer into thinking that he is getting at a buy which is not being made available to dealers.

The real reason why the advertiser puts 'No dealers' is very often because he himself is a dealer, and would be instantly recognised by any other dealers who might otherwise call. Alternatively or additionally, the reason may be that the vendor is asking a price which he knows no sensible dealer would pay, and to save himself the embarrassment of being told this, he tries to dissuade dealers from calling. The dealer placing the advertisement may sell the clock from his own home address, or more usually from a different address, perhaps that of a relative whose surname is different from his own. As often as not by advertising the item as a private sale, the vendor can avoid any redress should the buyer later find the item faulty. Also of course he can probably avoid paying tax on the sale. Naturally, there must be perfectly genuine private sales from time to time, but if you are thinking of buying a clock in this way, be very much on your guard.

Not long ago I was talking to a young couple who were very enthusiastically telling me about their newly purchased clock. They had been 'put on to' this by the friend of a friend of a friend. They had bought the clock from an eccentric old gentleman 'collector', who did not really buy and sell clocks, they assured me, but who had a large collection. Apparently, if this old gentleman took a liking to you, he might be willing to sell you one of his clocks. He must have taken a great liking to this young couple for not only was he prepared to let them have one of his clocks, but he was also willing to take in part exchange an old wall clock which they had and no longer wanted.

They asked me if it was possible to get the moon and date dials to function on their newly acquired clock, as they did not seem to be working. I arranged to call and see the clock, and when I did I found a very nice case, a very pleasant brass dial, and a nice enough movement. The only problem was that none of the three was made for either of the other two. The dial had been made for a one-handed clock, but it now had a two-handed movement which fitted so badly that the teeth had had to be cut away from about a quarter of the circumference of the date and moon discs to prevent the discs from obstructing the hands pipe. I explained this to them and showed them where the teeth had been cut off. They then asked me to value the clock. 'Which piece?' I asked. 'The dial, the movement, or the case?'

These people were a fairly prosperous, educated, and apparently sensible young business couple who could well have afforded to buy a clock from any local dealer. But instead of paying the going price, they had had to make a 200-mile round trip with the clock on the roof of their car, had been sold a faked clock as well as having lost what might have been a quite reasonable one taken by the 'collector' in part exchange, and heaven knows how much money they had been persuaded to part with at the same time. This story is absolutely true, and the incident took place fairly recently. One would imagine that anyone would have been slightly suspicious if two or three dials of a clock were not working, and when the simplest glance behind the dial revealed that half the gearing had been chopped away.

It is worth remembering that any dealer has some sort of reputation to maintain. Obviously, some are better than others, but with a dealer you always have some sort of redress. This applies especially if you insist on some sort of guarantee about a clock you are buying, and most of the better dealers will give this anyway, without having to be asked.

There is another side to the coin, however. There are many dealers and specialists who, far from cheating anyone, are genuinely enthusiastic about the goods they handle. They are usually pleased when a customer asks intelligent questions or expresses sensible opinions. There are customers who walk into a shop, ask which is the best clock, and promptly buy it with no further conversation. That sort of sale falls rather flat for an interested dealer, who likes to think that the customer will appreciate the item he is buying, and will ask questions about the clock, its age, its style and maker, as well as just signing a cheque.

It does not generally take long to appreciate which dealers are sincere and which are not. A good dealer is not some sort of high-powered salesman. He does not try to impress you with talk about how many clocks he sells in a month; how this one is a bargain; how the Victoria and Albert Museum are considering buying that one, so you had better be quick if you want it; how this one has just come into stock, and no one else has had a chance to see it yet; or any other gimmicky sales patter calculated to rush you, fluster you, embarrass you or cajole you into buying something that you don't want and which he wants to be rid of. You will often find that the most garrulous and ebullient salesmen are the ones who dry up instantly when you ask an intelligent question, and who will then hurriedly explain that they don't really understand clocks very well, but just sell the occasional one now and then.

Buying a clock is something you want to do pleasurably, unhurriedly, calmly, quietly, considering carefully the height, colour, style, period and price in relation to your pocket, your home and the setting for the clock. The final decision should always be a contented one. If you are not absolutely happy in your own mind about the prospective purchase, then don't buy it. When you see the clock you want to live with, you will know it.

I remember one occasion when I sold a clock to a customer who lived not very far from me. He was delighted with his purchase, so much so that later on he called in a couple of times to tell me, and eventually he brought round a friend and his wife to show them my clocks, as they had admired the one he had bought. He thoroughly enjoyed himself showing them the items, and they in turn were captivated. I hardly had a chance to get a word in! They chose a clock which suited them, I delivered it, they paid me: all was settled and done. A week went by. The telephone rang. Could I possibly agree to take back the clock? No, there was nothing wrong with it; it was very nice and going perfectly. It was just that his wife did not like it in that particular place, and he did not like it where she liked it; and he had had to move his stereo record cabinets, and then couldn't get to the electrical socket, and so on and so on. I collected the clock and gave him back his cheque. The trouble was that they had not given proper thought to their purchase. They had liked the clock and the idea of having it, but they had not considered how it would fit into their home; and the real answer was that it did not fit in. They had allowed themselves to be carried away on the tide of their friend's enthusiasm, instead of considering carefully and calmly. Don't make the same mistake.

There is one thing which you as a clock owner, potential purchaser or admirer owe to yourself, and that is to hold fast to your own tastes. By all means learn the 'whys' and 'wherefores' of clocks, but let no one tell you what you *ought* to like. A clock, more than any other piece of furniture, has a character, a personality, of its own. You have to live with it in your home, and a clock which you find attractive will give you many years of pleasurable company. Each day you will find yourself giving it a little nod of approval and appreciation from the sheer pleasure of looking at it. Therefore pay no attention at all to what someone else happens to like, whether or not he is an 'expert'. Do not let others hinder your judgement with their prejudices. Try to look with an open mind and you will recognise what you like as soon as you see it. A book may teach you how to look at a clock, what features to notice, and whether these features are well executed. It may try to advise you about 'quality', a much-used word in the world of antiques. So often this word is used to signify something which was difficult to make and costly in labour and materials, and therefore supposedly good. But however much of this kind of 'quality' a clock may have, this may by no means make it beautiful. All the 'quality' in the world cannot compensate for ill-conceived design, and of course the design is relevant only to the type of clock in question. It is quite unfair to compare a cottage clock with a palace clock as either would fail in the wrong setting.

90 and 91 Mahogany case and close-up hood detail with dial of clock by John Bancroft of Scarborough. This one dates from c 1815 and has a dial by Whittaker and Shreeve of Halifax with brass hands. The case is a very clean and handsome example with the Sheraton-style oval door panel, but here the door top follows a most unusual stepped-and-pointed shape. Height about 7 ft 6 in.

Similarly, do not be misguided in your attitude to white dial clocks by glowing descriptions of the slender and elegant case styles of the seventeenth-century London clockmakers with names like Tompion and Fromanteel. Beautiful as their case styles may have been, these clocks belong to an entirely different period and setting; and no white dial clock was ever intended to look like a seventeenth-century London 'coffin' clock. By all means learn to like clocks, but do not let others force their tastes on to you.

The one consideration that ought to be uppermost in your mind is genuineness. If the clock is not original then you are simply deceiving yourself by buying it. If you do not care whether the clock is genuine or a botched-up thing, then you are wasting your time reading this book for there is no earthly point in trying to date a dial if the movement and case do not belong to it.

Assuming that you do care, then your problem is in knowing how to decide whether what you see is genuine. Unless you are willing to devote a certain effort to that task, then the simple answer is that you cannot tell. Over half the clocks you see are likely to be 'wrong'. Armed with no knowledge you are at the mercy of every twister in the business and anyone who bandies a few technical words with you can soon blind you with science. 'In the kingdom of the blind, the one-eyed man is king.' If you wish to try to avoid buying a fake, then here are a few points to watch out for.

White dial clocks are so far the least-faked category, but with prices rocketing this is likely to change soon. The faker cannot afford to pull brass dial clocks to pieces in order to make fake white dials; indeed he tends to do the reverse. So all the faker can do today is one of two things—make white dial clocks from old scrap dials and movements or make them from new parts. As new parts would probably be obvious and could well be costly, let us assume that what we have to watch out for is an old surplus movement attached to an old spare dial. What do we look for to identify such a botch-up from a genuine clock?

Well, obviously we compare the retailer's name on the dial with the dialmaker's name (assuming we can identify the latter) and check that their working periods overlap. We also check that the dial style is consistent with that of its supposed period. Of course any name could have been re-lettered onto a restored dial, so we have to look out for possible alterations there, signs of old names that have been painted over.

Generally we have not yet reached sophisticated levels of faking in white dial clocks and if movement and dial did not originate together, the bodger who mated them up has not usually bothered to camouflage his work. Odd parts do not fit together easily and therefore such things that will usually be obvious are winding squares that do not centre correctly in the winding-holes; calendars where no drivework ever reached them; moon dials which have no motion-work; spare holes in the movement frontplate where other dial feet once fitted (or where other falseplate feet once fitted); falseplate feet or dial feet which have been moved to fit holes they did not originally fit. Those with experience of movements could recognise one of, say, 1750 if fitted behind a dial of, say, 1850 by the stylistic differences in the mechanics, but this is getting complicated for the beginner.

A more likely area of switching is where clocks are now in cases they were not originally housed in and in this respect the notes on page 148 may help.

18

Restoration

The basic principle behind the restoration of any antique object is to try to put it back into its original state, as far as possible by restoring the existing (if original) parts, replacing only those parts which are beyond restoration, and making any essential replacements in the correct style. If 'restoration' oversteps these limits it can soon become 'faking'. For instance, the converting of thirty-hour clocks to eight-day ones is not restoration, it is faking. It is furthermore a great pity, but it is widespread for all that, although largely confined to brass dial clocks. An essential feature of an antique, and one especially applicable to clocks, is the complete absence of a coating of dirt, grease, cobwebs and general grime: all of these, apart from spoiling the appearance of the clock, will grind themselves into the moving parts and help to shorten its life considerably. A clean clock is likely to work better and to last longer.

There are good clock restorers and bad ones. One would think that it would be quite unnecessary to point this out, but I am frequently astonished by the appallingly low standard of restoration which some people accept. As long as a clock ticks, that seems to be adequate for some. Often in conversation I hear about a clock which has just been 'restored' or repaired, but if I ask specially, I often learn that the date indicator does not work, the moon dial does not work, and sometimes even the strike does not work. I personally have seen very bad examples of this even from people who describe themselves as 'horologists' and who belong to trade associations.

Date dials and moon dials can be tricky things to put right, and if they do not function precisely they can cause the clock to stop. Hence some repairers do not wish to fiddle with dates. They may perhaps tell the customer that the date indicator cannot be made to work, and leave it at that.

The answer of course is that the customer should refuse to accept this. If one repairer cannot undertake to make the clock operate fully, the customer should take it to a better repairer who can. You would never dream of patronising a garage where they could repair engines but could not repair faults on, say, brakes or lights or windscreen wipers. One should be quite clear about this: if a clock was made with a particular feature, such as a moon dial, this was made originally to work and should be capable of being made to work today. Therefore do not be prepared to accept that a certain feature is irreparable without your being given a very convincing explanation. There is no such thing as a clock which cannot be repaired, though there are occasions when the cost of the repair work could be prohibitive.

Recently I saw a very valuable clock, the dial of which had an indicator for the (seven) days of the week and the (twelve) months of the year. Behind these sub-dials belonged wheels with seven and twelve points respectively. Incredible as it may seem, the original star-wheels had been put back behind the wrong dials by a 'restorer' who, having experienced difficulty in getting the seven-pointed wheel to fit behind the twelve-month sub-dial, had set about filing part of this away to make it fit!

Many good restorers, and there are plenty of them, will not take on repair jobs on dirty clocks unless they can also clean the movements. This is understandable, since a movement that is clogged up with grime and oil can hardly be expected to function well for long, and if it should stop by being clogged up with grime, the customer might blame the workmanship of the restorer. You cannot have it all ways. A repairer who is good will tend to be more expensive than one who is inefficient, but you get the workmanship you pay for, and it is probably cheaper in the end to pay a capable man once than an incompetent one several times.

If a repairer is a member of a professional association, you may feel that you could have more confidence in him. At least, if such an association member fails to give satisfaction, you have the opportunity of taking the matter up with the association concerned.

One word of caution: do not fiddle about with a clock. Left to itself a clock will often function happily for many years and, surprisingly enough, even sometimes when it is in a very dirty condition. Clocks do not often wear out under normal conditions. If a clock does not go, it is very often because someone has broken it. I have been told many times by people who have newly moved into a house that their clock used to go in the old house but will not go in the present one. Often it is simply not level, or else the fork holding the pendulum suspension spring has been bent during removal. When one hears of removal men tipping a clock on to its side and carrying it out lengthwise, it is hardly surprising that it will not go in its new home. Carrying a clock in this way without dismantling it is almost certain to break it. You must dismantle it by removing first the hood, then the pendulum and weight(s), and then lifting the movement clear of the case. It is a very simple operation, but if in doubt it would be as well to get a clock restorer to dismantle it for you—rather than have to pay him to mend it later!

Eight-day clocks almost always have a striking system known as rack striking. Some have repeating-work whereby the clock will strike the last hour whenever a cord is pulled, usually one hanging down inside the case. Repeating clocks were used in the same way as, for instance, a dinner-gong. If the household or visitors did not come in for tea at say four o'clock, then the lady of the house would send the maid to repeat the hour again, or would do it herself in houses where there was no maid. If you repeat the clock until you grow weary of pulling, it will still keep repeating the same hour.

Thirty-hour clocks are different and almost always have what is called locking-wheel striking, which system means that whenever it strikes it will strike one more blow than last time. If you accidentally trip a thirty-hour clock off, then it will be one hour out of sequence and will stay out forever unless you put it back into sequence again (which is done by lifting the arm which engages the countwheel at the back of the movement backplate). Every time you lift the arm (with the clock weight on, obviously) you will cause it to strike one hour later than the last. A thirty-hour clock will not correct itself if it comes out of sequence, as for instance it might do if it ran fully down and failed to strike as it lost driving power. So if a thirty-hour clock is out of sequence, you will have to correct it yourself, as explained above.

An eight-day clock cannot come out of strike sequence unless you break it, or unless you force the hour hand round on its shaft when you might find the clock will consistently strike a number that is different to the hour registered, but consistently different. The reason I explain this is because when you are re-setting the time if the clock has been stopped, you can damage the strikework unless you know how to handle it. Longcase clocks prime (ie get ready to strike) at about four minutes to—it varies slightly with each clock. It is important that you do not try to wind the hands *backwards* after the clock has primed—you will hear a slight click on priming. If you do wind them backwards at all, as you might wish to if for instance the clock has gained slightly, then you can safely wind the hands backwards from about ten minutes to the hour back until the previous hour, but it is important that you do not wind it back past the sixty-minute point.

In other words you can move the minute hand backwards as long as you do not cross before the hour point. When it comes to winding the clock forward, you may do this through the whole twenty-four hours if you wish without any harm, but if the clock is a thirty-hour clock then you must let it strike each hour as you do so, otherwise you will throw the clock out of strike sequence. If it is an eight-day clock then you do not have to wait for each hour to strike out as you wind forward, but you do have to let it strike the hour of twelve. This is very important because a high percentage of rack-striking eight-day clocks run a danger of jamming if they are wound quickly through the twelve-hour point without being allowed to strike twelve. If you do jam the clock in this way, you will probably find that not only have you upset the strikework but also jammed the clock's going mechanism too. By far the simplest practice is to make it a habit always to let a clock strike out its full hour whenever you have cause to wind the hands forward past any hour. That way you are far less likely to get into problems. I am deliberately trying to avoid getting into technical explanations as the average clock owner does not wish to become a mechanic.

White dial clocks sometimes suffer damage to the dial as a result of rusting from beneath the paint surface, and ultimately pieces of the surface may chip off like eggshell or even peel off. For those whose clocks have this problem there are specialist firms of dial restorers who can do remarkably good cleaning and restoration jobs. If you are thinking of buying a clock which has this fault, then bear in mind that such restoration is going to add to the bill. However, if the clock is a family heirloom, it can be saved and made to look just as good as the day it was first sold. In the same way, a dial on which some of the lettering or numbering has worn faint can be restored to its former clarity.

If a clock dial has reached such a state of deterioration that it would need to have a complete repaint from the backing upwards, then this is a serious problem, because even the very best restorer (and there are no more than half a dozen in the country) would have great difficulty in assessing what the dial looked like originally. Indeed it could be impossible for him to know. In the end he may have to 'invent' the dial decoration. If the best would have great problems doing this, the average 'restorer' would make a real mess of it. Some of the results of complete re-painting are diabolical. I have seen dials done with Dulux gloss with seagulls in the corners looking more like chipshop window decoration. If a clock dial has gone so far as to need a complete re-paint, I would advise against buying it as at best you are buying trouble and you may end up with a totally unsatisfactory result even after great trouble and expense. There are enough good examples left to choose from without buying the dregs.

As a measure of the better standards of restoration, those restored dials illustrated, such as the Deacon clock, give an idea of what can be done. None of the dials in this book had a re-paint in the sense of the background, but many had the coloured decorations touched up and even more had the black lettering and figuring re-done, not always carefully, as can be judged by the photographs.

Restoration of casework is exactly the same as for any other piece of antique furniture. An interesting aspect of case restoration is that of pine cases, or deal cases if you prefer the term. It was called deal in the past but today most people refer to deal furniture as pine, stripped pine or waxed pine—it is all the same thing really. A deal case was often designed for a less distinguished position than one in, say, oak or mahogany. It was for a clock case for a kitchen perhaps, or a farm cottage, or the servants' quarters in a larger house. It was the cheapest wood and was used for economy. As such, a pine case generally lacks brass fittings in the form of pillar caps and paterae, etc, and where possible, turned wooden alternatives were used, though not always.

This is not to say that a pine case is now regarded as an inferior item. On the contrary, it often has a particular charm because of its simplicity; and many pine cases are very attractively proportioned. In fact, in the absence of elaborate detail, proportion becomes a very much more important factor than in, say, a case where the beauty lies mainly in the veneers.

The interesting thing about pine cases, however, is that when they were made they were usually sold *painted*, or sometimes stained. I say 'usually' though I am tempted to say 'always', as I have never seen a pine case that does not show some signs of having been painted or stained, and very often some traces of red priming paint remain. Furthermore, the wood used is often knotty and the nailheads are crudely hidden with filler, making it apparent that the bare pine surface was never intended to be seen. Now stripped pine is very popular at the present time, both in antique furniture and modern furniture, and especially for kitchens. For this reason pine-cased clocks are popular, but they are not too easy to come by in good condition as pine cases tend to be prone to woodworm attack. Most dealers today who buy a painted, pine-cased clock would strip off the old blackened paint and sell the clock as 'stripped pine'. If you ever saw a clock of this type with shrivelled, blackened paint still on it, you would hardly take to it in that state.

If we were being strictly correct, what we dealers ought to do is to repaint pine cases. But what an outcry there would be if a dealer did this! We—customers and dealers—agree to the fair and sensible restoration of clockcases, except for pine ones, where we all agree that they should be stripped down to the bare wood and waxed, thereby producing an effect totally different from the one intended by the clockmaker who first sold the clock. It really is rather an odd situation. Ironically, it is often only because it was painted that a pine case has survived being devoured by woodworm. I do not mean to indicate that I disagree with stripping pine cases. I am simply pointing out that in treating them in this way we are breaking the rules of restoration. The cost of stripping is probably twenty times that of repainting. And as a final irony, in twenty-five years' time antiques dealers will no doubt get out the paintpots and repaint all the pine cases!

'Patina' is a word much bandied about in antique circles, especially if one is trying to sound knowledgeable. A clock case which has been sadly neglected may have lost not only its 'patina', but perhaps its colour too. You can obtain all manner of weird and wonderful waxes, and polish until you are 102, and you may be no nearer to restoring either the colour or the surface texture to a desirable state. An oak case may have been kept in a damp outbuilding: its surface has been attacked by moisture, which has broken through the wax coating and into the varnish beneath, and has attacked the original stain, causing the oak to appear now as a greyish white colour, maybe in patches. Where traces of varnish remain, these may be blistered into tiny bubbles and may well have turned white. You will be extremely lucky to manage to camouflage bad damp-staining by rubbing in waxes. The energetic application of brown boot polish is likely to be more profitable to boot-polish manufacturers than beneficial to clock cases.

I am emphasising two points. First, the oak case originally had colour applied to it when new. It was not, with very few exceptions, sold as plain white or yellow oak; it was stained initially to give it some richness and colour. Often it has a rich red tint to it. This colour may have improved through years of care, but the colour was put into it to begin with.

Second, after staining, the case was *varnished* prior to being sold. This was to keep in the colour and to provide a sealed base on to which one could wax. If you try staining without varnishing, the colour will gradually come out or be considerably weakened when wax is rubbed in. With later veneered cases the finish is often akin to a thin French polishing, perhaps a shellac coating of some kind. Scratch the surface with your fingernail and you will see this hard layer shelling off.

Grandfather clocks were not revered in the past as they may now be: 99 per cent of them stood in ordinary households and received every bit as much wear and tear as any other piece of furniture—and that, in most houses, meant vastly rougher treatment than most of us would give our possessions today. Our grandparents could renovate their old furniture, if they could afford it, by French polishing. For those of smaller means the varnish pot was the answer, and it seems that varnish was often used to 'brighten up the old clock a bit'. Both these forms of treatment are today considered to have been misdirected enthusiasm.

I am not advocating the rubbing down and repolishing of cases needlessly. However, if a part or even all of a clock case is in very bad surface condition, or treacled with several layers of varnish, it may be necessary to remove the old, shrivelled varnish, restain, revarnish lightly and then rub down with fine wire wool prior to waxing. This at least gives one a chance of working up some sort of surface texture which will improve with the years as the wax hardens.

19

Reference Books

Shortly after the publication of my book on Yorkshire clockmakers, I recall chatting one day to an antiques dealer about the book. 'Nay, lad,' he said, 'I've been buying and selling clocks all these years—what would I want with a book like that?' A down-to-earth question, for which I had no answer. As far as his interest went, of course, he was quite right. He knew how much to pay for particular types of clock and how much to sell them for. As to anything else, he did not really care who had made the clock or when. He knew from his own experience what no book could tell him: prices and saleability. Fortunately the majority of antiques dealers have a genuine interest in the objects they handle, additional to, and in some cases more important than, the daily business of buying and selling.

In pursuit of your interest in clocks, whether in buying, selling, or just looking, there may be times when you will wish to turn to some of the basic horological works of reference, and a few suggestions might prove helpful. Modesty does not prevent me from pointing out that the best general book you can buy is my own *Complete British Clocks*, which attempts to cover all that a beginner would want to know.

As basic background material for longcase clocks you ought to read E. L. Edwardes's *The Grandfather Clock*, 1980 edition. Another book for general background is Eric Bruton's *The Longcase Clock*. Both these books give considerable space to country longcase clocks, which one might normally meet with, as well as discussing top London-made clocks, which are beyond the financial aspirations of most of us. *Country Clocks and their London Origins* is another of my own books, concentrating on longcase clocks, especially provincial ones.

When it comes to reference books giving lists of makers to help in dating a particular clock, there are several works written specifically for this purpose. By far the most helpful and detailed ought to be those books which are purely about the makers in individual counties, and several counties have been covered in this way. Some of these county works are now out of print, but should be available through a library. Books I know of this type are:

Chester Clocks and Clockmakers by Nicholas Moore (Chester, 1976).
Clock and Watch Makers of Buckinghamshire by Edward Legg (Fenny Stratford, 1975).
Clockmaking in Oxfordshire by C. F. C. Beeson (Ramsgate, 1967).
Clocks and Clockmakers of Tiverton by Ponsford, Scott and Authers (Tiverton, 1977).
Colchester Clockmakers by Bernard Mason (London, 1969).
Cornish Clocks and Clockmakers by H. Miles-Brown (Newton Abbot, 1970).
Derbyshire Clock and Watch Makers by R. G. Hughes (Derby, 1976).
Devonshire Clockmakers by J. K. Bellchambers (Torquay, 1962).
Lancashire Clocks and Clockmakers by Brian Loomes (Newton Abbot, 1975).
Leicestershire Clockmakers by John Daniel (Leicester, 1975).
Shropshire Clock and Watch Makers by D. J. Elliott (Chichester, 1979).
Somerset Clockmakers by J. K. Bellchambers (Torquay, 1969).
Stamford Clocks and Watches by Laurence Tebbutt (Stamford, 1975).
Suffolk Clocks and Clockmakers by A. L. Haggar and L. F. Miller (1974).
Time in Exeter by Clive Ponsford (Exeter, 1978).
Westmorland Clocks and Clockmakers by Brian Loomes (Newton Abbot, 1974).
Yorkshire Clockmakers by Brian Loomes (Clapham (Lancaster), 1972).

Research into the clockmakers of a number of English counties is currently in progress.

In the meantime, for those areas not yet covered individually, one has to turn to one or more of the following: *Clock and Watchmakers in Wales* by Iorwerth C. Peate; *Old Scottish Clockmakers* by John Smith. For information on Scottish clocks Felix Hudson's small book *Scottish Longcase Clocks 1780–1870*, published by the Antiquarian Horological Society, Ticehurst, in 1977 is very useful and deals largely with Scottish white dial clocks, examining styles, etc.

The most comprehensive book on clockmakers, though each man is detailed only very briefly, is *Watchmakers and Clockmakers of the*

World by the late G. H. Baillie, which has been in print since 1929 and details about 36,000 clock and watch makers working before about 1820. As much new information had come to light since 1929, I compiled a companion volume to Baillie's book including such new names as I could gather and continuing the coverage up to about 1880, and my own volume contains 35,000 more names. *Watchmakers and Clockmakers of the World* therefore is now a two-volume work (Baillie's being known as Volume One, my own book as Volume Two) which covers more than 70,000 makers. When the first edition of *The White Dial Clock* was published, my own Volume Two had not yet appeared, and therefore earlier references to 'Baillie' should not be taken to mean both volumes. Britten's *Old Clocks and Watches and their Makers* also has a list of about 14,000 makers, but this has not been revised for many years and is not reliable in its accuracy.

There are some important factors that should be fully understood when using any horological reference books, and especially when using those books of a general nature. With the individual county lists the authors have frequently been able to ascertain the dates of birth and death of the makers listed, though not, of course, of every maker in such a book. Often, however, the lists may give a single date for a maker, simply a known year when he was working. A single date shown thus can be almost as misleading as helpful, since a clock by that man could have been made as much as fifty years distant from the given date. It is important to understand that unless positive dates of birth and death are stated, any date given should be regarded as only a rough guide to the period when the man is known to have been working.

Often when a single date is given, it is preceded by the word circa or the abbreviation c. This of course means 'approximately' or 'about', and is usually an indication that the date is simply a guess or an opinion as to the period of a clock. How valid that date is will depend very much on the competence of the person whose opinion it represents, and that could be a very variable factor.

If you were doing a crossword puzzle, you might later check your answers against the correct solutions. Similarly, after attempting to date a clock, you might then think of checking with a book such as Baillie to see if you were right. Where such an approach falls down is that the reference book you are checking by is simply another person's attempt at the crossword, not the definite answer. Learn to date clocks for yourself from your own judgement. If some reference list of makers confirms your dating, well and good. If it does not, this need not mean that you are wrong. One does not need to have been looking at clocks for long to realise that by no means all the answers are in books, and by no means all the answers that are in the books are the right ones.

Similarly, you should not feel that because a clockmaker's name appears in a reference book, this in some way means that he is a better maker than one whose name fails to appear in that book. It is in fact simply an indication that the writer may have come across work by the one man and not the other. The absence of a maker's name indicates, if anything, a failing on the part of the author rather than the clockmaker. Yet people *do* tend to have more faith in a clock whose maker appears in the standard lists. There is somehow a feeling that a clock by a known maker may be more genuine, or more authentic, or more safe, while an unknown name does not inspire confidence. In fact when you think about it, the reverse applies. There would be absolutely no point in *faking* a clock by an unknown maker, and if the buyer is to have any doubts at all, he would be far wiser to have them about a clock bearing a well-known name.

This concern with known names reminds me of a little incident of some interest. Some years ago I bought an eight-day white dial clock of about 1790 or so. The dial was very worn and the maker's name illegible. After about an hour of very careful examination under a strong light I was able to decipher the name, though only with great difficulty. It was important to me to know the name so that I could have it re-lettered along with the numbering when the clock was restored. Finally I made it out: Forster of Sheerness (Kent). I was very pleased to have been able to recognise the maker, and promptly, as I suppose many of us do on such an occasion, I looked him up in Baillie. The entry read: 'Forster, ... Sheerness, ca. 1790 CC'.

This means: Christian name unknown, working about 1790, member of the Clockmakers' Company of London. Having found this I was even more pleased, but there was really no reason for me to be. The magic letters CC had done it. The assumption (and of course it is a very wrong one to make) is that because a man was a member of the Company he was somehow a better clockmaker than one who did not belong to this body of London clockmakers. It was quite wrong of me to attach any more importance or value to this clock because of that fact.

The clock had a Birmingham-made dial and falseplate. It was no better or worse than a thousand others just like it. If it had been Forster of Plymouth or Manchester or Dundee it might have looked identical. And here is an even more interesting thought. If some unscrupulous dealer had arranged for that clock to be re-lettered, and had deliberately decided that it was to be by 'Forster of London', there is no one who would have known except that dealer himself. There was nothing about that clock, or thousands of similar ones, to say who had made it or sold it, except that name on the dial.

The real point I am making is that since an average white dial clock is almost identical, regardless of where it was made, with others of the same period and style, there is no good reason why a London-made one should be valued more highly than one from any other town.

There are times, I feel, when a person buying a clock wrongly hankers after 'quality'. He feels it would be better to have a clock by a maker who is said in some book or other to be a 'good maker'. So he reads a book or two, and perhaps sees, for example, that Thomas Lister of Halifax, Yorkshire (there were two, by the way—father and son), has a good name and that he made some clocks of very ingenious and fine workmanship. Having read this he sees a clock bearing the name of Lister and buys it, assuming that he has bought a *good-quality* clock. In actual fact, while it is true that this maker (the son) produced some very fine clocks, it is also true that his average clock was no better and no worse than anyone else's of that time. This is because a clockmaker made what his customers wanted; and the fact that a man made some good clocks by no means indicates that he did not make many very ordinary ones too. Look for a 'quality' clock if you wish, but do not assume that the quality exists because of the name on the dial. I am speaking here only about clocks by provincial makers. I am not competent to say whether or not the same applies to clocks by early London master-clockmakers. As we have just seen, the name on many later white dial clocks is hardly important anyway, but in this paragraph I am thinking of brass dial clocks as well. If it is a 'quality' clock you seek, by all means buy one, but make it one which you yourself consider to fit that description, not one that someone else tells you is good. Remember that no clock dealer will boast of selling clocks of *poor* quality!

One final point about checking on the dates of a maker. People often tell me that their white dial clock has no name on it. Occasionally they may be right but in my experience probably less than 1 per cent of the clocks are nameless. There may at first sight appear to be no name on the clock, but on closer inspection one can usually see that the name has been worn off by over-cleaning through the years. The way to decipher a very faded name is to get a torch or bright light of some sort and hold it close to the dial at an acute angle. Very often one can then make out the name of the maker and the town. White dial clocks almost always have the town as well as the man's name, if you have the patience to read it. There are occasions when dials have been *restored* very crudely and the names touched in incorrectly. In these instances skill and patience are needed in the deciphering. Finding out about the age and the maker of a clock is a fascinating pursuit for its own sake and half the fun of owning a clock lies in knowing about its history.

People all too readily accept dials as 'nameless', despite the advice in the previous paragraph. The name is almost always there (on British clocks) even if apparently washed away completely. To find it you first of all have to know on which part of the dial to look and, as the positioning of names on dials was fairly well standardised, familiarity with the dials in this book may help you decide where to look.

I know that it is not always easy to make out a name, even if you can identify a few letters of the word. If you can get access to one, then an ultra-violet lamp used in a darkened room is one very helpful method and will often make invisible letters stand out boldly on the dial as if by magic. If you know a friend of a friend who owns one, then ask if you can have a few minutes' use of it. Quite a number of picture dealers have them.

If you do not know anyone with such a lamp, very often the local art gallery or museum or the local archives department will have one, and a well-phrased request might see you taking your dial along for a five-minute session. I know museum staff are already busy with their duties, but there are plenty of busy people in the world (myself included) who spend a few minutes here and there helping out museums with their enquiries, and I find it hard to imagine a museum who would refuse outright to spend five minutes assisting a member of the public in trying to do a little historical research and preservation with equipment bought out of public funds in the first place.

If a museum is not there for the purpose of researching and preserving our knowledge of our past culture, then we might well wonder what it is there for, and one might forgive people for wondering whether there is not more merit in investigating the art in a clock dial with the use of public funds, than there is in buying and preserving for the nation piles of building bricks.

Still on the subject of worn names on dials, I was horrified to read in a recent book (*English House Clocks* by A. Bird) the statement that if the original name on the dial could not be made out, 'it may be proper' to write on the name of some 'unimportant' maker. The old-fashioned and incorrect implication in this is that 'important' makers did not make clocks with painted dials. Alternatively it is suggested that one might paint on a fictitious name and address. Thank heavens not many writers openly advocate a practice of this kind. If they did we might soon find that it was recommended standard practice for picture dealers to paint some 'unimportant' name on unsigned canvases or for antique furniture dealers to mark their pieces with some 'unimportant' name. Before many years had passed a whole literature would have been built up of names from such pieces, and actual examples would be on record as having been made by craftsmen who never existed. Enough problems exist for those of us who are interested in research into past craftsmen without these being multiplied by such scandalous forms of so-called 'restoration'.

So a vast literature on clocks is available, much of it written during the last fifteen years. It is futile to hope to learn about clocks from books written fifty years ago or more, as some of the old so-called 'bibles' of the subject were. More knowledge has come to light about clocks during the past fifteen years than in the previous thousand. The literature exists and if you expect to take a serious interest in clocks, then you have to use it.

Mr Kenneth Roberts has kindly helped to compile the following list of books which might prove helpful in identifying American clockmakers of this period:

The Book of American Clocks by Brooks Palmer (New York, 1950).
Chester County Clocks and Their Makers by Arthur E. James (West Chester, Pa, 1947).
Clockmakers of Lancaster County and Their Clocks 1750–1850 by Stacy B. C. Wood Jnr (New York, 1977).

Clocks and Watches of New Jersey by William E. Drost (Elizabeth, New Jersey, 1966).

Connecticut Clockmakers of the Eighteenth Century by Penrose R. Hoopes (Hartford, Conn, 1930).

Pennsylvania Clocks and Clockmakers by George H. Eckhardt (New York, 1955).

Six Quaker Clockmakers by Edward E. Chandlee (Philadelphia, 1943).

A Treasury of American Clocks by Brooks Palmer (New York, 1967).

Two Hundred Years of American Clocks and Watches by Chris Bailey (New York, 1975).

Acknowledgements

The number of dealers or even enthusiasts who can date a white dial clock accurately from the dial style alone is not large at the time I write this. Not because it is difficult to do, but simply because few have taken the trouble to look closely enough at the details. I have received little encouragement from some of the people I had hoped might be most interested, and considerable support from some areas where I least expected it. I must acknowledge the interest shown by many clock owners who have written to me during the preparation of this work. Mr W. A. Taylor, Birmingham City Librarian, went out of his way to be helpful. My colleague, Mr Peter C. Nutt, assisted with some of the genealogical research, as he has done on many occasions for me.

I must especially thank Mr E. L. Edwardes, author of *The Grand-father Clock*, for kindly reading through the manuscript and for his considerable interest and constructive suggestions. I must also acknowledge the assistance of Mr Kenneth Roberts, formerly of the American Clock and Watch Museum Inc, Bristol, Connecticut, for the same. Both these gentlemen are deeply and enthusiastically involved in horological researches of their own, and because of that I am all the more grateful to them for sparing time to help with mine.

Thanks are due also to my friends Brian Morison and David Barker for their enthusiastic interest and help; to Messrs Manby of Skipton, ironmongers, for allowing me to examine their old business records; to Miss S. J. MacPherson, BA, Archivist in Charge at Westmorland Record Office, Kendal, for assistance with the records of stock transfer of Jonas Barber III; to Mr A. Ankerson, Mr Eric Benton, Mr John Coker, Mr Jeremy Evans, Mr Bernard Mason, OBE, and Dr J. M. Plowman; and to many others too numerous to mention by name.

Most of the photographs were taken by the author and are of clocks which have passed through his hands. However, author and

ACKNOWLEDGEMENTS

publishers wish to thank the following for permission to publish plates of clocks in their possession: 32 and 58, Mr and Mrs K. Gooch; 35, David Barker; 7, 14 and 49, K. V. Flanagan.

Plates 63 and 39 were taken by Malcoms Photo Services, Otley.

Acknowledgements
to the Second Edition

In the preparation of the second edition the following people have been of great assistance: Chris Bailey, Stacy Wood, Ed La Fond, Roy Gault, Patrick A. Hewitt, John Pearson, John Daniell, Felix Hudson, W. A. Seaby, Leicester Record Office, Leicester Museum, Robert W. Snyder, John J. Snyder Jr., Stephen E. Kramer III, Granville Barrett, Keith Watson.

The following antiques dealers have helped with illustrations: G. K. Hadfield, Blackbrook Hill House, Shepshed, plates 17 and 51a; N. Geary Antiques Ltd, Richardshaw Lane, Pudsey, plate 19; John Morris, Gastrell House Antiques, Tetbury, plate 27.

All the other photographs were provided by courtesy of The Dusty Miller Gallery, Low Laithe, near Pateley Bridge, North Yorkshire, of which the author is senior partner.

Index